THE SOLWAY FIRTH

THE
SOLWAY FIRTH

BRIAN BLAKE

ROBERT HALE · LONDON

First edition November 1955
Reprinted January 1956
Reprinted January 1959
Reprinted January 1966
Second edition 1974
Third edition 1982
ISBN 0 7091 9747 0

PRINTED IN GREAT BRITAIN BY
KING'S ENGLISH BOOK PRINTERS LIMITED, LEEDS, YORKSHIRE
BOUND BY HUNTER AND FOULIS

CONTENTS

Chapter   *page*

AUTHOR'S NOTE AND ACKNOWLEDGMENTS   ix

I   SULWATH   1

II   SOLID FOUNDATIONS   14

III   THE LIVING COAST AND ITS BIRDS   31

IV   THE EDGE OF THE WORLD   52

V   DARK AGE CROSSROADS AND THE CHURCH IN SOLWAY   71

VI   FRONTIER AND BORDER   93

VII   FARMING   118

VIII FISHING   133

IX   INDUSTRY AND THE SPECIAL AREA   150

X   A JOURNEY ALONG THE COAST ROADS   169

POSTSCRIPT: 1973   216

POSTSCRIPT: 1982   219

BIBLIOGRAPHY   220

LIST OF PLANTS   221

INDEX   225

ILLUSTRATIONS

Between pages 70 and 71

1 "Rough Firth, typical of the northern shore, has a history of smuggling as well as a beauty of scene that has no equal across the water"

2 Scaurs and banks of the living coast dominated by Criffell

3 Netherhall, Maryport. Part of the Roman collection from Alauna, one of the greatest treasure-houses of the north

4 Moresby, near Whitehaven, has corn, coal and a lovely house. Around the church can be seen the ramparts of a Roman fort

5 Holm Cultram Abbey (Abbeytown) is still working as a parish church though it retains but a fragment of its former glory

6 Ruthwell Cross. "It is as though a struggling art form suddenly skipped the years of apprenticeship and adolescence . . ."

7 Dumfries. "A place to linger contemplating the swans under Devorgilla's bridge or watching the water curling over the Caul"

8 Grune Point "once sheltered half a hundred ships . . . but there is now no scene more typical of the wild loneliness of Solway and the texture of its surface"

9 Caerlaverock Castle. ". . . the dainty fabric of the dwelling-house"

10 Southerness, once Salterness. Paul Jones was born near here

11 Stones, sand and scaurs blend with jetsam under Criffell

12 Belted Galloway cattle. "This ancient and distinguished breed . . ."

Between pages 150 and 151

13 Salmon fishing. Stake-nets in Auchencairn Bay

14 Maryport Harbour. The town has turned its face from the sea

15 The Eden Bridge, Carlisle, pivot of Solway routes

16 The symmetrical slag of Risehow Colliery. "... coal from under the sea"

17 Hydro-electric Station, Tongland, Kirkcudbrightshire. "... the cleaner power of a later age"

18 Queen Mary of Scotland came to Solway through the gates of Dundrennan Abbey

19 "... to Fisher's Cross, just east of Bowness, which became glorified by the name of Port Carlisle"

20 The Solway Viaduct. "... a gallant monument to an age of reckless enterprise"

21 Workington. "... through quiet Portland Square with its cobbled roadway and dignified houses"

22 "Kirkcudbright ... is light and open, brightly painted and has a flavour of history"

23 "Dumfries ... retains a special atmosphere as the town of Robert Burns"

24 St Bees Head. "... so I turned back along the Solway and walked up over Tomlin"

Sketch-map of area   222-23

ACKNOWLEDGMENT

All the illustrations in this book are reproduced from photographs supplied by J. Allan Cash, F.I.B.P., F.R.P.S., London, N.W.3.

AUTHOR'S NOTE AND ACKNOWLEDGMENTS

FOR most purposes the Solway Firth can be defined as the inlet which both joins and divides the western coasts of England and Scotland. It is limited by the Mull of Galloway in Scotland and by St Bees Head in England. From some legal points of view the region is slightly larger than this, though a much smaller area has often been described as "the Solway", especially in the Middle Ages. However, I have not hesitated to abandon definition when I have thought that it would help understanding, and on the whole I have followed the opinion of the people concerned. For example, I have dealt less fully with those parts of Wigtownshire where there is little doubt amongst the inhabitants that they belong to Galloway rather than to Solway.

I have sometimes given to Wigtownshire and Kirkcudbright-shire the names of Shire and Stewartry respectively. These might not be well known outside the region but they are in common local use and have been since Archibald the Grim became Lord of Galloway in 1396 and appointed a Steward over the land between Nith and Cree.

I append a list of books and mention others in the text, but I feel that it would be appropriate to name here three sources which have been invaluable and constant companions. They are *Annals of the Solway until A.D. 1307* by George Neilson, *Transactions of the Cumberland and Westmorland Antiquarian and Archæological Society*, and the *Transactions of the Dumfriesshire and Galloway Natural History and Antiquarian Society*. I refer to the last two respectively as *C. & W. Transactions* and *D. & G. Transactions*.

If one were to acknowledge every source used in a book of this nature there would be more footnotes than pages. My first thanks therefore go to all the authors and scholars who must remain anonymous, although I have picked their brains in what I hope is a good cause. Also I wish to thank those Solway people who have allowed me to lead them into my text in an attempt to give it life. Their names will be found in the appropriate chapters.

A number of people have helped me in other ways and I am most grateful to them. They include Miss K. S. Hodgson of

AUTHOR'S NOTE AND ACKNOWLEDGMENTS

Brampton; Mr Ralph Birkett, Mr Ernest Blezard, Mr Tom Gray; Mr Robert Hogg and Mr T. L. Macdonald, all of Carlisle; Colonel Robert Armstrong of Langholm; Mr J. W. Herries of Edinburgh; Mr R. C. Reid and Mr. A. E. Truckell of Dumfries; and Sir Ifor Williams of Caernarvonshire.

Special help has come from Mr W. B. de Bear Nicol of Dumfries and Mr R. L. Bellhouse of Thursby, and I mention them separately so that I can add thanks for companionship and hospitality on both sides of the Solway.

Finally, I thank my wife. The author and the reader are both very much in her debt.

Scotby, Carlisle.   BRIAN BLAKE

Chapter I

SULWATH

WITH every tide the Solway Firth becomes a part of the great oceans, a sea for ships which sail its fairways and were once built in its ports. It is the haunt of sailors, a place of beauty and a frontier between two lands. With every ebb, half this sea disappears and its ships are gone away, except for those left wrecked, rotting in the silt. Then there remains an unknown Solway world of wet yellow sand gleaming over narrow channels. This part of the estuary, uncharted because daily different, is only familiar to those whose livelihood or pleasure is found by its shores. Seabirds and salmon, wildfowlers and fishermen share this wide but shallow valley with those who seek and find peace in space and beauty amidst the discipline of the tides. Against a backcloth of incredible skies, this tide-swept Solway sand forms a stage both for the pageant of history and for the satisfaction of everyday living. A strange beauty and ever-present danger, united yet distinct as the two sides of a coin, live together in the Firth.

Hills were my first love, and although this is not the story of hills, from the waters of Solway their presence is always gently felt. Criffell salutes Skiddaw to the south and dominates every scene, while Burnswark, neat and smaller, is always intriguing as it stands sentinel over routes to the north. These hills are always around and all around, but they never encroach or oppressively threaten as those of a mountain valley do—until you have topped them.

Skies come next as a mantle for the hills, seldom with the harsh blue brightness of the south, but always with a depth and texture. Clouds, building and breaking, send sunlight fleeting across each slope and harmonise weather and far turf into ever-changing patterns. You may come to these shores at any season of the year, and you will find movement and colour, both strong and delicate. Skies and hills dress the gleaming sand, and cloud or sunset-light the water.

Photographers will tell how skies and distant mountains are

completed and enhanced in a picture by the presence of water. When I stand on the English shore and see Criffell, snow-capped in winter, and burnished by the low western sun behind it, or from Scotland see a Lake District quite new and rare to English travellers spread out complete beyond the sea, I know exactly what they mean. You may remember Skiddaw's gentle slopes, and how you toiled up them, but you will wonder at the alpine profile it presents to Scotland. The best view of all, however, and the truest, is one that visitors rarely see. It belongs to the estuary, isolates one from both England and Scotland, and gives the essence of the Solway atmosphere. To see it, you would have to sail or stand with me in the very middle of the estuary at the ebb of the tide on a late September evening as every ripple is tinted by the dying sun. You would watch the night rise over the coasts until it covered even the profiles of the hills. On both shores, lights would flicker on to remind you—and you would need reminding—that human life still existed in this world of gentle wave-whispers and eerie bird-calls as they echoed against what is perhaps the loneliest silence in the world.

I repeat the warning that danger may lurk behind the loveliness of the estuary. Do not let me tempt you to wander too far from the shore unless you have great experience of this sea-bed, or have a good man to guide you. If you are sensitive to mood and atmosphere—and who on these shores could not be?—you need not fear that your guide will be matter-of-fact or unmindful of natural beauty. Almost certainly he will be a fisherman. The Solway fishermen know these sands better than all other men, and no matter how long they work in the waters, they never become matter-of-fact, for they know how great can be the daily and hourly changes. I think that in a long lifetime they never get over the sheer magic of this place; their eyes are clear with the spaciousness of sea and sky, their minds sober with its grandeur.

Regretfully, I shall have to tell you later how men and women of these coasts are being forced by events, mainly economic, to turn their backs on the Solway. Most of the bigger coastal towns have new living areas inland from the old harbours, and out of the sound of even the wildest storms. These new houses may shelter sons and grandsons of sailors and fishermen, but in a good many cases, though not all, the only fish they see are at meal-times at home, in factory canteens, or in paper after the pictures.

I am not disparaging fish and chips, nor certainly these men; they did not desert the waters until they themselves were deserted and found no living there. Indeed, today some of them work not in the Solway but under it, in coal mines five hundred fathoms deep.

I will postpone the economic story and its vicissitudes, but I must digress a little here so as not to give a false picture of the men of the Solway. It would take more than a few generations to get the salt water out of their blood. From St Bees round to the Mull of Galloway you will find many men differing in their accents as well as in their professions but united in the way the subject of fishing fills their spare time with action and even assails their working hours with dreams. They are mostly amateurs whether they fish in the Solway itself or the rivers that feed it, for the number who earn their living by fishing grows sadly less each year.

Such men are usually individualists and you may search in vain for one to call typical. When I lived on the Solway I knew one man who, although by no means typical of anyone but himself, epitomised the Solway to me. He lived in a small cottage and I thought then it would break his heart to change and have a brand-new council house, for his front door opened on to the quay and he lived almost in touch with boat and mud, with sea birds and salt spray. He was both an engineer and a sailor, and invariably mangaed to combine these interests. This was not difficult in the convoys of wartime but in the years since then he both tended factory engines and spent his off-time in his Solway boat. In 1955 Bob Fisher was Maryport's only full-time fisherman. He had succumbed to the lure of the Solway and escaped the pressure of noise and buildings. I guessed then that this burly blue-jerseyed seaman would always be out of place in a factory. Since this book was written pressures forced him to earn a living on land and he died a short time ago.

It is a true and not unduly sad reflection that wherever there are sailors and fishermen there are usually plenty of pubs where fishing-talk can be heard in as much quantity as football-talk elsewhere, though I must make an exception of the Cumberland coast around Workington, where pub conversation and even coal output is governed by the rules and fortunes of Rugby League. In many of the Solway pubs you will meet the wildfowlers. I have as yet only hinted at the bird life which is an integral part of the embrace of land and sea, and naturalists and wildfowlers, like fishermen, shall have space to themselves before this survey is finished. Very few of them are professionals, but all share that love of a solitude which is never lonely when it is the centre of a calling flight of duck or geese.

For centuries past, the wildfowlers and fishermen have trodden the shores of the Solway, have waded its waters and pushed their punts along its creeks, but many of the older stories concerning these shallows are about neither of them. They tell of people who have used the tracks through the water as a way to travel between England and Scotland, sometimes in boats, but much more often on foot.

Our best-known stories are really about two separate regions, the two sides of Solway now called Scotland and England, at odds with each other. These stories of wars, of diversity, tend to hide the longer traditions of unity and similarity between the people who look south across the water and the people who look north. Rivers notoriously make bad frontiers. People on both banks insist on trade and on love even in the face of national decrees; and an estuary like ours, with its secret crossing-paths, is much like a river in this respect.

These paths have joined the peoples even when the water has divided the two countries, England and Scotland, or at the worst, they have provided the routes for battle. It is about these paths or fords across Solway and its rivers that I first write in detail, because the adventures associated with them belong to some of the most exciting aspects of our history, and because one of the fords has given the estuary its modern name.

Let me begin at the eastern end near the waters of Eden and Esk. There is a dark, straight road shining in winter from the lights of many trunkers roaring along between England and Scotland; it stretches between Carlisle and Gretna and is now by-passed by the M6. Millions of Britons, and more millions of tons of goods, have travelled it. Strangers on their first journey always note the sign at the little bridge over the Sark that says "England" from the north and "Scotland" to those driving from the south. Who is there, travelling north along this road for the first time, who does not also watch for the first of the blacksmiths' shops? Even seasoned travellers feel that home is not far away when they see this national signpost. This road was the creation of that gifted Dumfriesshire engineer, Thomas Telford, who built the Caledonian Canal and many British roads and bridges. It is almost an interloper in the history of Solway, for it did not exist until 1826. I shall tell stories of thieves and kings, as well as of gentle and ordinary folk, passing between Scotland and England—not only crossing the border but making it, moving it and fighting over it; but the road they took was an older one, less straight, unhurried, a pleasant road. Two hundred and fifty years ago that intrepid and altogether delightful young woman, Celia Fiennes, went by this old road·

"for Scotland and rode 3 or 4 miles by the side of this river Emount,★ which is full of very good fish. I rode sometymes on a high ridge over a hill; sometymes on the sands, it turning and winding about, that I went almost all the way by it and saw them with boates, fishing for salmon and troute, which made my journey very pleasant; leaving this river I came to the Essex (Esk) which is very broad and hazardous to crosse even when the tyde is out, by which it leaves a broad sand on each side which in some places is unsafe—made me take a good Guide which carry'd me aboute and acrosse some part of it here and some part in another place, it being deep in the channell where I did crosse, which was in sight of the mouth of the river that runs in the sea;"

If you have leisure on your way to Scotland, you can still take this old road for most of its way, and delight with Miss Fiennes in the sight of men fishing in these pleasant rivers. When you have left Carlisle over the Eden bridges (there is only one now, but older people still say bridges; it is only a century and a half ago since the second one was removed) swing left from the main road and aim for Rockcliffe through landscape that still has the feel of the old in spite of great sheds and hangars which at least imply continuity of military function in the district. After you have walked down to the river and enjoyed its views, both back along the red cliff to the church and village, and over the marsh to the open sea, and perhaps reflected on its history, you can meander through Floriston between chocolate-purple hedges to join the main road again not many yards from the Metal Bridge over the Esk, with its attendant inn of the same name. The present

★ Celia meant Eden; she was usually bad on rivers, but the maps of her time were not much better.

"metal" bridge is built of reinforced concrete. Telford's original structure was of wrought-iron, but it was not strong enough for the great munitions traffic from Gretna during the First World War, and had to be replaced. A section of the original Metal Bridge is kept in the gardens of Tullie House Museum in Carlisle, and on it you will find the date, 1820.

The fords over the Esk in the region of the Metal Bridge have been one of the two key strategic points of the main Solway river systems. This Esk is the more northerly of the two major rivers, and although its home-stretch is now in England, it was for many years the frontier between England and Scotland, a distinction which moved to the Sark in 1552. The other key to the strategy of the Solway is the ford, long-bridged, over the more southerly river, the Eden. This vital crossing is guarded by Carlisle, which acts as the pivot of the whole region. The Eden bridge is the master-key to the whole system of Solway fords. It is still—see photograph number 15—the first road bridge across the river inland from the estuary, but the traveller who uses it must not object to going through Carlisle. In the past, thieves, armies, raiders and smugglers *have* objected, and have chosen to take their risks in the waters. Secondly, the journey from shore to shore via Carlisle is patently too round-about for the busy traveller. Whereas today his laziness and his car allow him to do it more rapidly than in the Middle Ages, his predecessor chose a route across river or estuary, depending on his destination, and walked or rode when the tide was low. Once only in its history has the modern traveller been able to take the short cut across Solway without facing the dangers of the waves. There was a railway viaduct from Bowness to Annan between the years 1869 and 1934. It became unsafe, and its repair not economically worth while, so it was pulled down. The embankments remain, as you will see from photograph number 20 in the second section of illustrations.

Eden and Esk are partners in the route between north and south. Both must be crossed; they are fairly close together, and are both tidal for some miles inland. Timing is essential, but not too difficult except under conditions of pursuit and retreat. *Expert* timing would no doubt be relied upon to put a barrier of water between pursuer and pursued. Three examples of this will demonstrate possible situations. Cattle-raiding is a fairly slow business, and while the beasts were being prodded across the ford at the hour after ebb that left a slight margin of safety, the more militant thieves could remain as a rear-guard to cover the crossing, trusting for their escape to the swimming ability of their horses over a river rapidly becoming dangerous. Or consider a plundering army whose retreat had been delayed by unforeseen action; they would be tempted to brave the torrent rather than the pursuing sword. Sometimes they would be lucky, but in 1216 almost two thousand Scots were drowned in such a retreat over the Eden. In more recent years, a more domestic picture enlivens the river banks, and one can imagine a beautiful daughter and brand new, if not approved, son-in-law rejoicing on the north bank of the Esk, while father's impatient coach was held up on the south by the flood. It is little wonder that out of all Scotland where clandestine marriages were possible, only Gretna has achieved lasting fame.

So far I have been writing generally about the fords, and it is time to be specific, for there were several, each with name, character and history. Taking the rivers first, Eden winds for miles from Carlisle to the estuary, and a great choice of crossing-places was offered. Quite near the city was the Etterby wath, near the site of the bridge that carried the Roman Wall. (The exact position of the wall-crossing was a mystery until tooled masonry was discovered as recently as 1953 during work on the river banks.) The next two Eden fords that have made a mark on history are those named after Grinsdale, south of the river, and Cargo to the north. In my mind I link them together and associate both with the Jacobites. The Old Pretender's army failed to cross at either of these in the rising of 1715, and had to trudge the banks inland for many miles. Prince Charles Edward's army which followed thirty years later was more successful, and splitting, crossed at Cargo, Grinsdale and Rockcliffe further west before re-forming to assail the city. There is an ironic parallel between the two invasions. The first went inland almost to Brampton before it could cross; the second retired to Brampton, where the Bonnie Prince received the surrender of Carlisle. Both were finally unsuccessful.

These fords are historically known as waths, a word which has been spelt in various ways, according to both Old English and Old Norse antecedents (wæth or vath), and as we move westwards, as

Miss Fiennes did along the pleasant Eden banks, we come to three famous waths bunched close together at the most convenient point on the track from the south shore of the Solway to the north. Two of these are Rockcliffe wath, used as I have said by the Jacobites, and the Stonewath, a few hundred yards to the west (sometimes called Stonywath, an accurate term for those with tender feet). A quarter of a mile further to the west, opposite Old Sandsfield, is the most famous of this trio of fords—the Peatwath. The Scots I mentioned earlier met their deaths herein. Edward I's army frequently used it, and his coins have been found along its approaches, mainly on the southern side; in fact, the camp that saw his death was but a short stroll to the south-west of Sandsfield and there you will find his monument.

All these groups, having crossed the Eden, would find one more river, the Esk, an equally difficult obstacle. Esk crossings were kept within a limited stretch close to the estuary in order to avoid two crossings. The River Lyne joins the Esk about a mile from the beginning of the medieval estuary, and somewhere along this mile was the greatest crossing of them all. This was the Sulwath, the muddy ford. Unhappily, we do not know exactly where it was; but because of this, the search for the early Sulwath has provided an intriguing problem for scholars. To two of these scholars in particular I must acknowledge my debts, as I have used their information and I travel some way with them in their respective arguments. One is W. T. McIntire, whose work is to be found in the *Transactions of the Cumberland and Westmorland Antiquarian and Archæological Society*, and the other, George Neilson, in whose scholarly book, *Annals of the Solway Until 1307*, you will find sources, maps and arguments on these and many other subjects.

Let me begin with my conclusion. The name of the Solway Firth comes from a ford, the Sulwath, across the River Esk. This conclusion was not always accepted, although it generally is today. Camden, in Holland's 1610 edition, says the Solway is a fordable arm of the sea at low waters called after a village by the mouth of the Nith. I think he was wrong, as no one has ever traced this village, and one suspects a careless correspondent. At one stage in my own wanderings, I was told of a tiny district still called Sulwath, but this red herring appeared to be standing on its head. The "district" was a house, and the house had been

named after the historic ford, not vice versa. Another view can
be heard today that relates Solway with Silloth; this I fear takes
things too far, as wordmongers, unscholarly variety, often tend
to do. Silloth was the sea-lath, the barn on the coast, of Holm
Cultram Abbey. Although no village, Solway, has been discovered, the earliest Solway (in the thirteenth and fourteenth
centuries) was definitely a specific place and not a huge estuary.
People arranged to meet there, as when King Reginald of the
Isles was escorted into England. Court cases were tried there, and
someone bought the right to collect the tolls *at* Solway. There are
many more indications besides these brief ones from which
Neilson and others have argued inescapably that Solway was a
point on the Esk. In one of the law cases mentioning Solway,
cattle were tested by swimming across the Esk; the ford toll I
have mentioned was linked to land between Esk and Arthuret. The
branches of argument dovetail together so easily that there is no
doubt that the ford across the Esk was the Sulwath, and that it has
given its name, modernised as Solway, to the greater stretch of
water. Neilson has gone further by pointing out that old maps
show that the mouth of Esk would be somewhere near where
Metal Bridge is today. He pointed out that in, say, 1400, the long
promontory known as Rockcliffe Marsh did not exist. About
three miles of land has grown in the intervening years. This
growth of marshland can easily be estimated by a comparison of
the modern map with older ones. There is a good selection in
the *Annals*, and others can be seen in Camden, hanging on the
walls inside Carlisle Castle and elsewhere. I have tried to indicate
on the map at the end of this book, from a study of such sources,
three successive stages in the development of this part of the coast,
and the present One-Inch Ordnance map shows an embankment which can be followed on the ground curving seawards
from Castletown and back in a semicircle to Metal Bridge, which
is indicative of one stage in the marsh growth. I am going to
suggest that the argument could be taken a step further. You will
remember that the ford taken by Celia Fiennes was within sight
of the mouth of the Esk. She did not name the ford, and it is only
in the last two centuries that the name Greenbed, alternatively
called Willie o' the Boats, has become popular. I suggest that
about the time of Miss Fiennes the name Greenbed was taking
the place of the name Sulwath for one and the same place. To my

mind what has happened is that as the name Sulwath or Solway gradually extended to the whole estuary, the alternative name for the ford would be used more and more to avoid confusion. There is another and better-known case of the name of a ford spreading to a larger inlet, for King John's wath has, with the passage of years, become the entire Wash.

Before leaving this subject I ought to mention that I have seen in recent books the Sulwath equated with a ford over the Sark. There is only one incidental point to support this, and at least two big ones against it. Historically, the minor ford over the Sark has been known as the Loan wath. Secondly, I doubt if the Sark has ever in historic times been a big enough river to merit an important crossing. A mention of both Sark and Sulwath separately —which to my mind clears this issue—was made in 1448. At the great Battle of the Sark many of the Percies who had been defeated by the Douglases were drowned *in retreat* over the Sulwath. The one argument that may but does not necessarily associate Sulwath with a Sark mouth ford brings in one of the most historic, if least beautiful, stones of the Solway. A few yards to the west of the Sark mouth, standing on older and slightly higher ground than most of the marsh hereabouts, is the Lochmabenstane. In historic times this stone gained fame as a meeting-place of the Wardens, Scottish and English, of the opposing West Marches. Here the trials were held on days of truce, and here decisions were made, sometimes affecting the whole troubled border. Neilson equated, I think sensibly, the Lochmabenstane with the visible terminus of the great Sulwath. To me it seems no difficulty that the stone stands not on the banks of the Esk. In the medieval landscape, the stone would be quite visible to parties crossing Eskmouth, and the further distance past the mouth of the Sark would be a negligible step forgotten in the excitement of the great meeting between two nations.

The Lochmabenstane is not only historic, it is *prehistoric*. I see no reason to doubt the scrupulous writers of the new *Statistical Account of Dumfriesshire* when they described a dozen or more stones, of which Lochmaben was the greatest, standing as part of a circle. Only one other is now left—half-hidden, by the gate—but in 1840, stone circles were not protected by a ministry, and more than one farmer has followed the example of the Gretna landowner and broken or buried or otherwise removed parts of an ancient monument. I hasten to add that the present owner of Old Gretna farm, where the stone may be found, is rightfully proud of this ancient monument.

Lochmabenstane was first Clochmaben, and there are so many suggestions as to the origin of this name that your guess is as good as mine. Neilson quotes Cloch, a stone, and Mabain, a cluster from the Old Gaelic dictionary. Arthurian legends give Mabon as one of the Knights (and there is much to suggest that Arthur fought hereabouts). The British inhabitants of Roman Solway worshipped the god Maponus, sometimes called Mabon, equated with Apollo, and altars to this god have been found at several settlements in the vicinity; but, whatever the origin of the name, the circle of which our stone is a remnant saw worship in the Bronze Age, before any of these other heroes were heard of.

So far I have only discussed the river crossings, but crossings on foot were also made over the wide sweep of the estuary. A certain amount of practical experience has led me to believe that protracted estuary crossings may be safer than short dashes across a swollen river-channel; and, in fact, when I have been in doubt in other places, I have often walked down bank to the delta, formed when the river is slowed down by its impact with greater waters, and there found a longer and colder but less hazardous track. In the Solway, as the map will show, an estuary crossing could save hours of winding land-travel. The most dramatic crossing is from Bowness to Annan Waterfoot, foreshadowing by centuries the route of the viaduct. The English called it the Bowness wath; and, of course, it is the Annan wath to Scotsmen. This wath, too, is giving its name to a greater part of the estuary and I note the present edition of the One-Inch map of the Ordnance Survey has the words "Bowness Wath" writ large *along* the deep channel in the middle of the Solway. A fine wath, starting, traversing and finishing in deep water! Bowness wath found fame during the campaigns of Wallace and Edward I, not merely because the army used it, but also because of the adventures of a certain peacemaker. Robert of Winchelsea, Archbishop of Canterbury, was perhaps not a willing peacemaker. His instructions and his letter ordering Edward to stop the war came direct from the Pope, and Pope Boniface VIII's peacemaking was not altogether altruistic. Edward was in Scotland and gave no help to Robert. He probably guessed the contents of the letter. But the

Archbishop persisted, and for the first time in history, and almost certainly the last, an Archbishop of Canterbury forded these wet and shining sands. His own words give a vivid description of his trials.

"... I lurked in certain secret places near the sea, which divides England from Galloway, and taking the opportunity of the ebb of the tide, under the guidance of those who had a perfect knowledge where to cross, I made the passage in the course of four tides, with the horses and their trappings, there being great danger in entering and departing, not more by reason of the depth of the water than by reason of the shore and the quicksands."

I think that the Archbishop's four tides would be better understood if more freely translated as four *channels*. The reckless wanderer should note an illustrious precedent for obtaining guides.

Edward's army was already retiring, not having been able to make effective contact with the enemy. His stalling answer to the Archbishop could therefore be made without inconvenience. The war went on in later years.

It is interesting to plot Edward's return route. On 30th August he was at Dornock; on the 1st September at Drumburgh (pronounced Drumbruff). Dornock is a little Scottish village a few miles east of Annan, and Drumburgh, equally small, lies east of Bowness on the English side. In other words, Edward used the second favourite ford of the estuary, the Sandywath. The English end of this wath is sometimes given as Sandsfield, on the south bank of the Eden. This would make a much longer ford, and if a mistake has not been made in the study of sources, I suggest that this route was rarely used. A later raid found Dornock–Drumburgh useful for retreat. Thomas Dacre's party, plunder-laden in 1332, were evidently hoping for a quiet crossing of the Sandywath from Dornock when they were surprised near the beach by the Scots and had to fight their way out. Perhaps the modern name, Battle Hill, is the site of this Battle of Dornock, and nearby Swordwell tells its own gory story. This same ford may have seen a desperate escape by Edward III's puppet, Edward Balliol, as on an unsaddled horse he galloped in haste from Annan Castle across the sands of Solway to his master's territory; but I cannot find details of his exact crossing-place. He probably didn't even notice.

Sometimes these estuary waths cannot be sited exactly from historic sources, but I can personally understand how errors arise and locations vary. It is all right for the historian in his study to talk of a crossing from Annan to Bowness, but in the first place, Annan is a mile up an estuary with a choice of short-cuts over-land; and in the second place, one does not walk on a line chalked across the sands. We do not know what the bottom sand was like, and where the channels were in 1300 (except that Robert of Winchelsea passed through four of them), but I do know that if the steps in front and to the left tend to lead into deeper water, on to softer sand or into a faster swirl, then one goes to the right. It is worth saying again that the Solway changes daily, and as much as the man makes his route, so the route tells him where to make it.

The nicest story of the Solway crossings is one that belongs to the days of raid and counter-raid; and it is a story that has not yet ended. On one of the raids from Scotland, the bells of Bowness church were not only stolen but dropped in the middle of the estuary. I think the pursuers must have been catching up. The English of course regarded this as a challenge, and you will see in the porch of a little church at Bowness-on-Solway two ancient bells, one dated 1612. They are said to come, one from Dornock, and one from Middlebie, a nearby Scottish parish, signifying successful revenge. When I first heard this story, I thought with suspicion "Another pleasant legend"; and then I saw the bells and finally I heard how the minister of Dornock makes it a duty to write to Bowness for the return of the bells whenever a new rector is appointed. I rather envy the English vicar who can write back, saying "Certainly—when ours come back from the sea."

There is a later edition of this legend, which describes how the English bells can be heard ringing over the water from their home "the Bell Pool" in mid-channel in the quiet of evening. I suspect that this is pure legend. I have crossed this ford both ways and heard wonderful sounds of night in the waters, but no bells—yet.

CHAPTER II

SOLID FOUNDATIONS

THE shores of Britain act as a display case for the rocks and soils of the island, setting them off against the waves that help to give them shape. The Solway shore is itself a microcosm of coastal scenery descending along both shores from high cliffs thrusting towards Ireland to low mysterious flats and marshes in the east where the fresh water joins the salt. I used to neglect the low coasts, having a passion for cliffs, half-cousins to beloved hills, but the Solway has taught me much since then. Although I shall always enjoy the exhilarating wind on high cliff-tops, there is a peace and beauty and a world of subtlety about the low shores far from the hills.

All grades and textures are classified as rock by the geologists, and they are all part of the same eternal process. The harder and more solid rock usually represents the earlier phases of geological history, and it is with this foundation structure that I shall begin my brief survey.

Solid rock has practical and symbolic contacts with life at many points. The climber has a private and vividly remembered world where the texture of rock becomes intimate and important. Rock too forms the world of the miner and quarryman who, like climbers, often make good amateur geologists. Climbers, miners, quarrymen and geologists all have associations around the Solway which I could sum up by telling how the best climber I have ever partnered began his working life as a miner under the Solway in Risehow pit and later became a geologist. A more symbolic analysis has been provided by Norman Nicholson from his home near the Solway, who based his fine religious drama on the stone of cliff and mountain and called it *Look to the Rock*.

The archæologist and the historian also look to the rock. The story of man, his religion and art, would be so often lost were it not for the clues of the megalithic tomb, the carved altar and the sculptured cross, all stones which grow from the ground like living rock. The Lochmabenstane, to me most symbolic of the history of the Solway, is a perpetual reminder of the link between the granite of geology, the transportive power of the ice, the hardly understood religion of the Bronze Age, the frontier struggles between English and Scots and the thoughtlessness of a generation of farmers who destroyed its companions. When man alters scenery, he carves the rock into stone. His fields are limited by it, and when his home is built of local rock it fits without strain into the landscape as do the New Red Sandstone towns of Solway mellow in the evening light. On his less material levels, man finds stone in which to worship in our abbeys and cathedrals, and worshipping stone achieves its truest glory in the carved sandstone of Ruthwell Cross, near Solway's northern shore.

Rock is seldom isolated, even when natural. It is clothed with soil, particular plants adorn it, and especially in Solway, it is the home of birds, but in long ages past, when the oldest rock was born, there was no life. We tend to find the geologist's millions of years hard to comprehend, but when once the dynamics of change are seen in present action, the process leading to the modern scene can be imagined whole. In few places in Britain is it easier to see this change taking place than along the coast. When geologists talk of eras, enormous and long past, when great seas covered our region, and silt and sand from the now vanished continent in the north-west poured into them to build the rocks on which today we stand, I like to think that this is just the same process, with a variation in size and time, as now when silt blocks Kirkcudbright's Dee, and still jams tight the gates of Senhouse dock at Maryport.

The whole process is but an extension of the inevitable movement which takes soil from slopes of the world eventually to the sea. Whilst India's great rivers each second carry tons of material to build some future Himalayas, a raindrop on the slope of Eden bank spurts grains of dirt which drop, gravity-pulled, further down towards the river. The wind-churned waters of the Nith and the Esk, swirling soupy with mud, are always giving a little of their burden to the plants at the water's edge so that, when they are gone, the marsh of Rockcliffe or Glencaple merse are a little bigger than they were before. The same rivers can steal from the land, taking as well as giving, perhaps with compensatory action. Over six centuries the sea has given up hundreds of acres of land in Moricambe (the "Bay" is redundant as in Lancashire's greater inlet) and in parts continues to do so. Elsewhere in the same bay, land has been lost to a lesser extent but measurable even in present lifetimes.

The geologists divide their rock into hundreds of different types, and usually give them dreadful names. I shall have to use some of their names, but first I will try to simplify the subject for the non-technical. In very general terms, the sightseer need only think of three kinds of rock: sedimentary, igneous and metamorphic. Most sandstones and limestones are formed from sea-bottom sediments laid like the dregs of an inferior beer. Some limestone sediments of shell and skeleton are already often in the water, while the sands and muds continuously wash down from the solid land. Sandstone can also be dry-laid by wind, and one of Solway's rocks is formed in this way. Of the other two kinds of rocks, the igneous can never be forgotten here, for Criffell watches over the Solway as an intruder from a past volcanic age. These igneous rocks spoil the regularity of the sedimentary layers by thrusting through, powerful and molten, from just under the earth's shallow crust where the hottest (radio-active) rock abounds. Finding weaknesses, they spread, sliding as sills between sediments or bulging as granite masses beneath the shallow covering of the surface rocks; or they spurt through all above them, falling as ashes through the air, and pouring as lavas where fast air-cooling makes them smooth and compact compared with granite's slow-cooled crystals.

The third type of rock is a bastard kind. Hot igneous rocks and the upheaval that accompanies their eruptions alter (or metamorphise, as the books say) the rocks around them. Miles of rocks are compressed, sometimes into complex shapes like the bellows of a concertina. These you can see in the cliffs or imagine under the landscape of Wigtown and Kirkcudbright. Sometimes heat or pressure, or both, squeezes them into slates, which in Cumberland, south of the Solway, have a worldwide fame for roofing. At other times such action may change a sedate limestone into a glamorous marble. Veins and arteries of metals, precious or useful, come into being at these times of crustal revolution, and placid sediments that have long slept horizontally may be twisted and turned, cracked and faulted.

This geologist's term "faulted" describes the curse of the collier.

The Solway coalfield has more than its share of faults. Geologists and planners consult together and drill their bores until the precious dust is found. Then capital is invested, great roads are blasted under the land as big as an Underground tunnel, and for a similar purpose. Rails are laid, conveyor belts are hitched and locomotives run, squat and heavy, between the muddy paths. Men's helmet-lamps fight the acrid fog of explosions swept by the ventilation winds, and the mechanical cutter slices into the seam like cheese, filling air and pores with more black dust. All this goes on to win our coal, but plans go wrong in Cumberland, and quite suddenly stone, or "metal" as they call it, blocks the way. A crack and a slide in past ages—for that is all a fault is—and who knows whether the seam continues fifty fathoms up or fifty fathoms down, as the Main Band does at Solway pit? In these last few years they have found Main Band several times, only to lose it again in the contortions of the earth. West Cumberland coal-seams are thick, compared to some, although the miners do not always admit it, but the coal is difficult to work. The faults are not always fifty fathoms, but there are far too many of them.

The several thousand million years of the earth's history are difficult to comprehend, but by a certain slightly artificial knack, one sees them whole as a succession of more or less clear-cut periods, the later ones topping the earlier, if undisturbed, and identifiable not only in themselves and by position, but through the fossils they contain. What we may call the revolutionary periods, when the sedimentaries were tormented and the volcanics surged, seem to have occurred with a natural rhythm, five or six with an interval of about two hundred and fifty million years between each. The earlier ones we can ignore, but the last but two, called the Caledonian, made the foundations of Lake District and Solway and saw Criffell and Skiddaw rising to watch each other across the new-formed hollow, later to be our firth. The Tertiary period saw the last or Alpine upheaval which completed the uplifting of the Lake District, and perhaps the shaping of the Solway apart from the trimming of the surface deposits.

Over the long aeons this pulse of the earth might be also associated with Ice Ages. There have been several of these ages, but only the last (called Pleistocene) concerns us. It probably lasted more than half a million years, and within itself had smaller throbs of warmth and cold, of melting and spreading of great ice sheets. Ice too lays down sediments—*dumps* would be a better word. On the English side of Solway we find that scrapings from the hills and valleys of the Lake District alternate with those from Scottish lowlands and clothe the bones of the bare rocks beneath our feet. English and Scottish ice anticipated man, and fought its battles over the estuary before it disappeared finally from our islands. Foreign stones in unexpected places, erratics, show the pattern of attack and the sway and sweeps of victory.

Starting at the beginning, we can dismiss the first two-thirds of the history of the earth by calling it Pre-Cambrian. There are Pre-Cambrian rocks in the north-west of Scotland and the Midlands of England, but nowhere near the Solway, and likewise, we have none of the rocks of the Cambrian period which followed. The story of the next two periods does concern us. These are called Ordovician and Silurian, and their old hard rocks are typical of the Highland zone. Named after two Welsh tribes, these rocks should serve to remind all Solway Celts of their true and ancient ancestry. Laid in a great sea that crossed where now is Solway, a close examination of the rocks tells the detective geologist the fortunes of this trough which buckled and squirmed in ages following. English Solway has neither of these rocks, though the slates of Skiddaw, Ordovician in age, overhang the Solway plain, and many lowland dwellers spend their week-ends on Gable in the sight and feel of the Borrowdale Volcanic Series.

The fact that one side of Solway only, the Scottish shore, is made of these old hard rocks gives a great contrast in landscape, and has in secondary ways helped to make differences between the lives of those who look south over this water and those who look north. The low plain, the gently sweeping bays on the English side give an atmosphere quite different from that of the intricate outline of the Scottish inlets with their myriads of hidden coves and fringing islands. Rough Firth, typical of the northern shore and shown on the photograph facing page 70, has a history of smuggling as well as a beauty of scene that has no equal across the water.

In south-west Scotland, both Ordovician and Silurian were strained and stretched, pleated and bent, soon after they were laid. More than sixty synclines and anticlines have been counted within a mile close to the Isles of Fleet. The rock of the Rhinns of Galloway, the Machers and the Kirkcudbright lowlands with their ragged coasts and islands show faces of Silurian rock for mile upon grey mile. Whilst this rock is of the sub-type called Llandovery, there is a later band of Silurian called Wenlock at Burrow Head, west of Wigtown Bay, fringing the shores of Kirkcudbright Bay and appearing eastwards to the Nith in intermittent stretches. Where it runs along the Colvend shore close to Criffell granite, the rock was much altered by its igneous neighbours.

The upheaval we call Caledonian was beginning in the Silurian period, but one or two volcanics in south-west Scotland sometimes associated with Silurian folding may be much earlier—in fact Pre-Cambrian. They may form part of the bed over which the Silurian was wrinkled like a pushed tablecloth. However, the peak of the upheaval was in the next period, and because of the climatic changes it inaugurated, it caused the world to be a very different place.

This geological period, more than three hundred million years ago, is called Old Red Sandstone. In sections of this rock, in Solway tiny and only to be traced in the Kirkbean district, we see evidence of great arid deserts in the dry sparkle of its grains. An alternative name is Devonian, and this rock is best seen in south-west Britain. In the first part of this period came the intrusive granites of Skiddaw on the south, and Cairnsmore of Fleet, Loch Dee and especially Criffell on the north of Solway, thrusting through the Silurian strata, and in cutting and changing it, providing the evidence of their age. They were called intrusive because at this stage they were still encompassed by some surface strata. The Criffell-Dalbeattie mass is perhaps sixteen miles by six, and over two thousand feet high, and the granite is coarse-grained, classified Tonalite for the specialist. It brought an industry to Dalbeattie, and has provided strength for lighthouses the world over, beauty for London's embankment, and respectability for banks and civic halls. If *you* want to handle it, West Cumbrians, look on your beaches, where the ice dumped enormous blocks, and in your walls, especially round Crosby, where the farmers carried it. Speaking of walls, what a magnificent granite wall with blocks up to five feet tall encircles Sweetheart Abbey!

During the second part of the Old Red period, the continued upheaval, together with enormous denudation, resulted in the

geography that shows the beginnings of a Solway Firth. A broad
depression was outlined across mid-Britain from north-east to
south-west, from the North Sea to the Irish Sea. The western
section of this persistent pattern has remained throughout many
changes as the basis of the Solway Firth, while to the north-east
its lines are mirrored in the Merse of Berwickshire.

Shallow lagoons in this embryo Solway formed the resting-
place for the next depositions of sedimentary rocks that go under
the general name of Carboniferous. What a general name this is!
The Carboniferous lasted for some fifty million years during
which limestones, sandstones, coals and grits were laid down
under varying conditions of erosion and in varying depths of sea.
First came Lower Carboniferous, of course, and a strange thing
about Solway is that while most of the Lower Carboniferous in
Britain is mountain limestone (which I always link with ramblers'
scenery from Cheddar Gorge to Pennine pot-holes) most of our
Lower Carboniferous comes within the sandstone series. It was
laid in these lagoons, whilst from Durham to Cumberland and
through to the Isle of Man there was still a peninsula waiting to
be submerged. This Lower Carboniferous fringes the Solway
between the Nith and Kirkcudbright Bay. There is a good
patch near Arbigland and it is well exposed around Southerness,
where Mr Cash took photograph number 10 which shows its
appearance when waveworn. From Barlocco Bay to Abbey
Burnfoot are interesting samples, some of them conglomerates,
which, as they contain pebbles of Criffell granite, show that Criffell
was already exposed and eroded in Carboniferous times. East of
Port Mary Bay the conglomerates are cut by veins of barytes.
But by far the most fascinating of these Lower Carboniferous
rocks is a limestone group around Arbigland Bay which is rich
in beautifully preserved fossil corals. There is a fine example south
of Carsethorn. Lower Carboniferous limestone near the English
Solway is less extensive and less picturesque but it is the chief
source of hæmatite, which, being non-phosphoric, is the best iron
ore in the British Isles. The ore belt lies inland from Solway
around Cleator Moor.

With the Carboniferous, Solway has become united once
again, and we find coal measures as well as limestones on both
sides of the estuary. Coal measures do not always contain coal,
otherwise there might be a pit at Gretna where the barren

measures have been found by boring. There is coal in south-west Scotland, however, and not far from Solway. The Canonbie coal measures are up to three thousand feet thick, and although most of this is non-productive, seams up to five feet thick (of which the Main Coal is the best) have been found in the past, and there are signs that Canonbie coal will soon be dug again, for the Coal Board are (in 1954) doing further exploration and a tall derrick now stands by the main Langholm road. The detailed study of coal measures shows to the expert how the seas and lagoons shallowed into swamps of luxurious vegetation, for coal is merely the end product of a recognised family tree (here somewhat over-simplified).

From the decay of swampy vegetation, through the ageing and compression of peat, past soft brown coal which is also called lignite, it goes on through the stuff burnt in grates, and changes finally to the fashionable anthracite. If it is difficult to think of a tropical lagoon where Workington now stands, remember the coral island at Arbigland, and stretch the imagination further to roof all Cumberland with coal measures now long eroded and gone.

After the tropical lagoons came great rivers spreading deltas of tiny pebbles in huge heaps that were later to be consolidated into wedges of millstone grit, still Carboniferous, and a rock of great personality as Lancashire and Yorkshire know. None is left in Solway, though geologists have doubts about one or two sections on the English side which we can ignore in a general survey. The fact that millstone grit normally follows immediately on coal has in other districts given rise to its wistful name of "Farewell" rock—the farewell being to coal. Once he has struck the millstone grit, the miner knows he has "had it".

The rocks called Permian are sometimes classified as the last of the old hard rocks, and indeed may be taken as the dividing line between the regions of Highland and Lowland Britain, a division I shall often stress. In character and personality, however, the Permian is quite a young rock. It is usually a pale red sandstone, though a streak of magnesium limestone of Permian age runs across Britain and a narrow band can be seen in undistinguished cliffs south of Whitehaven in Saltom Bay. Permian sandstone often looks like its successor, Triassic sandstone. Both suggest a hot, dry land, and they used to be grouped together as the New

Red Sandstone. Many learned papers embodying fine practical and theoretical work have sought the dividing line between the two in Cumberland with doubtful results. The old title of the New Red for both seems wisest here to an amateur like myself. However, the New Red again unites the Solway. On the Scottish side, there is little doubt about the separation of Permian and Triassic, for the Permian, which lies in the upper part of Annandale and most of the lower basin of the Nith, is a true relation of that English Permian which leads past, and builds, Penrith Beacon, although they may have been laid in separate basins. This Permian rock was laid by wind. Its fragments of highly polished rounded quartz grains are very similar to those now being formed on a modern desert by the action of wind on sands and pebbles. The bedding of the strata, too, is similar to that found in a modern sand-dune (the geological term is false-bedding). To complete the tie-up with known Permian rocks, you will find examples in the Observatory Museum, Dumfries, of this sandstone still bearing fossilised reptilean footprints of Permian age which can be paralleled in Tullie House, Carlisle's museum.

The Triassic of the Solway is much like the Permian. At its most obvious, you can see it at St Bees Head, ribbed against the Irish Sea, mottled white with droppings and beautiful in summer crowned with a wreath of pink Armeria. At its most gentle, you can see it in the smooth curves of low weathered outcrops on the beach north of Maryport where the local people go to swim. There are varieties of Triassic sandstone distinguished by names which for some odd reason often amuse. These are Bunter and Keuper. Keuper—subnamed Stanwix Shales—reaches from Allonby Bay to Carlisle, and outside it is a ring of Bunter from Maryport round the head of the Solway almost as far as Annan. This ring has an offshoot up the Eden Valley and the St Bees sandstone is Bunter too.

You can see both of these red rocks, shaped into buildings by the hand of man, in every town and village from Annan to Carlisle, then west to St Bees. The Romans used them for their altars and knew how to choose and handle the rock. Their inscriptions after eighteen hundred years are still plainly readable, and this cannot be said of all the carved red sandstone of Carlisle Cathedral. Stone must be chosen with care and handled with love. Sir Christopher Wren let his blocks of limestone lie for years to dry and mellow before he used them in St Paul's. The micro-fragments of this Trias are sharp and angular, and the rock was laid in water that must have submerged the Permian deserts. It is quarried on both sides of the Solway, and there is a direct continuity between Annan and Maryport.

Coal lies under the New Red off Maryport and coal and coal measures lie under the New Red between Annan and Canonbie. This New Red stretches under the Solway, and coal is now mined up to two miles under the sea, a distance governed by ventilation and transport, especially the former. Is there a possibility that, should new techniques permit it, a new vast reservoir of coal could be mined from pits sited in the middle of the estuary, or outside the known limits of the coalfield? The short answer to this question, which has fascinated many and which has great economic importance, is that no one knows. Coal-seams sometimes continue, sometimes they are lost by faulting, as we have already seen, and sometimes they just die out. I have not the space to go into detail, but for those local readers who may be interested in this problem, I would recommend *The Geology of the Carlisle, Silloth and Longtown District* (1926), published by H.M. Stationery Office, Chapter VII of which provides a good summary of the problem and gives detailed references since 1859.

At the end of the Triassic submergence, a sea called Rhætic flooded the district and probably allowed an extensive settlement of younger rocks which themselves may have been followed by an even younger series such as one finds in the true Lowland zone of south-east England. However, the Tertiary earth movements intervened and were accompanied by great denudation. Nothing is left of these later rocks but, as a brief reminder, a little plateau of Lias about Great Orton to the west of Carlisle.

The drainage pattern of south-west Scotland probably originated on this now lost surface. The Cree, Ken-Dee system and Nith seem to belong to a past geography rather than the present one. They trench the mountains in a way that suggests that from early higher sources in the Western Islands they have stuck to their original directions, cutting the later-moulded southern uplands, rather than being diverted. The fact that the Solway bays tend to decrease in size from west to east—Luce (main river now gone but valley obvious), Wigtown, Kirkcudbright, Nith—suggests that the original (Tertiary) landscape was higher towards the west than it is today. The Tertiary earth movements, spectacular only in the south of England, raised the Lake District into more or less its present form, and finished the shaping of the Solway basin apart from the dressing of the Ice Age and more recent cover. There is just a faint trace of the vulcanism associated with Tertiary earth movements in our region. Many dykes, vertical walls of igneous rock, sweep like curved spokes from the Island of Mull, and one of these, stronger and longer than the rest, crosses the Solway from the Nith to Moricambe and eventually reappears to continue its curving travels as the Cleveland dyke of Yorkshire. It does not affect the scenery, but is mentioned purely for geological interest.

With the Lias, we leave what the layman would call rock, for we have nothing younger in Solway except soil and sand, silt and clay. On the skeleton of solid rock the Ice Age and the work of waves and weather, of rivers and of man laid a mantle for landscape. If this mantle did not exist, the Solway coast, like many other parts of Britain, would have a very different appearance, especially around the head of the estuary and for some miles inland from the shore on the English side. In the neighbourhood of Abbeytown there is nearly a hundred and eighty feet in depth of this superficial layer, and over the coastal district generally the depth of this cover, mostly of sands and clays, varies from ten to three hundred feet. If it were not there, the sea would be.

Most of the mantle is the rubbish of the Ice Age. Ice has a double action, take and give. It scrapes and carries material from the hills and high valleys, carving the mountain scenery as it goes. Peaks, corries, lochs and lakes in the Lake District to the south, and in the uplands of Dumfriesshire and Galloway to the north, were robbed to make the plain of Solway. Ice cannot carry for ever; it eventually melts and dumps its debris in assorted heaps and layers on the lowlands. The main ice-laid mass is known as "till" or boulder-clay. Sometimes it has no boulders, but here they are found too often for farmers' tools, and when you see them sticking out from the sides of pits or cuttings, you can easily tell that dumping was their means of formation for in general the boulders have been neither smoothed nor sorted into sizes by the action of water.

I have said that there were several cold periods interspersed with warm within the last Ice Age. On the Continent four, perhaps five, can be distinguished with some certainty, and in parts of England, especially the south-east, a tremendous amount of work has gone far towards proving a similar separation of these main stages, and they can be correlated with the continental scheme. As far as Solway is concerned, the second half of the Ice Age has hidden or removed traces of the first half, and the only suspicions of advances one and two are in doubtful fragments of ancient, weathered boulder clay that were discovered in the upper Caldew valley.

The *third* glaciation of the east of Britain is therefore probably the one represented by the *first* of the boulder clays in the Solway. This boulder clay represents the dumping of debris carried far by powerful expansion of a great ice flow, which even took its fragments past the Solway and up the Eden Valley to Stainmoor, whence the Romans came later, and through the Tyne gap to the east where the Romans built their Wall. This ice came from south-west Scotland, and left its boulders of Criffell granite like cairns to mark its route. The text-books call it "the Early Scottish glaciation". Its retreat is marked in the valley of the Eden by sands and gravels and lake-laid clays. It was followed by the "Main Glaciation", equivalent to the fourth in eastern England.

The "Main Glaciation" saw Lake District ice at its maximum extent meeting the threat from Scotland. The two ice barriers met about the Solway. Both were deflected right and left; the Scottish ice field split, possibly about Criffell, and one flank was forced east to the Tyne, and the other west, where it continued down the Irish Sea. The English ice suffered in a similar way; its eastern wing joined Scottish ice to sweep across Carlisle, and its western wing was forced to travel not only across the Solway plain, but further round in a complete half-circle to join the Scottish flow along the coast of Cumberland and accompany it south down the Irish Sea. This great advance ended with the waning of the ice sheets and the usual deposits of sand and gravel were left by the melt waters, which themselves cut overflow channels from ice-dammed lakes. One of these lakes was Lake Carlisle, and its shores have been traced by careful field work. Other lakes were to the south-west, and I must mention one overflow channel, for the road that takes you into Whitehaven from

the north passes through it at the top of Bransty Hill. This inter-
glacial period seems to have been long and exceptionally warm,
for between the boulder clay of the "Main Glaciation" and that
of the one which was to follow, have been found fragments
of peat, implying settled warm conditions, in a section near
St Bees.

Scottish ice seems to have had the last word. The last cold
period is marked by the "Scottish Re-advance", which, although
not very powerful, managed to lay another covering of boulder
clay on the English Solway plain as far as the foothills of the Lake
District. In recent years, an arctic type of crustacean has been
found in Lake Ennerdale; its ancestors probably owed their
existence to the Scottish Re-advance. The clays of the last two
glaciations are known in the books and technical papers as the
Lower and Upper Boulder Clays, and are either greyish or
reddish, depending upon whether they have been derived mainly
from the coal measures or from Triassic sandstone. Erratics found
in both the types of clay provide a record of the source and the
path of the ice.

On the surface of the main mass of boulder clay are smaller
legacies from the melting of the ice. There are so many around
Solway that books could be filled with descriptions. I shall content myself with a few generalisations and examples. Melting ice
and its associated water laid down formations in many and strange
shapes. Geologists have studied, sorted and classified them and
given them odd-sounding names. Eskers, for example, still mark
our landscape. They were created as melting caused the front or
snout of the ice to retreat. Sand and gravel carried by water
through the internal caverns of the glacier were left stringing
behind in long, writhing heaps. Today they exist all over our
district, often avoided by farmers and crowned by clumps of
trees. There is one opposite my front door, and others stretch for
miles towards the Solway shore. Eskers are recognisable even
from the train as it threads its way from Carlisle to Wigton.
Another neat one is interesting for reasons not geological. It
appears at Arthuret (near Longtown) and is in two long ridges
separated by the road that passes the church. It is pleasant in the
sun, and rooks dash from the trees as you walk its leafy crest.
From a flat plain it rises, visible for miles around, and is associated
with the early days of the Dark Ages as a possible site of a famous

battle. The western knoll was certainly inhabited in an early period, as the remains of earthworks show on its slope, and I have come across a piece of fourteenth-century pottery kindly excavated by the rabbits. No archæologists are ever likely to excavate this interesting hill. The bulldozer has beaten them to it. Eskers often make good sandpits, and the last war saw thousands of tons removed from this one. A good windbreak was also removed; the church is now unprotected from the western gales which sweep up the Solway and a new line of trees is to be planted. King Charles's jester, who sleeps in the churchyard, might well smile again at the follies of a later generation.

Similar to eskers, but smaller and neater, are the pleasantly-named drumlins. There are literally thousands on the lowlands dropped from the interior of melting glaciers, their long lines, as seen on a careful map, marking the direction of the ice-flow as clearly as a signpost. The English Solway plain, the Kirkcud-bright lowlands, the Machers and the Rhinns of Galloway are all solid with drumlins varying in size though all shaped more or less like a half-egg, cut longwise and lying on the flat. In the Rhinns they often seem to come in twins, and in Kirkcudbright the "Drums", as they are called, are now valued sites for plough-ing although once they were much avoided. The Solway itself has carved a drumlin in half at Glasson, near Port Carlisle, and has provided an opportunity for investigating its structure, as the bulldozer later did for the Longtown esker.

I always have an affectionate interest in eskers as I happened to be a member of a party of students in Norway who came across perhaps the first recorded example of one that was alive and growing. It was thrusting from the cavern in a glacier, and was definitely being laid in and by the flow of water. It was just a baby one, but as with small corries in the same region, I find that to see a living process in a modern Ice Age makes the present scenery more comprehensible. There are other manifestations of glacial activity, but the two I have described are typical of Solway, and for further details I will refer the reader either to the excellent text-books that exist or to the memoirs of the Geological Survey of Great Britain. The very interested reader who goes about things the right way and takes a geological map on his holiday, should be reminded that these maps come in two forms, solid and drift. The drift edition hides the skeletal rocks, but for a region like Solway is much more interesting to the walker.

In the years since the Ice Age another complication has affected our coastlines in a remarkable and fascinating way. First of all there is the problem of changes in level between land and sea. These changes have come about as a result of several factors. The most obvious is that the formation of ice from snow over large areas of Europe took water, and, by the taking, lowered the level of the sea perhaps three hundred feet at the maximum glaciation. It also raised it eventually in degrees as the ice melted. This process may be still going on in an infinitesimal way as the Ice Age still lingers around the poles. This simple fall and rise of water is complicated because the land was not a fixed, immovable standard against which to gauge it. As the masses of ice grew, so the crust of the earth slowly sank under the weight, and as the ice melted, so recovery began. The process was not instantaneous, and parts of Europe have not even now recovered fully from the depression caused by the weight of the ice of a million years ago. The whole subject is complicated. If land sinks, there is flooding. If land rises but water rises faster, there is also flooding. Land emergence can similarly be the result of a variety of changes. All I want to do at this stage is to point out some of the evidence in which the Solway is rich, and to mention some general conclusions, including one to the effect that the Solway shores are probably still rising out of the waters. Whenever there has been an effective fall of sea-level over a long period, there has been time for land plants, especially trees which may be preserved for centuries, to grow in a region now covered by water. A submerged forest is the descriptive term. There are several round the coasts of Britain and Solway is again particularly rich. Sometimes one has been found by digging near the shore, for example, when Silloth dock was built or the railway taken to Port Carlisle. In this latter case, some of the timber was good enough to use again. More imposing are the glimpses of submerged forest revealed by particularly low tides. In Scotland the stumps of trees *in situ* and prone can be seen off Redkirk Point, and in England in Allonby Bay, from Cardurnock west of Bowness, and especially off Beckfoot, a mile south-west of Silloth. Occasionally, this is said too easily. I should warn the reader that he may be unlucky in months of observation when all conditions do not favourably coincide, and the stumps are hidden by water or sand. Mr Cash went to Beckfoot, in one way unluckily; the submerged forest was not visible and I regret to say that the residents he inquired from had not even heard of it. He consoled himself with a typical piece of Solway flotsam which although not submerged has, I think, created a picture giving a mood of the estuary so typical that I have retained the photograph— number 11 in the first section of illustrations.

When the water-to-land-level rises, for whatever reason, the waves carve themselves a higher platform and cliff, and often leave traces of beach-material at its foot. In a term technical and simple, we get a raised beach. The longer the standstill at any particular level, the more marked is likely to be the beach and its wave-cut platform. If you travel from Maryport to Silloth along the coast road, you will be driving for much of the way on the twenty-five-foot beach, and you will be able to see the old line of the cliff a few yards to your right, that is, inland, as you drive north-east. This is the most obvious example perhaps, but not the only one. Almost every inlet, and especially the major river-valleys of the Annan and Nith, shows quite good stretches of this twenty-five-foot beach, and the careful searcher may find evidences at higher levels of other carved beaches. The twenty-five-foot beach is a title not a description. The tilting of the land and other complications cause it to be found at varying heights from sea-level upwards.

Whichever way sea-level changes, the rivers have a new base on which to align their flow. If the sea rises, the river slows and its sediment fills the old channel; if the sea falls in relation to land, the river cuts a new and deeper channel to make a smooth grade to sea-level, and often leaves bits of its old flood-plain as terraces on either bank. Traces of such terraces may persist for ages, and the study of their levels and composition offers many clues to the detailed geographical history, not only of the river, but of the sea-level, for they may often be correlated with raised beaches, submerged forests and sea-built sediments known as "warp". You can see such terraces along the river-banks that lead into the Solway. Sometimes they are obvious, but I admit that at other times the expert eye and the spade of the geologist together with a touch of imagination are required. Most of the classic studies on river-terraces in this country have been made on the

Cam and the Thames, and the reader is referred to Chapter V of *The Unstable Earth*, by A. J. Steers, for the best résumé of present thought on this subject.

The curious mind can combine with the practised eye to make every landscape reveal something of its history. There is a cause-and-effect relationship about every slope, every hill and every plain that can be seen. Even the solid foundations on which I shall build the whole of this book are not inanimate and can tell a story of continuing change; but to see the pulse of the earth and its throbbing most vividly, you must come to the living coast of Solway.

CHAPTER III

THE LIVING COAST AND ITS BIRDS

MANY of the changes that began in the Ice Age are still going on. It may be that the whole of Britain is slowly tilting about the Midlands so that the land in the north is rising while that in the south sinks. Some of London's Roman levels are now "drowned", and the corresponding information about this rocking (which can only be estimated in centimetres per century) has been obtained from a study of the raised beaches of the Solway and the fact that Grune Point is still extending in a particular way that shows slight terraced steps. Such movements are subtle and doubtful, but we can see in the Solway Firth changes which are quite obvious to the eye of the layman today.

First let us select a few of the sand-dunes round the estuary, and see how they grew up in the drier periods of the present post-glacial era. There are greater expanses of sand-dunes along other British coasts, but they are very characteristic of our holiday stretch between Allonby and Silloth. The westerly wind picks up sand from the shore and the flats and banks uncovered at low water and blows it inland until it is trapped by the groins and plants of the shore. If you wander about this shore on the long stretches that are seldom covered by the tides, you can watch the whole process. You will see the sand piling up against a bunch of sea-couch grass * or even a heap of stones. Gradually the sand becomes more permanently held by the grass, which itself grows higher through the hillock of sand. When these hillocks are but a foot or so high and collecting plenty of fresh sand, marram grass takes the place of the sea-couch grass and from then on the process is generally rapid.

This newish group of dunes is generally settling down and gradually aligning itself at right angles to the dominant winds. An older set of dunes can be found inland from these most of the way until they both end near Silloth. The more seaward range

* An appendix gives botanical and alternative names for all plants mentioned in this chapter.

protects the older ones from the blowing sand so that they are not growing and moving, and in addition are fixed by the grasses and heather that they now support. The soil of an older generation of dunes is usually darker and in parts here it is almost brown. There are remnants of dunes in Maryport just south of the loop of the river that may be the oldest in the Solway.

The Scottish shore has its dunes as well, and although it is unnecessary for me to go into great detail, I should like to mention two groups of sand-dunes with personal affection. The first group is in that pleasant district south-east of Gatehouse-of-Fleet and the other the sand-hills fringing the mouth of the Luce, which have sheltered my tent from the cold west winds.

I wrote earlier about the give and take of the Ice Age, and the modern day brings another and more obvious example. On both sides of the Solway we can travel east from the dunes, and if we stick to the shore we shall eventually be amongst the salt-marshes characteristic, to many, of the Solway scene. Salt-marsh can grow yearly; almost from day to day can you see it change. Sometimes the tide is its ally and sometimes its enemy. The tide feeds the plants that build the marsh when it is not tearing them up and washing them away. Marsh can grow outwards on the sand-flats that fringe a low-lying coast, or inwards from the shelter of a sand or shingle bar especially, on the east coast, between its recurves. It may grow in both directions if conditions are right, but on the Solway there are no true shingle bars apart from the spit at Grune Point, and the marsh grows outwards or fills in the estuaries of our rivers.

Different coasts around Britain support different kinds of marsh. Plants are the deciding factor, and they in their turn depend on the salinity of the water and the composition, that is, sand or mud, of their foundations. Several good modern books give typical successions for east, south and west coast marshes, those by Steers and Hepburn being the best. The marshes on any one coast do not follow these ideal successions in every detail, and in an estuary like the Solway quite big differences can be found not only between one inlet and another, but even between different stretches thirty yards apart. Some marshes have been surveyed in great detail, especially the ones within striking distance of the older Universities, but the Solway has not, and as I am no expert and the task is indeed a monumental one, I shall content myself with a very general and superficial study checked wherever possible by observation but obviously leaving great gaps for study locally.

It is worth considering first how much marsh exists around the head of the Firth. The most striking stretch is that Rockcliffe Marsh which can be seen on the introductory map as the long promontory growing out into the waters between Esk and Eden. There are quite wide stretches of marsh at various points to the west on the English coast from the banks of the Eden to the Silloth side of Moricambe and especially in that bay itself where Long Newton marsh has grown considerably during the last century. Two factors have brought the marsh of the English Solway to the notice of a wider public. Its fine surface, called Cumberland turf, of short-cropped fescue is exported far for lawns and bowling greens and has the unique distinction of providing the Centre Court at Wimbledon. Secondly, the association of this marsh with the Herdwicks from their heafs on the Cumberland fells provides an example of transhumance often quoted in the text-books of human and animal geography. I shall mention this aspect again when I am writing about farming. On the Scottish side there are great expanses of merse land fringing the coast and lining every estuary and shallow bay well into Galloway. The merse lands of the Nith are most interesting and have the advantage that as far as I know they are the only section that has been studied in much detail. I am greatly indebted to this study by W. L. Morss which was published in the *Transactions of the Dumfriesshire and Galloway Natural History and Antiquarian Society*.

In the open estuary a growing marsh has a difficult life and sometimes there is great local scouring and erosion. Off the shore by Burgh,* you will find great blocks collapsed by the cutting current of the Eden channel which has been steadily swinging to the south since about 1910, but even here you can see wide sandbanks exposed at low tide and striving in vain with a scattering of vegetation to build an embryo salt marsh. In the river estuaries and in the sheltered bays, the process is speeded up, and Rockcliffe is the most striking example of all. It is not obviously sheltered, but at low tide is fronted by acres of sandflats and in addition collects great quantities of river silt as the Esk and Eden are slowed down by the salt water of the Firth.

* Pronounced Bruff.

As with sand-dunes, vegetation is the prime factor in salt-marsh building. Whereas the grass of a dune traps little piles of blown sand, the seaweed and rubbish of a sandbank or mud flat collect each tide a minute quantity of silt and sediment, sand and seeds. These are normally carried in suspension in the moving water, but when the short period of slack water at the turn of the tide occurs, particles may drop, collect round the obstacles and begin to build the foundations of a future marsh. Shelter is important too. The casualty rate among plants struggling to get a foothold against the wash of the water is tremendous, but once they have got their roots in, they are, like all true pioneers, extremely tenacious.

In the soft mud of Southampton Water a variety of rice grass is nowadays the main pioneer, but although a few plants were introduced into the Solway some years ago, I do not think it has become established. The west of Britain in general provides a sandier coast than the east, and the Solway demonstrates this rule by having a greater proportion of sea-manna grass than the eel grass which likes an anchorage of mud, although meadows of waving eel grass can be seen in the Scottish bays. Another early pioneer in the Solway is the jointed glass-wort, known locally as sandforth, which sometimes comes first as in Moricambe, where you will notice it even at a distance as a thin scattering of stems green or red according to season, branching and cactus-like in appearance. In the Nith the sea-manna grass is generally already present to greet the glass-wort. These two or three plants, if we include the eel grass, spread fairly rapidly, and even on new sand-flats their seeds are caught by the lying green seaweed and the marsh begins to grow. At this stage one sees fairly compact circles of green revealed when the tide has begun to ebb, and as more plants settle, more sand and silt is trapped and even dead roots assist the process. The micro-fauna, too, helps the growing marsh at this stage by its aerating activity as it burrows between the roots, and as the marsh gets settled and grows in height, the pioneer plants are often joined by annual sea-blite.

From this stage the process is self-accelerating and the marsh soon grows so high that only the highest tides can cover it for a short time each day. The water tends to flow round the hummocks keeping certain channels clear of plants and these may persist as permanent creeks. Plants that can stand less salt now

begin to take root. After the soil material has set the pattern and
the marsh has raised itself, salinity is the master factor, and thrift
—the most beautiful of them all—sea-plantain, sea-aster and
later scurvy grass tend to replace the glass-wort. That tough
pioneer, the sea-manna grass, continues well into the life of the
marsh even after other grasses of the fescue community grow to
the edge of the established marsh. The tidal water rarely covers
the grown marsh at this stage, and its passage is restricted to the
many creeks that thread their way about it. The edges of these
creeks are thus watered by the sea much more than the interior
zones, and because of this develop a different assortment of plants.
This aspect is more marked on the Norfolk salt-marshes where
obione invariably paints the banks of the creeks with a lighter
green. In the Solway, sea-manna grass and arrow grass still seem
to dominate this border zone. In the drier creeks on Solway you
often find a concentration of scurvy grass, its white flowers in
summer unseen from a distance, but marking the creek like a
paper trail when seen from above. This is particularly true of
Rockcliffe marsh, where the scurvy grass does not get much
chance to live on the main marsh where the grazing of sheep and
cattle is intensified by that of thousands of wild geese.

Once the water is restricted to channels, the marsh grows little
in height except when extraordinarily high spring or storm tides
cover it, but if it is sheltered enough it continually grows outwards. Two aspects mark the later stages. The first is the filling
in of creeks or the closing up of parts of them to leave isolated
stretches of water, called pans or "floshes" locally, in the body of
the marsh. These pans may persist for years as excess salt due to
evaporation keeps the plants at bay and occasionally kills enough
of them to allow two pans to run together. Sometimes, of course,
they are reflushed with normal estuary water when an exceptionally high tide is backed by a south-westerly gale and even the
oldest and the reclaimed marshes are flooded, to the dismay of
their farmers. One is often surprised, even on an oldish marsh, to
find the ubiquitous Solway flounder living apparently happily in
an isolated salt pan not more than a few square yards in area. In
the summer heat when little rain falls, a concentration of salt will
no doubt end its life if the children have not got it first.

Once an old marsh is really established, it supports mainly a
grassy vegetation group dominated by sand fescue-grass, a

variety of red fescue, interspersed with great bunches of thrift which tends when grazed to grow in a rosette form, compact and low instead of loose and straggling. Its bunches of leaves, glaucous-green generally but with a purple tinge in winter, can be distinguished at every season. Amongst other plants found in varying percentages is buckshorn plantain, especially near Rockcliffe and on Longnewton Marsh where joined with sea-plantain it is very characteristic. Sea arrow-grass is common on many marshes in the waterlogged creeks.

Speaking of creeks, a word of warning is essential to those who wander these marshes. It may seem easy to clamber across a creek on the fallen blocks eroded by the rushing water if you strike the marsh when the tide is low, but as the tide gradually rises, or at worst rushes wind-backed, the creeks are suddenly full and a gentle scramble becomes at least a sloppy rush and at worst a desperate panic in an effort to reach safety. It is surprisingly difficult to scramble out of a muddy creek when the water is swirling about your legs. The creeks have their uses, of course. They are so convenient that they might almost have been designed to shelter and hide wildfowlers and bird watchers.

Sharing some of the mystical atmosphere of the marshes, but less useful to man, are the mosses and flows around the Solway. These are low-lying areas of peat that have slowly developed through the centuries, and are usually found occupying hollows in the boulder clay or on the marine alluvium. They are smaller now than they were, a fact which is shown by the "black top", the dark soil light in texture and rich in humus, which makes valuable farming land around their margins and which has been won from the peat. This lowland peat, by the way, is easier to reclaim than its moorland counterpart and gives softer, less acid soils. There are half a dozen or so big mosses of which Lochar Moss, south-east of Dumfries, is the largest, and Solway Moss, north-east of Gretna, the most famous, having given its name to a battle. The mosslands have a flora and fauna and therefore an atmosphere that are absolutely their own. Rushes and rough grasses lead to heather, gorse and bracken and the whole is shrouded invariably with a scrub of silver birch. I shall deal later with the more economic aspects of the mosses and flows, but Solway Moss has had one natural event—as well as the military one—that brought tragedy in its wake. Peat can hold a tremendous amount of water, and on the night of Saturday, 16th December, 1771, after torrential rains, the mound of Solway Moss burst and spread on the east side from a gullet at first but one hundred yards wide. By morning two hundred acres of the best land in the north were flooded with up to thirty feet of horrid peaty mess. As more rain followed, the peat spread to cover five hundred acres, and thirty families were made destitute. It was estimated at the time that the centre of the Moss subsided twenty-five feet as a result of the eruption, whilst the desolated houses were covered to the eaves.

We shall tread the moss and marsh again when we search for the birds of Solway, but before I leave "the living coast", I want to consider the bed of the estuary and the waves that wash its shores. I shall be brief and cautious about the submarine geography. It is quite impossible to dogmatise about the channels. They do change frequently, almost daily in places, as I pointed out when talking about the fords. The specialist, whether pilot or fisherman, will know much more than I do about these channels, and I hope the general reader will be satisfied with a brief description.

There are in the main two deep channels stemming from the mouths of the Esk and the Eden. These often join to form a single one in the upper reaches of the estuary before splitting again somewhere between Dornock and Drumburgh where the estuary narrows and the more swiftly racing waters easily cut new routes. The banks that are most permanent are, of course, charted and named on various maps. The map in this book would become too crowded if I tried to name them all, but the brief description that follows will be made more clear if the map is used for reference.

Starting at the east of the estuary, we have the Middle Bank, a great stretch of sand looking like dry land at the ebb dividing the channels of Esk and Eden. It continues the line of Rockcliffe Marsh. These channels swing of course, a movement that is of great and international importance as it decides whether the majority of the salmon are caught by Scottish or English fishermen. These channels run together somewhere about (and that is as near as I dare say) the Whan Scaur on the north and the West Scaurs to the south. Where Bowness viaduct sticks out, is Herd Hill Scaur, making a right confusion in the water. From here there may be two main channels to the west, but the most reliable one sweeps north past Powfoot and Priestside Bank, which is offshore from Ruthwell. The Priestside Bank has a variety of small scaurs, Powfoot, Howgarth, Brewing and Rough from east to west, while on the south of the estuary, Cardurnock flats fringe the coast from Herd Hill Scaur to Moricambe. The local name for this part of the estuary is Hudson's Bay. Quite a number of aircraft ended their days in the Solway sand when the district was a wartime training ground. Around the mouth of Moricambe is Tickhill Scaur and out to sea Stenor Scaur leads to Brow Scaur to the north-east and another Middle Bank. The channel here off Cardurnock, the Swatchway, threads its way through tricky scaurs. Scaurs and sands fringe the coast south-west from Silloth to where the lightship used to be anchored a mile and a half to the west of Dubmill Point. But I go too fast. Nith mouth has the Carse sands on its western bank and the three-mile sweep of Blackshaw Bank on its east off Caerlaverock. Southerness Point with its lighthouse divides the Carse sands from the Merse Head sands off the Criffell shore, and these are paralleled a mile or two out by the Barnhourie Sands, which are sometimes called the Goodwins of the Solway. The deepish water between these Goodwins and Maryport has its shallow parts, amongst which I can name the Dumroof Bank and Robin Rigg which is separated from Allonby Bay by the buoy-marked channel of Pillar Fairway, a route for all those ships that have avoided Three Fathoms Bank, the main obstacle seawards in the rest of the estuary. People always like to talk about wrecks and I am no exception, but though the Solway is full of stories of heroism and tragedy, I must be very selective. Many of the stories are mainly of local interest and too many tell the same sad story of gales and sandbanks and all hands lost, though some have been preserved in oils by Cumberland's painter, William Mitchell. Such a one was the story of the *Estrella de Chile*, which was lost on the Robin Rigg I have just mentioned, and I choose this one, from dozens, because it brings England and Scotland together against a common danger. A lifeboat sailed from each side of the estuary and in high seas all the crew were saved except the mate who had been washed overboard.

From 1299, when the *Holy Cross* went ashore near Silloth and its cargo of wine was "salvaged", to years within memory have

Solway folk benefited from "washed-up" cargoes, but they have done their share, too, in caring for the shipwrecked from the days of the Spanish Armada when the coasts from Solway to Clyde saw the desperate ships. A record from Ayr tells how £10 was spent on the "pure Spanyardis" (the adjective is old spelling, not modern meaning).

With mist and even, I regret to say, without it, ships have lost their way in the Solway and more than once in history mistaken it for the Clyde, but it was definitely misty for the nicest story. Some ship was "wandered" in fog too near the Colvend coast when suddenly land and a solitary workman were seen and hailed. "Where are we?" was answered calmly by "within twa hundred yairds o' Jenny Black's yaird". Not finding Miss Black's yard on his chart, the skipper asked for advice, was told to "steer for the sun" and got away safely through banks and scaurs.

I have used the word "scaurs" rather a lot and I had better explain it. They are hummocks, boulder strewn, lurking under the surface or exposed at low water like the baby one you can see behind the tree stump in the photograph facing page 103. They were formed from the boulders of glacial boulder-clay ridges, and their long narrow shape may show the direction of glacier movements. The sea both removes the clay from the boulders and sometimes hides them with sand. This boulder clay probably reached well out into the bay in early prehistoric times before the sinking of the land that continued until the Bronze Age. Scaurs are the equivalent of the "sarns" off the Welsh coast. The banks that I have referred to require less explanation as they are typical estuarine sand-flats. Both banks and scaurs provide feeding- and resting-places for thousands of sea birds and waders, and unhappily in the history of the Solway they have proved the last resting-place of many a fine ship. Fishermen, too, know the paths of the salmon as it skirts the Solway scaurs.

Having dealt with the stones and the sands, we come again to the waters. First I must deal with the tide that shapes and reveals Solway, and which influences in one way or another most of these chapters, whether they be historical, economic, geographical or holiday-making. Again I am going to generalise. The tide is roughly one hour behind Liverpool. It ranges from about fifteen to twenty feet at ordinary neaps and springs, but it can, of course, be higher, as many a drowned sheep could bear witness, when a thirty-foot tide is backed by a south-westerly gale and folk have been known to row home down King Street, Maryport.

The wanderer around the Solway shores and marshes might some day benefit from a reminder of his schoolday lessons on the subject of tides. The spring tides, when the sun pulls *with* the moon and the tidal range is greatest and most dangerous, are roughly at their highest two days after full moon and two days after new moon, and most pocket diaries will provide the necessary information. The notices in certain places around the Solway do not exaggerate when they warn bathers (and naturalists) of swift and dangerous currents.

That tidal phenomenon known as the bore, which receives its best publicity quite deservedly in the Bristol Channel, can sometimes be seen when conditions are right in both the estuary and the rivers of the Solway. As far as the rivers are concerned, the Scottish Nith and English Wampool seem to provide the most regular performances. In each of these, when the right combinations of tide and wind are prevailing, the observer who has timed his visit well can see a wall of water not very high, perhaps a foot or two, but very regular, moving slowly and steadily up and over the surface of the river. The speed of these river bores is estimated variously at anything between four and twenty miles per hour. As far as I am concerned, the lower figure seems to be the more accurate. I am told that a similar manifestation can be seen on the Eden around Sandsfield, but I have not been lucky enough to be at the right place at the right time for a good example. The open estuary itself can show a bore. A neat and tidy one like its Severn counterpart is rare, but can be seen where the estuary narrows between Annan and Bowness. It is not as high in its steep front as the Severn bore, but it is much more extended. The storm bore of the Solway estuary, ragged, threatening and extremely dangerous, has perhaps been described in literature with more grandeur than accuracy, but Sir Walter Scott's words about the waves "three feet abreast" give a picture of the strength and power behind these elements.

Waves are, of course, formed by wind, and as the dominant winds in our region blow in from the west and south-west, the waves break obliquely from west to east along the Solway shores of Scotland and England. Many older books speak of material being swept along the shore by tidal currents. This is only true when small and floating particles are being considered. For the bigger items, which can vary from tree trunks, pebbles and rocks to empty tins and bottles of all varieties as well as chunks of coal, wave action is responsible for beach drifting, in the particular way revealed in the last few years by the work led by W. V. Lewis. In brief, the power of the waves, both the on-shore swash and the backwash that follows, can transport tremendous masses of material, but they do it in different ways. A wave breaking at some angle against the shore, and here they break from the west on both sides, carries material with it obliquely. The water draining back from the slope does not reverse the direction, but runs down at right angles to the coast under the pull of gravity, not the push of wind. Any material therefore carried by this wave on the edge of the water would be moved steadily from west to east in a zigzag or saw-toothed motion, and over the years may be carried far. As this movement covers the shore on the English side from St Bees to Rockcliffe, it naturally carries large quantities of coal and slag varying in size from powder to boulder and strews them unhappily on the Solway shore. The worst effects are seen north-west from the coalfield, in the Allonby Bay region. The proof that the process can be extensive has been found by Scottish fisherfolk who have combed the beaches at Gretna for coal in time of shortage. There is a similar drift, west to east, on the Scottish side, but there the greater intricacy of the coast with its promontories and hidden bays acts as a filter to the drifting material. The promontories act as enormous groins and the material piles up on their western sides. The bays round Kirkcudbright, especially Brighouse Bay, are quite well known for their collecting power, but the ultimate and most untidy dump of material from both sides of the Firth is the coast between Esk and Sark. Here reclaimed marsh is protected by a great dyke which is strengthened both by human tipping and by a buttress of wave-carried debris beyond which new salt-marsh is gradually building its own additional buffer. There is, of course, no great coal drift on the Scottish side to detract from this lovely coast, but in fairness to the English Solway, I must say that compared with the tar and seaweed fly problems of some of England's southern beaches, the worst of Solway provides an object lesson in cleanliness.

Scotsmen may think that in some parts of this book I do not

treat the northern shore with sufficient accurate generosity. I hope that what I write next will well offset my sins in this respect. It may also in the long run cause me to emigrate. Leaving the marshes aside as common to both, the Scottish Solway coast is by far the more varied and the more beautiful of the two. It caters less for one type of holiday-maker than the English side with its pleasant resorts of Silloth and Allonby, although it has its Kippford and its greater length of coastline shelters many more and grander hotels as well as small friendly inns and delightful quiet villages. Having said that, however, I must reaffirm my faith in the Solway taken as a whole, where every kind of coast and sky sweep broadly down to the sheet of water that is common to both countries. The beauty of the district is centred on the Firth after all.

Therefore having taken the Solway to pieces, I am going to end this section by considering it once again as a whole. The reader who is not acquainted with the district may consider that the strong claims I have made for its unique beauty are exaggerated by some form of local prejudice. I do not think this is so. Firstly, because having been lucky enough to travel fairly widely I have many memories of other beauty spots as a yard-stick, and the Solway loses nothing in the comparison. Secondly, I can give half a dozen good reasons, coldly scientific and topo-graphical, for its uniqueness. Solway is like a gigantic saucer. One stands on the shore and beyond the flats and marshes merging with the water the hills are a gentle circle three-quarters of the way around. This sets the stage. The Solway coast at the head of the estuary is a dry zone averaging under thirty inches of rain per year. It is well known and frankly admitted that the westerly winds are heavy with moisture as they approach this part of Britain. They do drop a lot of rain, but not in Solway, and as the hills of the south-west Scottish Uplands to the north, the Lake District to the south, and the northern Pennines to the east, force this damp and moving air to rise, there is crystallised out an ever-changing moving picture of cloud forms, growing and towering and shifting to the east over both sides of the estuary. Add to all this the fact that one generally, from the head of the estuary on both sides, looks to the setting sun over the hills and you have the perfect picture which only needs one small refine-ment for its evening glory. The sunset glow of almost any sky is accentuated and enriched when the air contains just the right amount of suspended particles of microscopic dust and dirt. We have no London fogs in Solway, but from the industrial belt of West Cumberland comes a north-east drift of pleasantly thin, hazy smoke. This is the refinement which, when added to the western hills beyond the water, the clouds and the dying sun, floods the sky with colours unbelievable.

This living shore of the Solway is the home of a vast population of birds, some permanent inhabitants, others migrants who touch down in passing or spend some season of the year around these waters. They are as much a part of the Solway scene as the landscape itself or the people past and present who make its history. You need the trained eye and expert knowledge of the ornithologist to sample to the full the feast that Solway has to offer. If you would penetrate safely into the haunts of the shy geese, you need, too, some knowledge of the habits of wind and tide, for a south-westerly gale driving the waters before it can turn the shallow creeks into rivers and in early spring transform the grassland of the marshes into a foaming sea.

You need not, however, be an expert to get great pleasure from the birds of marsh and cliff and shore, and there are several places where the reward is out of all proportion to the effort needed for getting there. An afternoon's stroll will take you to the top of the cliffs at St Bees, from where you can look down on colonies of herring gulls, kittiwakes and fulmars, guillemots and razorbills, and far below, nearest to the swirling waters, an occasional small group of puffin. The cormorant has begun to nest here in recent years, and, offshore, gannets can quite frequently be seen busy with their fishing, though for breeding gannets you must go to the Big Scar Rock on the Scottish side of Solway. The warm red cliffs are streaked with the droppings of all these birds, and the air vibrates with their shrill calls. Their perches on ledge and in cranny are unbelievably narrow and the casualty rate for their eggs must be high. In the strong winds which so often beat against these cliffs, these ledges are no easy landing-ground. As the birds stall, the uprush of air catches them and whirls them out over the sea again. The most hardened sceptic will find it difficult to tear himself away and escape the mounting tension as the birds try again and again to find a lodgment.

Another point easy of access by car or bicycle, again on the south shore, is the stretch of road between Bowness and Cardurnock known as the East Whins. Here, if you choose your time carefully when the tide is high, you will see a great variety of waders, birds of marsh and estuary, sometimes in remarkably large numbers. Common among these, especially in autumn, when the local inhabitants are reinforced by visitors from Scotland and the far north, are the oyster-catchers. These distinctive birds, with their black and white plumage and long orange bills, can be seen in flocks of many thousands; in fact, Solway has one of the biggest concentrations of them in these islands. Here, too, can be seen the occasional greenshank, the more numerous redshanks, dunlin and ringed plover, gulls and cormorants, lapwings and curlews. Here, as in other parts of Solway, you may see the handsome but predatory great black-backed gull, the least common of the gulls that reside in Britain. Of these birds of the shore, the most characteristic of the area is the curlew, whose clear bubbling call is familiar to those who live near the coast, and indeed far inland among the moors and fells where they breed. So common is it, in fact, that it forms a dominant part of Cumberland's coat of arms. The curlew, by the way, uses his other call for broadcasting.

Interesting though this roadside bird-watching may be, he who ventures no further will see little of the geese which come each year in great numbers from their breeding-grounds in the far north. These birds shun the haunts of men and live and feed far out on the marshes, where bird watcher and wildfowler, shielded by the deep and tortuous creeks, stalk them with field-glasses and guns, or await them in hides, chilly at dawn. It needs skill and infinite care to approach a feeding flock, and most people see them only in flight or hear the strong beat of their wings over the quiet towns at night as they sweep in in migratory flight or move from feeding-place to resting-sites on the exposed sandbanks. These geese are the wildest of the wild creatures that live in this region and seem to epitomise the spirit of the estuary, a spirit which exists independent of man and even perhaps in spite of him. The soul of the Solway is revealed only to the very few fishermen and wildfowlers who have been absorbed into its utter loneliness and have become a part of its almost tangible silence. The silence of the marshes is unique; it is not absence of sound, but a blending of the primitive sounds of nature, of bird-call and flight, of lapping water and soughing wind, as white is the blending of all the colours of the spectrum.

The Scottish shore of Solway is not so accessible for the casual bird watcher. The main road runs further inland and is screened from the sea in places by higher ground, but a detour will well repay the time and trouble it takes. The stretch of rocky coast from Rough Firth to Kirkcudbright Bay is as lovely as any in all Solway. It is seen at its best from the sea, and it is not surprising, perhaps, that little places like Kippford are a-clutter with sailing craft in the summer months. If you sail past Almorness Point to Balcary, you will see a changing view of the coast that it would be hard to surpass in beauty anywhere, first up Orchardton and then Auchencairn Bays, with Screel and Blengairn rising in the background. Secluded bays like Horse Isle, seen behind Rough Island in the photograph facing page 70, are famous for wildfowl, and the cliffs of the mainland and the small islands lying off the coast are the home of a wide variety of seabirds, particularly gulls, guillemots, razorbills and cormorants, and in addition the rock-dove, though serious doubts have been cast upon the purity of the blood of this latter. The fulmar has been increasing in numbers on the cliffs as far east as Colvend, and Balcary Cliffs have followed St Bees, with the fulmar having at last decided to nest (1952).

The most interesting part of the upper Solway both from the point of view of birds and atmosphere is Rockcliffe Marsh. Its sea-washed turf makes wonderful grazing, and on it winter the Herdwick yearlings from the Lakeland Fells and literally tens of thousands of ducks and geese. Few people wander on the marsh beyond the Castletown boundary fence these days, and the wild-fowl can feed in isolation and comparative security. By day the ducks rest on the open sea a few miles down the estuary or on lochs in the hills, but as darkness gathers they stream in to feed on the marsh. I have watched them on an evening of great calm as the sun slipped low over Criffell and flooded the wet mud with an orange light that picked out each stone as a separate gleaming entity, flighting east into the advancing darkness first in small bunches, then as the momentum quickened, in skein upon skein until the air was full of their wing music. Sheld-duck, teal, mallard and widgeon—the last two called grey duck and loughs in Solway—preponderate, though they are not the only ducks you will find on the marsh. The whole of Solway is, in fact, rich in varieties of duck. Among the winter visitors are pintails in considerable numbers, scaup particularly on parts of the coast rich in mussel beds, and less numerous though regularly seen on the Firth, the golden-eye and long-tailed. The Common Scoter is also a regular winter visitor, but can also be seen on occasions in quite large numbers during the summer. Of the nesting duck, in some places on the Scottish side shovellers greatly exceed teal, while both goosander and merganser breed regularly up most of the Scottish rivers. Evidence of breeding of these last two in Cumberland has only recently been found and that in the far north of the county in the region of Esk and Lyne. At the beginning of the century, ducks were reared for sporting purposes at Netherby, and this has probably done much to establish some of the rarer species in the Solway area.

To return to the marshes, from inland feeding-grounds come the gulls, too, in the evenings. The scavenging herring-gull and lesser and great black-backed gulls, who have learnt to appreciate the amenities of civilisation in the form of refuse dumps, fly in from the towns along the Solway coasts, and from the arable land around come the common and black-headed gulls, tumbling over each other in a positive ecstasy of pleasure when the weather is fair.

Geese, however, are the great glory of the winter saltings. Pinkfeet predominate on Rockcliffe Marsh, and are indeed ousting their less gregarious cousins throughout the Solway region. In the last half-century there has been a significant change in the distribution of species of geese here. Formerly Solway was the haunt of Grey Lag and Barnacle, but they have been steadily retreating before the Pinkfoot invasion, pushed westward by the sheer weight of numbers. The expedition sent out to Iceland by the Severn Wildfowl Trust in 1951 has added greatly to our knowledge of these birds and appears to suggest that the majority of the world's population of Pinkfeet come to Britain in the winter, and that of these a large proportion come to Rockcliffe. Some of them do not stay, but after their preliminary mustering disperse to other feeding-grounds, only to gather again before departing to their northern breeding-areas.

The Pinkfeet have not, however, driven the other geese from the area altogether nor even from Rockcliffe itself. Small groups of Grey Lag can almost always be found grazing among the thousands of Pinkfeet, and a recent report suggests that the Barnacles are returning to Rockcliffe from marshes in the Moricambe area.

The geese that winter on the Scottish shores have as yet been touched only by the fringe of the Pinkfoot invasion, yet here, too, there have been notable changes of location. The Grey Lag geese have left the neighbourhood of Annan where hundreds used to winter and now their headquarters are in the estuaries of Nith and Cree, though there are indications that their days on the Nith are numbered. The Pinkfeet have moved into East Park or more exactly to Blackshaw Bank and Blackshaw merse, and Kinmount with its flighting thousands is now a kind of sanctuary. This has caused a westward migration of Barnacle geese which has been accompanied by a change in feeding habits, for they now inhabit a stretch of coast where no salt-marshes exist, and they have begun a practice, formerly rare, of flighting inland at dawn to feed on arable land. This would not be remarkable in grey geese, but Barnacles normally show a marked disinclination to feed far inland. They tend to keep to the seaward edge of the salt-marshes, only venturing as far as the sea wrack marking the limit of the highest tides in exceptional weather conditions, and only then after a careful reconnaissance by an advance party.

The little Brent goose has for long been known in Solway, but recently seems to be a more regular as well as more numerous visitor to the Scottish shores, although it is not as predictable as the pinkfooted goose. It is thought that present movements of the Brent goose are related to the decline in *zostera* over recent years.

The last of the grey goose family, the Bean goose, has now almost disappeared from the English shores of Solway, but still winters in considerable numbers on the Scottish side. The Solway is, in fact, one of the chief centres in Scotland for the wintering of this goose.

Coupled with the geese are the swans. The mute swan is of course everywhere, adding dignity to the landscape whether on that silk-smooth stretch of water above the weir on the Nith at Dumfries, sailing majestic across the red reflections of the low cliffs at Rockcliffe on the Eden, or leading a family of cygnets solemnly and somewhat incongruously in the lee of slag heap and pithead gear on Siddick Pond.

To digress for a moment, this tiny stretch of freshwater bounded by two railway lines and a main road and lying on the fringe of industrial Workington is extraordinarily interesting for those with a knowledge of birds. Its unusual accessibility has made regular observation possible, and a very excellent survey * has been made of its bird life by a group of amateur ornithologists living in the neighbourhood. As the sea is only a few hundred yards away on the other side of the road and railway, it is not unusual, particularly in rough weather, to see little waders and other birds more usually associated with the shore congregating here out of the reach of wind and wave.

But to return to the estuaries and swans; apart from the mute, to which it sometimes seems difficult to attach the epithet "wild", even though it depends little on human bounty, the Whooper and Bewick's swans are both winter visitors, the latter particularly on the Scottish side. The Whooper seems to have been increasing in numbers while the Bewick's has decreased and, in fact, become scarce, not only in Solway, but in the whole of Scotland. Whoopers are fairly regular visitors to freshwater close to the coast on the English side, and have been noted, for instance, at Siddick and on Thurstonfield Lough, near Kirkbampton. Swans on water, though decorative, have not the impact on the emotions that swans on the wing can produce. The Whoopers, noisiest of the swans, herald their coming with trumpeting call, and the mutes with incessant singing wing-beats, so that by the time they come upon you in powerful direct flight out of the dusk, you are excitedly prepared for their beauty. The flight of swans is un-common for most of us, though my friends from Gretna will remember how they delighted and surprised our inspection of a Roman fort, and Dumfriesians are lucky in the regular evening flight of the swans that live on their river.

To my mind, the most engaging birds of the Solway are the waders. I have already mentioned them in passing, but to look at them in more detail will bring us back to the coast. All along both shores you can find them, easier to approach than the geese but often more difficult to see. The commonest of the small waders is the ringed plover, a busy little bird seeming always to be in motion as it makes little dashes among the shingle to pick up the molluscs and insects that form its food. Against the background

* Published in *Lakeland Ornithology* by the Carlisle Natural History Society.

of shingle it is difficult to distinguish, and its eggs, lying in a shallow depression on the shore, are so like the pebbles that surround them that they are almost under your feet before you detect them. In Scotland these little birds commonly breed up all the rivers for quite a distance inland, and this inland spread has lately been noted too in Cumberland.

Companions of the ringed plover are the dunlins, though they feed lower down the beach on the edge of the sand left wet by the receding tide, probing with their longer beaks. Some of them go like the curlew to the higher hills to nest, but there are always others to nest on the marshes or on the peat mosses near the coast.

With them you may see turnstones, which feed on the mussel beds or in the litter of seaweed left by the tide, running forward with head and beak plunged into the material likely to yield them food. Somewhat similar in feeding habits if not in method are the purple sandpipers, but they are generally seen lower down the Firth, as they prefer a rocky coast.

Sanderlings, which complete this group of small waders though they do not exhaust it, are extraordinarily active little birds running on the very edge of the tide-line almost chasing the receding waves. They are not quite as common on Solway shores as might be expected, but each year are with us generally as passage migrants.

Of the larger waders, I have mentioned the extraordinarily large numbers of oyster-catchers, curlews and redshanks that congregate on our coasts. These three nest with us, redshanks frequently on the marsh itself though they are not conservative about their place of nesting and can be found equally well, like the dunlins, on the mosses and flows or in the hills. Resident too, of course, are the lapwings which breed so extensively and stand so solemnly on arable land in the British Isles that you are apt to forget that they are waders until you see the great flocks gathering on the winter saltings.

Among the more common passage migrants, too, are greenshanks, now happily increasing in numbers in Solway, and whimbrels and godwits, and the little knots which cover such vast distances in their migratory flights. Perhaps I should mention, too, the dotterel, for though it is a rare visitor to the coast, it does nest in the hills of both the Stewartry and Cumberland. Its

49

nesting-sites are a closely guarded secret of the few, lest the curious should frighten it away and our hills know it as a nesting species no more.

Another group of birds which nest on Solway takes us back in general to the dunes. The terns come back to us in spring to lay their eggs in shallow depressions among the marram of the dunes, on the sandy shore or shingle banks. Common and little terns nest on both shores of the Solway, the common in a number of large colonies. In Scotland the roseate tern has been increasing in numbers and distribution, and has been noticed among the flocks of common terns gathering after the breeding season. The roseate frequently breeds in a colony of common terns, so that observation may eventually confirm its breeding on the northern shore. The sandwich tern also breeds on the Scottish side, though not in large numbers. The southern shore knows it not as a nesting species, but just south of our region at Ravenglass there is a sanctuary where sandwich, arctic and common terns nest in a very large colony of black-headed gulls. Common terns nest too on the marshes, where the earlier clutches are often lost when high tides unexpectedly cover their nesting-sites. There is no need to go to Ravenglass to see the arctic tern. The little island of Hestan off Balcary has a unique colony of these aggressive birds which adds to the fascination of this lonely island, an island we shall meet again.

Many hazards beset the nesting birds of all species. Wind and tide take their toll on cliff and marsh. Fire may sweep across the dry heather of the inland mosses and flows. Men may rob the nests or crush the eggs with clumsy and heedless feet, but as well as this, nesting birds are constantly harried by the predators among their own kind. Gulls are notorious egg thieves, and the terns often suffer from the depredations of their black-headed neighbours. Great and lesser black-backed gulls steal each other's eggs and pay the penalty of the lawless in fear for the safety of their own, so that they are reluctant to leave the nest once the eggs have been laid.

Besides these unprincipled opportunists, the Solway provides a fruitful hunting ground for the true birds of prey, the short-eared owl, the peregrine and the kestrel. The peregrine quarters the marshes for prey, swooping on sitting tern, knocking a single chosen bird out of the sky from among a cloud of oyster-catchers, or when satisfied with food, harrying a flight of lapwings for the sheer joy of the tumbling chase. The lovely peregrine has its enemies north and south of the border. Scottish gamekeepers have long waged war against it, and in Cumberland wordy battles are fought by ornithologists and miners who swear it takes too great a toll of their cherished racing pigeons. Despite persecution, however, like the kestrel it still continues to nest on the cliffs of the northern coast, and now, too, the pair at St Bees are believed to have nested.

How much there is to tell of Solway birds and how much must of necessity be left out. To include them all, an account must either degenerate into a list or expand into a book. The latter is outside my purpose and my capabilities and I have tried to avoid the former, for in a list there is no magic, and birds are at the heart of the magic of Solway.

CHAPTER IV

THE EDGE OF THE WORLD

In distant centuries this living coast provided an unsteady stage
for the earliest men. Alterations in sea–land level re-drew the
coastline repeatedly in the years following the great Ice Age. This
geographical factor might have been a partial cause of certain
differences which we shall notice from time to time in the prehistory of the two sides of Solway.

As far as earliest man is concerned, there is no difference for
there is no man. Palæolithic man has not been traced so far north.
The cold and miserable climate of the dying Ice Age in that birch-
and-pine period ten thousand years ago is blamed for this absence.
I find it hard to believe that a few hardy pioneers did not penetrate north in summertime at least, having myself found warm
sunshine at the foot of many a cold glacier in parts of the world at
present arctic. However, the total population of these times could
probably be counted in hundreds, and as most of these would
prefer the lowlands on the one hand and most of the searching has
been done there on the other, it is not surprising that if any came
here their traces have not been discovered.

The Solway has always had its hunters and fishermen, and their
earliest prototypes belong to the age called Mezolithic. Many
micro-flints, small, exquisitely worked arrowheads and harpoon
blades have been found between the Mull and Gretna, though
rarely on the English side, and these are evidence of these first
fishermen. You can see some of their implements in Kirkcudbright Museum. From their middens—found near Oban—we
know they hunted seals and sharks, ate shellfish and haddock and
utilised the antlers of deer and the bones of whales. Their harpoon
method of fishing was again in vogue in the Solway Firth after
seven thousand years. There were two branches of the Mezolithic
family, each named after a site on the Continent. Harpoons from
the Dee near Kirkcudbright tell of Azilian settlement along the
shores, whilst elsewhere core and flake axes in Maglemosean style
imply the presence of the other branch, one that tackled the forests

rather than lived solely on the shore. These latter are traced to
Ireland, and it is more than probable that the Solway was their
halting-place on the route from eastern Britain.

Leaving these hunters and fishers, we come to the first farmers.
Two separate branches of Neolithic man are distinguished
(ceramically and architecturally) as Windmill Hill and Peter-
borough people after the type sites in the south-east lowlands.
Pottery and monuments of both have been found round the
Solway. The Windmill Hill people were part of that great
religious movement from the Mediterranean that filtered via
Brittany up the seas of western Britain. As Neolithic peoples,
they represent a revolution, a transition from savagery to barbarism, from wandering and gathering to growing and taming,
although lagging centuries behind the original economic and
urban revolution that slowly spread from the fertile crescent of
the Middle East. These changes in technique allowed the population to increase and prosper and finally to support a class of people
concerned in secondary and tertiary occupations. Stone-masons,
priests and clerks would all be involved in the building of the
great cairns which contained their ritual tombs, and which are
found on the hills of all our western shores. The Galloway hills
come down almost to the sea, and in them are hidden these tombs
—called Megalithic—some with typical horned forecourt. In
Cumberland we note a difference for none are found on the plains
of Solway. However, cairns are not the only evidence of these
Neolithic people, and even wooden implements (as well as stone
axes and pottery) were found at the wonderful settlement beside
Ehenside (or Gibb) Tarn * between Beckermet and the sea just
south of Solway in West Cumberland. Ehenside Neolithic
pottern is related to that of the same period from Glenluce in
Scotland, but the southern site was occupied well into the Roman
period.

About this time, 5,000 years ago, land was low and water high,
and it is possible that no settlements on the English coast of
Solway have been found because this land, flatter than its Scottish
counterpart, was under water to a greater extent. There is yet
another reason, one that accounts frequently for the richness of
finds on the north compared with those on the south. The bays
of Galloway reach out into the sea like a gigantic stake net and

* This was a tarn but now is cultivated land.

tend to catch more of the traffic passing before south-westerly winds up the Irish Sea from the south. In many ages was this tendency repeated.

After the Neolithic period, metal came to Solway with the folk of the Bronze Age who were at first, however, still overwhelmingly using stone. Neolithic and Bronze Age cultures met and fused in this part of the north-west. Fusion is one of the key words in the study of prehistory, especially hereabouts, and involves a whole collection of ideas first formulated by Sir Cyril Fox, to whom all later writers are indebted. He divided Britain not as we shall do at Solway or even Roman Wall, but into highland and lowland zones. South-east Britain, with its young softer rocks and drier lowland plain, is akin to the lands of western Europe of which it was a part until some seven thousand years ago. Being the most attractive farming land in the country, it has continually received waves of invaders across the short sea passage to settle and drive out or master the existing population. The highland zone contrasts in almost every way. Old hard rocks give mountainous country and consequently heavier rainfall. It is superficially less attractive and lends itself to a more pastoral or ranching type of agriculture. It has been the refuge over many ages of men escaping from the lowlands, and has tended to absorb and preserve their traditions, traditions which were usually completely replaced by new ones in their original home zone. This conception is sometimes exaggerated, and one modification springs to mind immediately where we are concerned. It is useful to think of the head of the estuary and the lowlands of the Solway, with their modest rainfall and flatter scenery built of younger rock, as a part of the lowland zone that has got itself lost or rather isolated from the rest. It is a zone which has been found by typical lowland peoples under pressure of peril or accident and, in more recent centuries the call of employment. The division between highland and lowland zones traditionally persists in our attitude to the Southerner and vice versa. The Southerner is still made welcome as in Bronze Age times, particularly when he brings the skills or materials of a civilisation more developed economically, if less spiritually rich.

There are sufficient clues for the Bronze Age in the north-west to be divided into its different periods. The first metal users, known from their ceremonial and drinking vessels as Beaker folk, arrived in the Eden Valley from the east through the Tyne gap. It is just possible that they formed the foundation of a traditional and linguistic conception, that of the Celtic peoples, which lingers in the west up to the present day. We shall hear much more about the Celts; sufficient to say now that nothing is really known of any linguistic identities at this early date. The Carlisle Museum and Dumfries and Galloway collections have many examples of their drinking vessels and in general we can imagine that the Beaker folk imposed themselves on the older Neolithic stocks. Some of their barrow burials, particularly in Yorkshire, certainly imply a wealthy type of leader, who used amber, jet, bronze and gold. It is believed that the Beaker folk were responsible for the great circles, which developed from wood to stone, that mark the landscape in various sizes. None exist on the southern shore, though fell Cumberland has fine examples near Penrith and Keswick, but the moors that run down to the Scottish side of the estuary have many and various circles, some of which we shall pass in later travels.

The Beaker barons in Britain bought the products of the Irish metalworkers, and the Solway is well to the fore as one of the routes along which this trade passed. I cannot reproduce them here, but the distribution maps of some of their products prepared for *The Personality of Britain* by Miss Lily Chitty are as clearly indicative of major routes as erratics were in the Ice Age and milestones are at the present time.

In the record of pottery, food vessels replace beakers, and as they have a flavour of Neolithic design, they probably represent a further fusion of cultures around the Firth. They certainly represent by their numbers a vastly increased population. There are many food vessels in the museums of Solway, and a very strange manifestation of the culture of the Food-Vessel people is found in the simple carvings, normally on living rock outcrops, of what are called "cup-and-ring" marks, circular hollows and associated groups of concentric circles—or occasionally spirals—all shallow yet still clearly discernible.

The people who followed the food-vessel users are also described by their pottery which is of a more sepulchral kind. They cremated their dead and buried the ashes in cinerary urns. The Urn folk migrated to Ireland again, via Galloway and Solway, and the evidence of their pottery can be seen in our museums, often complete with bones. These people absorbed the Food-Vessel societies. Subgroups can be distinguished by the decorations on their urns, and the two types round Solway are known as encrusted and cordoned. Although one cannot be dogmatic, the encrusted urn is generally found south from the water and the cordoned type to the north, showing the regrettable tendency the estuary occasionally has to separate cultures. The Urn folk could trace their ancestry back to European warriors who used battle-axes, and a variant of this type of axe became so popular in one district of Ireland that it is called the Bann axe. If I stress a single instance it is because there is a lesson hidden in a personal experience. A Gretna man brought to me recently one of the finest examples of Bann-type axes ever found, sharp at one end, rounded at the other, beautifully smoothed and perforated; it was a joy to handle. If expert opinion had been consulted when the axe was found and its site and associated sediments carefully noted, it might have provided a major link in the study of Solway settlements and prehistoric trade routes, but it was found many years ago "somewhere in Solway Moss". No one now knows exactly where, and much of its value has been lost while it has been lying in someone's lumber-room. It is now in Tullie House Museum. Similar cases lead me to believe that many finds must go unrecorded, and with the passing of time become entirely detached from associated evidence. I mentioned this during a lecture and two axes were later unearthed; perhaps this book will lead to more disgorging or at least prevent some recurrence of hoarding.

There must have been quite a settlement of the Urn folk around Dumfries, as one cemetery excavated there produced ten urns. That the Urn folk were a numerous population is evident, and it is a possibility that their language persisted in spite of later invasions. If this is so, it might be that it represents the earliest gaelic Celtic that can be speculatively traced in these islands. I have no space to write in detail of the development of metal weapons and implements, although I am tempted to do so as there are many examples from Solway in our museums, and the dating and typing have been done to a fine degree. However, I leave this as a subject of study worth following up.

It would be easy to say that the Iron Age followed the Bronze Age and quite misleading as far as Solway is concerned. Replacement of culture if not of peoples was the order in lowland Britain, but penetration of ideas and folk was slow in the highlands, and some people lived a Bronze Age life in Solway, lagging behind the rest of Britain until well into the Roman period. I am not saying that the Iron Age did not reach Solway. Imposition by chieftains and example by refugees would again lead to fusion, and there are many bits and pieces of the Iron Age as fragments in a complicated chain of evidence.

Let me try to be technical without too much complication. Speaking generally, the five centuries before Roman times saw three main Iron Age invasions. The first is known as Iron Age A or Hallstatt and had not much direct influence on the Solway.* The second was Iron Age B or La Tène, an invasion which introduced a culture vitally important in the further history of the western peoples. The La Tène invasions interrupted the Hallstatt and divided them into A1 and A2, but I can dispense with these finer divisions after making this point. Iron Age C or Belgae peoples do not concern the Solway directly.

The La Tène people are divided into several different groups, each of which influenced the Solway in a different way. Perhaps first were the people, sometimes called the Abernethy folk, who built the Gallic forts of Scotland of which Solway claims several examples. We shall visit one near Gatehouse. These people may be the ancestors of the Picts of history, and even of some present Scotsmen. There is a difference of opinion about their place of entry. Some think they landed on the east coast of Scotland, around Moray Firth and pushed down the great Glen to Lorne and also in Tay and Forth from where they spread to Clyde, Dumfriesshire and Galloway. They are distinguished by their manner of building, and Gallic forts (the name was Cæsar's) with fire-fused walls are usually termed "vitrified". The walls had cavities, timber bonded, and whether the fires were started accidentally or on purpose—by builders or attackers (most likely in the time of Agricola)—the effect was the same. The draught through the particular cavity construction allowed temperatures high enough to fuse the stones to be developed, as Childe and Thorneycroft have proved experimentally. The presence of a few similar structures in North Wales and the Midlands plus a related form of building in Cornwall has given rise to the alternative

---

* Although the line dividing A and B cultures is not always clear-cut.

suggestion that these people came up the western seas to Gallo-way, Clyde and Lorne and then spread to the north-east. A La Tène people, similar in some ways, came from the Marne to Kent, Wessex, perhaps the Isle of Wight and certainly to the York-shire coast north of the Humber. They used chariots and from a little village near Hull, where great numbers of burials have been found, are sometimes called the Arras charioteers. They are great in our history as the finest early exponents of the Celtic craft of metalwork.

We are now sliding imperceptibly out of prehistory into the Roman period. When the Romans came, they met several great risings of Iron Age Britons. Sir Mortimer Wheeler has drawn a vivid picture of what might have been the last great battle of these troubled years when King Venutius and his allies fortified Stanwick for a last gallant stand at the strategic gates to the north. The British were defeated and fled. Stanwick is near Scotch Corner, and some refugees may have gone north up the Great North Road, but no doubt others went west over Stainmoor and came through Penrith and Carlisle on to the Solway plain where they might be guaranteed a few years of comparative peace, until Agricola brought the Romans amongst them once again. I have given an imaginary picture, but there are evidences of isolated Arras chieftains on both sides of the Solway, and two finds at least are beautiful. The jewel-decorated sword found at Embleton in Cumberland, and now in the British Museum, is an isolated find, but when we get to the Scottish shore the links are more common. Fantastically striking is the chamfrein from Torrs in Kirkcudbrightshire that once adorned the study of Sir Walter Scott and is now in the National Museum of Scotland. This horse's mask, beautiful with its scrolls and weird with the two curved horns ending with the beaks of birds, once had a partner on the other side of a chariot pole, a pole incidentally along which the warrior could run and fight whilst his driver stood in the open-fronted platform. This mask is unique, even though doubts have been expressed about its present form, but from Yorkshire to Ireland (the old route again) there can be traced a series of horse trappings, especially bits, which indicate more than a transitory visit.

All these Iron Age people were Celtic, and another branch built the mysterious and inspiring brochs of Caithness and the

Northern and Western Isles. Whilst the point is not proved, it is reasonable to relate the broch builders with the Iron Age B people who settled in round stone forts and lived in courtyard houses in Devon and Cornwall and spread their duck-stamped pottery to the Cotswolds. This would provide another example of migration over that oft-used path, the Irish Sea route.* I would suggest that some of these migrants might have been tempted or blown, as many of their predecessors were, into Galloway bays for there are three or four suspected brochs around the Glenluce area, "suspected" because they have not been excavated well enough to prove their relationship to the true broch further north. The true broch was built around a central circular court-yard, perhaps roofed in timber, in the form of two concentric walls inwardly battened like a modern cooling tower and honey-combed between the walls with passages, steps and small alcoves. The Solway brochs are not up to this standard. I think they are true brochs myself, especially the one I know best south of Stair-haven near Glenluce. It is sited on a rocky shore by a tiny creek useful for smuggling or piracy; the outline is clear and the cavity well defined even though the ruins rise only a few feet. To my inexpert eye, the one at Teroy overlooking Loch Ryan is less broch-like, but it is both circular and Iron Age and so may be related. These Galloway brochs might never have towered to forty and fifty feet like those in the north (Mousa in Shetland still rises to forty-three feet). Sir Lindsay Scott has recently suggested that only a few of the hundreds of known brochs would rise above one storey. The majority would house small farmers and this argument does away with the necessity of imagining some hundreds of wealthy chiefs.

The broch culture is related to another south-west Iron Age B group called after its type site of Glastonbury. The people in that amazing collection of lake dwellings—which may have been the British emporium mentioned by classical continental writers—used the same type of implements for weaving and the same dice for gaming as have been found in Scottish brochs, and this gives additional strength to the suggestion of a south-westerly source. The Solway brochs might be an indirect development from this

* Some may have travelled overland, and a bone dart-head from Carlisle and textile appliances from Borness cave in the Stewartry hint at the last stage of their journey into the Solway Firth.

south-west source built by people thrusting back from a settled northern population rather than being the homes of some small group fallen by the wayside on the migration northwards.

Scottish Solway has its Iron Age crannogs (lake dwellings) too. Many have been excavated up to the latest in Milton Loch near Dumfries, and the *Transactions* are full of descriptions and catalogues of finds. Carlingwark Loch in the centre of Castle Douglas, for example, was well inhabited.

The numerous multi-vallum hill forts in the southern lowlands of Scotland on the slopes above Solway, and the headlands overlooking it, are also Iron Age B. Their occupants seem to have respected the frontier-to-be for they rarely appear south of the border on the English side. They probably also came from the south or south-west, perhaps by sea as Mrs Piggott has suggested, and it is probable that they were just not allowed to settle in the huge area under "Arras" control that later formed the state of the Brigantes. The Brigantes had fewer hill forts, but the great structure at Stanwick revealed in a classic excavation by Sir Mortimer Wheeler is a fine example.

The Iron Age C people can round off this part of the story, although these Belgae had little to do with the Solway. They only arrived in Britain about 75 B.C., but they brought with them the tools that were to make this country sufficiently prosperous to tempt the Roman Empire builders who were already struggling with their kinsmen on the European plain. Briefly, they introduced the heavy plough that shaped the pattern of Celtic agriculture in the lowland zone that can even today be traced beneath the Saxon or enclosed landscape. They brought the potter's wheel and three things which really changed the state of barbarism to one of civilization—cities, coins and kings, one of whom has passed as Shakespeare's Cymbeline into our literature and through Roman reporters into our written history.

Without a break, prehistory ends and the story of the Roman Empire picks up the thread of history. The Empire stretched from the Sahara and the Near East across Europe to the Solway which it joined to the North Sea first by a road and later by a wall. This was the first of many frontiers we shall meet. In Cæsar's trial invasions in 55 and 54 B.C., and in the successful invasion of Claudius in A.D. 43, the short crossing from Gaul was taken to lowland Britain. The lowland zone was again defined, this time

as the civil zone in which the Romans worked and farmed, settled
and lived a cultured life. Once again defeated occupiers retreated
into the highlands to be pursued and pacified in what we can call,
when ·the Roman supply lines were organised, the military as
well as the highland zone.

The Romans practised two dissimilar policies in northern
Britain. Some tried to extend their influence as far as it would go
and conquer the whole of the land. The others combined the
demarcation of a frontier at a suitable point with an attempt
to win to active co-operation the tribes north of the frontier
as a buffer between the Empire and the barbarians without.
Under two emperors, the frontier-plus-buffer-state idea was
stressed and in both cases the line was drawn from Solway to the
Tyne.

Hadrian's Wall, built by the legions under Aulus Platorius
Nepos, has given to the border the greatest Roman monument
in the west. Severus much later renewed the Wall as a fixed
barrier (he was once thought to have built it, so extensive were
his repairs) but his approach to the adjacent tribes was not like
that of other emperors. Instead of a cushion of friendly people, he
apparently attempted to create a cushion of people crushed and
cowed. In this respect his policy was one of expansion and attack.
Two others had attacked before him. Lollius Urbicus, the
governor under Antoninus Pius, had pushed far enough into
Caledonia to build a second frontier from Clyde to Forth. This is,
of course, *The* Wall to present-day Scotsmen. Antoninus Pius was
following the policy of Agricola, governor under the Flavian
emperors, and the Antonine armies in the field followed in his
very footsteps. Agricola had the best eye of any Roman for the
most suitable road, fort and camp, and excavators generally find
that Antonine forts in south-west Scotland overlie the remains of
earlier ones built by Agricola.

Of all the Romans in Britain, Agricola comes most easily to
life as a result of his biography by Tacitus. Tacitus's *Agricola* has
quite recently been suspected of more inaccuracies than was
previously thought, but his writing is vivid and terse and makes
good reading for its own sake as well as for its historical value.
One must make allowances for the fact that Tacitus was writing
about his own father-in-law and would rather praise Agricola
than put names to the sites of his camps and battles. This has

caused confusion and much speculation, but the confusion is in the light of recent discoveries being partly resolved.

So much work has been done on the Romans in the north that new discoveries are both surprising and exciting. As often, they have come about as the result of the application of a modern technique, in this case, aerial photography. This photography, combined with the ever-necessary spade-work, has given a completely new picture of the activities of the Romans in south-west Scotland. A great deal of this new information makes sense of statements in Tacitus's *Agricola* which were until recently doubted. Two expert comments will emphasise the change. As recently as 1932, Sir George Macdonald questioned whether the Romans had ever mastered Annandale and the country to its west, and he criticised their plan in leaving their main eastern routes and midland occupation threatened by the Achilles' heel of south-west Scotland. Sir George Macdonald was, of course, expressing an opinion based on the then known archæological evidence. It can be seen how the evidence has been changed when I quote from another eminent archæologist, Professor Ian Richmond, writing on the discoveries at a Roman site just north of the Solway in Kirkcudbrightshire. He has said "they imply the existence of nothing less than a trunk road through Galloway and the thorough penetration of a district hitherto considered as beyond the Roman pale ".

Let me try to blend Tacitus's history with the latest scientific archæology. Agricola's governorship lasted for seven years from A.D. 78 (or 77). His first task was to quell a revolt of British in North Wales led by refugees from the south-east who had settled in Anglesey. In his second year Agricola reached the Solway apparently without much fighting. The archæological evidence makes it fairly clear that he moved north through Cumberland and then across to the east coast of Britain constructing as he went a road supported by signal stations, side roads and forts. The route he took, from Carlisle across the isthmus as far as the main route north along Dere Street into Scotland, was again used by later Roman generals, especially under Trajan, and is generally known as the Stanegate.

Agricola's third year of campaigning

"opened up new nations, for the territory of tribes as far as the estuary named Tanaus was ravaged. Our army was seriously buffeted by fierce storms, but the enemy were too terrified to molest it. There was even time to spare for establishment of forts."

So speaks Tacitus. In other words he conquered much of southern Scotland by land and sea attacks.

The next chapter in Tacitus sums up Agricola's successes in southern Scotland although it does not specify what was happening in the south-west. He describes how districts already overrun were secured, and how a halting-place was found at the narrow neck between Clyde and Forth. He says that "the whole sweep of country to the south was safe in our hands" but I suspect that penetration into Galloway, if any was made, was superficial until his fifth year of campaigning.

Until recently, responsible opinion confined Agricola's advance to the eastern part of southern Scotland. This advance was made along the great road from Corbridge through Cappuck and Newstead to Inveresk on the Forth and across to Castledykes near Lanark. The discoveries made by Dr St Joseph and his colleagues have satisfied most of the authorities that this advance had another prong in the west. In brief, that Agricola was no mean general and that his pincers had two claws. From Carlisle a Roman road goes through Annandale and has been traced in many sections. The fort of Birrens, known for years as an outpost of Hadrian's Wall, has now been shown to have been built on an earlier Agricolan site. Agricolan forts have been found in this valley also at Burnswark, Torwood, Milton and Littleclyde, covering a line up to Inveresk where it would meet the road from the east. There was probably a main branch to Castledykes as well which then split into two, the north arm leading on to Bothwell-haugh and the Firth of Clyde, while the other branch led south-west from Castledykes to the Loudon Hills and probably on to the west coast to a port in the neighbourhood of Irvine (this last coastal section is pure guesswork, but an obvious conclusion).

This, however, is nothing like all the story. Further west, in the valley of the Nith, a whole new series of forts has been discovered and partly excavated. Most of them belong to a later period, that of the Emperor Antoninus, but in two places at least are traces of an Agricolan settlement, the main one being at Dalswinton just north of Dumfries.

This is quite sufficient evidence to alter the known picture, but even more exciting was the discovery in 1949 of the large Roman fort of Glenlochar in Kirkcudbrightshire, just north of Castle Douglas, obviously part of a road system to Galloway and first occupied in the time of Agricola. There is even evidence of a road going north from Glenlochar and although up to the present traces of a road to the west have not been found, a small Roman fort was discovered at the crossing of the Fleet above Gatehouse which is probably part of the same system. Prophecy is unwise in archæology, but it is more than reasonable to hope that somewhere round Stranraer will be found a Roman seaport to act as the logical terminus of this system, Ptolemy's *Reregonius Sinus*.

Archæology does not tell us exactly when Agricola built these forts, so we must now return to Tacitus who says:

"In the fifth year of campaigning, Agricola began with a sea passage,* and in a series of successful actions subdued nations hitherto unknown. The whole side of Britain that faces Ireland was lined with his forces. But his motive was rather hope than fear . . . I have often heard Agricola say that Ireland could be reduced and held by a single legion and a few auxiliaries."

For decades archæologists have tried to interpret Agricola's actions on the basis of these sentences. R. G. Collingwood argued in the light of then available evidence that "that part of Britain which faces Ireland" meant the Cumberland coast, but even from Tacitus it is awkward to reason that to get to, say, Maryport or Ravenglass from his base fort, which might have been Chester or Carlisle, Agricola should begin with a sea passage. This was not impossible—from Chester—but rather unlikely. It is even more difficult to believe that the West Cumbrians were "nations hitherto unknown" when Agricola's armies had already passed their territory more than once.

He could have easily taken a sea voyage across the Solway and landed on the Galloway coast, which most definitely "faces Ireland". There were many places from which he could have left, and indeed there is some evidence to support the view that at some time Ravenglass and less certainly Maryport harboured the Roman fleet. Recent work has given him one possible landing-place, and it is conceivable that others will be found. On the hill

---

* An alternative if less understandable translation of "*Nave prima transgressus gnotus*" gives: "Agricola crossed by the first boat".

just north of Caerlaverock Castle is a native British settlement. This has long been known. On the side of the hill is a Roman fort. This has long been suspected. In 1772 that great traveller Pennant wrote in his diary:

"Visited Wardlaw, a small hill with a round British camp, surrounded with two fosses on the top, and on the south side, the faint vestiges of a Roman camp now much ploughed up. The prospect from this eminence is very fine." *

Pennant observed well, except that the fort is actually north of the camp. About twenty years later this fort was noted again. The Old Statistical Account speaking of Caerlaverock says:

"Not far west of this castle rises the hill of Wardlaw, on top of which are yet visible the vestiges of a Roman encampment conjectured to be the Uxela of Ptolemy." *

This little district must have a strange effect on compasses because Wardlaw with its obvious tree-crowned outline is due north of the castle, not west. However, this site has now been accurately surveyed, though not completely excavated. It was resurrected by air observation, and an aerial survey in 1945 revealed more details. Excavation has proved that this fort was both big and permanent though it has not provided any evidence of Agricolan building. However, Wardlaw is sited in a wonderful position to command the Solway and the entrance to Nithsdale, to receive signals from the south Solway shore and perhaps to guard a harbour (R. C. Reid has suggested a possible site for this harbour near the castle) which would be the Scottish terminus of an oft-made Solway journey. Just as the medieval castle near by saw the massed armada of Edward I crossing the Solway for an attack on Galloway so might the British occupants of Wardlaw Hill have seen Agricola's fleet twelve centuries earlier.

So far as the Solway is concerned we have little more to do with Agricola, but I will finish his story for the sake of completeness even though it has a sad ending. Agricola advanced into Caledonia, saw a revolt of Usipi tribesmen from his army (who quite probably escaped on a ship from Solway) and in his last year in Britain fought a decisive battle against the north British at

* My attention was drawn to these extracts by *The Roman Occupation of South-Western Scotland*, edited by S. N. Miller.

Mons Graupius, wherever that might be. After this victory Agricola was recalled and, although such action was not without precedent, was much depressed. His son-in-law went further and hinted darkly that Agricola's death which soon followed was the result of poisoning by the Emperor Domitian.

Agricola had the whole of Britain within his grasp, but it was "let slip". Under Trajan, the next emperor who concerns us, the Stanegate was strengthened to meet a worsening situation. There is much evidence of Trajanic work, but things must have been pretty bad when the next emperor came himself to Britain in A.D. 122 and decided to build a wall from Solway to Tyne as a permanent barrier against the north.

Hadrian's Wall was built under Aulus Platorius Nepos who was legate of Britain in the years immediately following 122. The eastern section of the Wall, which was seventy-three English miles from coast to coast, was built in stone from the beginning, but owing to lack of materials the western half was first built in turf as a temporary measure and later replaced in stone. The whole Wall was first designed as an elevated sentry walk with a castle every mile to hold about fifty men, and two turrets between each castle for the Roman equivalent of the inevitable platoon and sergeant. The bases at first would be the forts on the Stanegate to the east of Carlisle, and perhaps Carlisle, Old Carlisle and Papcastle, inland from Solway, but it is thought that opposition to the building caused a change of plans which involved the building of forts on the Wall itself to house the fighting garrison. The Wall was built by the legions but manned by auxiliaries. I often wonder how the Spaniards at Maryport reacted to the Solway's colder westerlies—and in open sandals too!

There are really four parts to the defences; first a ditch facing the north, then the Wall incorporating forts, milecastles and turrets, and behind it the great earthwork of the vallum which seems to have been designed as the political frontier distinct from the military one (there *are* more recent theories about the vallum, but lack of space prevents me from discussing them in detail, and the one I have given, which is largely due to Professor R. G. Collingwood, does not—to me at least—seem to have been completely demolished). Finally, there was a network of supply routes. Magnificent though the Wall is, particularly to the east where it marches on the crest of the Whin Sill, it does not belong to the Solway except for a few miles between Carlisle and Bowness. I shall return to this stretch in a later chapter, but here I just want to remark on the factors which led the Romans to end their Wall at Bowness-on-Solway. Camden put his finger on the main reason. The Solway and its rivers are fordable, as we have seen, between Bowness and Carlisle, and armies crossing this water could turn the Wall had it ended at Carlisle or along the Eden. Personally I think there is a little more to it than that and that a major function was to control raiding. The elevated sentry walk that I have mentioned (the phrase is Collingwood's) would be an excellent means of stopping loot-laden raiders, especially those driving stolen cattle. Cattle as well as men can ford the Solway. The Solway can be crossed easily enough to the west of Bowness, but only in small boats, and no reiver in his right senses is going to indulge in cattle thieving using small boats. It is a pity that the Wall was destroyed in this western section. It would have been useful in later times, and in fact a similar contraption was once suggested to Queen Elizabeth.

However, the western flank of the Wall, even ending at Bowness, could be turned by determined seaborne attackers, and some defence system was obviously necessary to the Romans along the Solway shore. I shall describe this in a little more detail as it is more a part of the Solway scene than the Wall itself and also because it has had less publicity. First of all, there was a road along the coast running for most of its length probably on present coast roads, although a new twist has been given at Bankend, north of Maryport, by an inland scallop. Stretches of this road are completely untraceable, but there is little doubt of its existence and parts have been reported from time to time, particularly by Camden. The patrolling troops were given quarters similar to those of their colleagues on the Wall, but these coastal buildings have been named fortlets and signal towers instead of milecastles and turrets. Many of them have still to be found although there is a sufficient amount of archaeological evidence to imply their location with a high degree of certainty.* The system probably stretched from Bowness to St Bees and was then linked south by road to Ravenglass.

As on the Wall proper, the main garrisons were put in forts on this front line, and the three forts have been investigated over the

* See p. 68.

past few centuries in varying degrees. They are at Beckfoot, south of Silloth, revealed anew in 1947 by an aerial photograph which shows great detail; Maryport, known for years and with its civil settlement one of the greatest treasure houses of the whole system (a few of the finds now preserved at Netherhall are shown in photograph number 3); and Moresby, north of Whitehaven, the outline of which can be clearly seen on the lower distant plateau in photograph number 4. Again in parallel with the Roman defences on the Wall and elsewhere, these forts are linked by a system of roads to supporting forts in the rear. The two main inland forts were Old Carlisle (the name is confusing; the site is near Wigton) and Papcastle near Cockermouth. Although the roads are not traceable along all their length, it is almost certain that Old Carlisle was connected to both Beckfoot and Papcastle, whilst the latter had branches to Moresby and Maryport.

Since this book was written and sent to the publisher I have had the pleasure of doing a season's work with Mr R. L. Bellhouse, an amateur archæologist living in Cumberland. We have had sufficient success to necessitate rewriting the next few hundred words and risking the wrath of the printer. We have also had some grand days by the Solway.

I have space here for but a brief summary of the work. A full report will be published in the *C. & W. Transactions*. I have already told how years of work have established the sequence of the structures of Hadrian's Wall. There was a milecastle for thirty to forty men every Roman mile (1,620 yards) with two turrets, each externally about twenty feet square, spaced equidistant between them, i.e. every 540 yards. These structures, with local divergencies, were built with the Wall itself, and soon after, great forts, sometimes obliterating a turret, were added *on* the Wall to house the patrolling garrisons. For reasons already mentioned the Wall was ended at Bowness-on-Solway.

To the south-west of Bowness the marshy inlet of Moricambe divides the smooth curve of the Cumberland coast into two sections, which are usually dealt with separately. Fairly recent work has shown that from Bowness to Moricambe the 540-yards sequence of milefortlet and signal towers—the Solway equivalent of milecastle and turrets—was continued, although the Wall itself was not. South-west of Moricambe the position has been vague.

The major coastal forts that I have already mentioned have long been known, and in the nineteenth century Joseph Robinson of Maryport discovered four isolated signal towers exactly equivalent to the Wall turrets. A fifth tower was observed in 1937 but was destroyed in gravel quarrying. In the 1920s Professor R. G. Collingwood surveyed the whole coast and on the evidence of his own observations and Robinson's towers deduced that this section of the Solway defences as far south as St Bees had been planned *tactically* with the signal towers sited on intervisible high points. Last autumn Richard Bellhouse attacked the problem from a different angle. Combining the known evidence with some new observations and a piece of brilliant reasoning, he searched selected points each some multiple of 540 yards from Beckfoot fort, assuming the latter had replaced a signal tower. His assumptions were proved correct, and weekend digging in October added three more towers (and a host of smaller finds) to the five already known. These eight towers are sufficient when plotted on the map to illustrate the existence of the same sequence that has achieved an almost ritual significance along the line of the Wall, although to complete the picture at least two milefortlets are still required. At the end of the year none had been found, although one can be seen plainly at the base of Grune Point in an aerial photograph. It has not been possible to test this with the spade.

This work, therefore, left two questions: the first concerned the existence and situations of milefortlets, the second the extent of the system to the south-west.

Burrow Walls, Workington, was chosen as a site that might, when excavated, throw light on both questions, and a week's holiday dig was planned there for Easter 1955. This site had medieval remains (see page 210). It fitted into the calculated sequence, had already been suspected as the position of a milefortlet by Professor Collingwood and others and was on the land of a most co-operative farmer. Mr Bellhouse, Mr Iain McIvor and myself established a camp there in the shelter of the ancient walls, and were joined by students and volunteers.

In planning the dig the history of the site was studied. It gave hints of a structure much larger than our suspected fortlet, and when aerial photographs of the site were supplied by Dr St Joseph these hints seemed to crystallise with exciting definition. We therefore surveyed the whole area and opened those squares on our grid which might test the existence not of a fortlet for forty men but of a full-sized fort for perhaps a thousand infantry. The remains we found were very near the surface, and this perhaps explained the absence of dressed facing stone, but the medieval stone robbers had left complete the cobble in clay foundations of the rectangular rampart and could not destroy the evidence of the protecting ditches. Here was a fort 290 feet across the ramparts along the coastal axis and perhaps 360 feet at right angles to the coast. This latter figure is an estimation, as erosion by an ancient channel of the Derwent has destroyed one end. The rampart was protected by two ditches and the inner ditch still contains fallen stone and timber. A complete investigation was not possible, due both to shortage of time and abundance of water, but the finds indicate that this fort was built in the time of Hadrian and was a partner to Beckfoot, Maryport and Moresby both in size and function.

Close inside the rampart foundations on two sides was another ditch, unexpected and out of pattern, which gave up pottery of the fourth century. Whilst it is too early to be certain, the evidence and parallels elsewhere suggest that the Hadrianic fort was reconstructed on a smaller scale, and that this ditch belongs to the later fort. This point will be investigated in the future, but the last six months have seen the Wall sequence proved in the Beckfoot sector and the addition of the major fort of Burrow Walls to the Roman defences of the Solway Firth.

For most of three centuries the Solway Firth shared with Hadrian's Wall the distinction of marking the northern boundary of Imperial Rome. There had been many changes over this period. The Romans left behind, on both sides of the Solway, a Celtic people to whom the ways of imperial civilisation were no far-off fairy tale but a commonplace of their daily lives. Romano-British settlements continued to exist on the south of the estuary at least, and one, Old Carlisle, which had already had experience in local self-government, seems to have been prosperous many years later. Probably this corner of Britain saw a continuity of tradition which lasted in some form or other for centuries.

1. "Rough Firth, typical of the northern shore, has a history of smuggling as well as a beauty of scene that has no equal across the water"

2. Scaurs and banks of the living coast dominated by Criffell

3. Netherhall, Maryport. Part of the Roman collection from Alauna, one of the greatest treasure-houses of the north

4. Moresby, near Whitehaven, has corn, coal and a lovely house. Around the church can be seen the ramparts of a Roman fort

5. Holm Cultram Abbey (Abbeytown) is still working as a parish church though it retains but a fragment of its former glory

6. Ruthwell Cross. "It is as though a struggling art form suddenly skipped the years of apprenticeship and adolescence . . ."

7. Dumfries. "A place to linger contemplating the swans under Devorgilla's bridge or watching the water curling over the Caul"

8. Grune Point "once sheltered half a hundred ships . . . but there is now no scene more typical of the wild loneliness of Solway and the texture of its surface"

9. Caerlaverock Castle. "... the dainty fabric of the dwelling-house"

10. Southerness, once Salterness. Paul Jones was born near here

11. Stones, sand and scaurs blend with jetsam under Criffell

12. Belted Galloway cattle. "This ancient and distinguished breed . . ."

CHAPTER V

DARK AGE CROSSROADS AND THE CHURCH IN SOLWAY

THE decay of the Roman Empire was a twofold action. As the heart weakened so the extremities rebelled. The north was neg-lected on more than one occasion, but almost always the gar-risons returned. Forts still show the marks of destruction and repair. Almost always; when Maximus withdrew his men in 383, there was no return. This, by the way, is the traditional view. It has been suggested in the light of recent coin finds that certain forts might temporarily have been reoccupied until nearly A.D. 400. The exact date of the going of the army is not important to us, however, for the army was not the only contribution of Rome to the Solway district. They left Britain a disorganised country with the troubles of the Empire reflected in attacks by Caledonians from the north and by Saxons from the east, and in internal unrest caused by wandering bands of freed slaves, who caused havoc in the countryside, especially in the lowlands. The Romans left, however, a native British (linguistically Welsh) population very different from the Iron Age Celts they had found four hundred years before. I have pointed out that as far as three of our local settlements were concerned Romanised life continued for a long time. Roman influence still persists in the language—especially of Wales—as well as on the landscape, and the British of the year 400 were proud citizens, still part of the Empire, if temporarily neglected. Even nearer Hadrian's Wall, the Chester-holm stone, inscribed in capitals of the end of the fourth century, implies a continuation of Roman traditions. It also takes us from the material to the spiritual, for it records the burial of a Christian. Whatever else collapsed with the military Empire, Christianity survived and even grew stronger.

In all Britain, it was first on a little promontory overlooking the northern Solway that the seeds of Celtic Christianity took root and grew to flavour not only Britain but the whole of western Europe. It seems as though, for once reversing the

71

atmosphere of centuries ahead, we here had peace, while much of Britain was suffering from anxious havoc.

The geographical distinctions noted in earlier parts of this book show how natural it was that while war and replacement of peoples went on in the lowland south-east, the preservation of the old stock and the traditions of Rome should be strongest in the highland zone of the north and west. It is symbolic that it is about the north-west district that were written the majority of the old stories which preserve in a mass of legend some grains of truth pointing to the preservation of old ways of living as well as to an active defence against new invasion.

Native resistance was sustained by a hard core of Welsh principalities under local rulers both north and south of the estuary and in Wales itself. These men kept in touch for as long as possible with an Empire not yet dead. They founded ruling families which lasted for generations, and were so important that, under the title "Men of the North", they almost monopolised that earliest Welsh poetry which is one of our chief sources for this period. The earliest known of these kings, Coroticus, seems to have ruled from Altclut—the Rock of Dumbarton. He was Romanised and at least nominally Christian although he has a niche in history as the recipient of St Patrick's letter chiding the "citizens" for their lapses. His successors concern us more directly. One of the greatest of these, Coel the Elder, ruled south-west Scotland from his capital in Kyle, which may, like the nursery rhyme, preserve his name today. It is a possibility that Coel, working under the general strategy of distant Rome, was the central figure responsible for moving the military leader Cunedda from his own district near Edinburgh to resist an attack on Wales by the Scots (at this date confined to Ireland). Cunedda's sons founded dynasties in Wales, and it is more than probable that his allies were gathered from the shores of Solway. Legend may approximate to truth when it tells how Cunedda stopped in Carlisle on his journey south to gather compatriots (Cymry) for his struggles. Whether he did or not, the name of his Cymry is still to be found in Cumberland. This migration to Wales from a district in Scotland between the Walls—incidentally a common Roman tactic—indicates that the central authority considered that the north was fairly safe at this time, the beginning of the fifth century. This suggestion is echoed in the fact that a young

Romanised Briton called Ninian returned about this time from his studies in Rome and Gaul to be the founder of the first Christian church in Scotland.

In passing, I should mention St Patrick, an almost contemporary great Christian. It is believed by some authorities that his early adventures—he was kidnapped when a boy by Irish pirates under King Niall—began on the shores of the Solway. This is not proved. Bannavem Taberniae, his birthplace, has not been identified with certainty though it must have been on an arm of the western sea in a Romanised district. His father was a church deacon and a Roman official. When Patrick returned to visit his family, he apparently found no great changes, although the Romans had been gone some years.

There is more evidence about St Ninian's activities in the region, although much of it is as shadowy as a Solway mist. It consists in the main of a Life, written some eight centuries later and rather unreliable although based on an earlier source now lost, a number of inscribed stones, Bede's account of a legend and a poem, both of the eighth century. Archæological evidence proves at least that Christianity was established in Galloway very early. The Latinus stone found at Whithorn marks a Christian burial and is inscribed in Roman fourth-century style. St Ninian is supposed to have founded the first church in Scotland about the year 397. This church was probably discovered in 1949. I can say this because of the whitewash.

About Ninian, Bede wrote: ". . . and this place pertaining to the province of Bernicia is commonly called 'ad candidam casam' because there he made a church of stone after a custom strange to the Britons". *Candida casa* means literally "the white house". Now, the local stone is greyish, and the Britons of that district would be no strangers to stone buildings, having seen plenty of the activities of the Romans. Therefore we can assume that Bede's description indicates that the church was plastered or whitewashed.

On the tiny Isle of Whithorn, bridge-distant from the Machers thrusting south from Galloway, is an Iron Age promontory fort and a thirteenth-century chapel, probably built for pilgrims—kings and commoners have made the pilgrimage to Whithorn *—but no traces of an earlier chapel have ever been found on the

* James IV made many pilgrimages, from Edinburgh, on foot.

Isle. At Whithorn itself, some miles away on the mainland, are the ruins of a Premonstratensian abbey founded by Fergus of Galloway in the thirteenth century. In 1949, in the course of excavations, a much older building was found incorporated in the southern end of the abbey foundations. These most ancient walls appear to have been covered with a white cement or plaster. Knowing the habits of early monastic builders, it seems probable, and this is all that can be said at the moment, that they built their altar on top of the original *candida casa*. Perhaps Ninian's bones were once preserved therein as holy relics. One of his arms travelled and was revered throughout Europe until it finally disappeared from ken at the time of the Reformation.

There is no doubt that the church of Ninian was a great centre of missionary work and of learning in close contact with the Celtic church that soon grew up in Ireland. Its continuity is indicated in the writings of Bede and others who tell us that it was the centre ot an Anglian bishopric some four centuries later.

There has always been a minor sea state in culture, if not political organisation, surrounding the Irish Sea: in this context I might call it the Celtic sea. Small boats can still ply these channels almost as quickly as a modern railway travels from part to part. Try this by going by train from Stranraer to Land's End calling in at St Bees, Anglesey and Pembrokeshire on the way. I imagine such a journey would be worthy of an inner circle to Dante's Inferno. By sea, these Dark Age Britons speaking Welsh (P-Celtic or, as it used to be called, Brythonic) would be in contact from Galloway to Brittany, whither there had been migration from south-west Britain. Ireland, on the other shore of the Celtic sea, spoke the other Celtic form, Gaelic or Qu-Celtic (Goidelic), which they later took to Scotland, but the monks were either bilingual or relied upon their common Latin. At any rate, the Solway was a focal point, and just as Irish gold of the Bronze Age was traded along the Solway, so the religious ideas of the Dark Ages took the same route into the heart of Britain.

The Celtic peoples lived a precarious life with little in the way of material civilisation, but their intellectual and imaginative life was sustained at a high level. Even their art, which, inherited from the La Tène charioteers, had slumbered for centuries and been overwhelmed by Roman mass-production, rose anew and to its greatest height during these ages. Shadows of the Celtic personality still persist around the Irish Sea. Peoples of these lands are noted for their storytelling. Lethbridge has suggested with point that the Norse sagas only grew to glory after the blending of Celtic influence. Stories of Cumberland (even Will Ritson's exaggerations), the romances of Galloway in Crockett and lesser-known writers, the ancient poetry of Wales and the modern poetry of that country up to the richness of *Under Milk Wood* may be all part of the same inheritance that lingers in the tales of Ireland and the wealth of *Juno and the Paycock*. Belief in fairies and wee folk persisted (still persists) around the Celtic seas later than anywhere else in Britain.

The Celtic church had two more serious aspects to its personality. The first was the love of learning that helped preserve the traditions of Classical Greece and Rome during an age when profane literature was banned and almost wiped off the face of western Europe. Secondly, this church won lasting respect by its simple yet strong missionary spirit that converted the west, then the north of Britain, and had already extended into western Europe, where it was to influence the revival of the Roman church.

Leaving for a time religious developments, we find an interesting political situation in the fifth century. Two well-known individuals in Wales and the south-west had parallels in the Solway. Vortigern of Wales was a great chief of the west and possibly its early central authority. He it was who welcomed the Saxon fifth column and may have lived to rue the day. Let us hope that the modern policy of rearming the Saxons' descendants in Germany is not one of history's repetitions. Vortigern was a general title meaning "high lord" as well as this man's name, and the Dark Age settlement (Palmcaster) that succeeded to the site of Roman Old Carlisle was ruled by a lesser Vortigern, a minor lord of Solway. The other parallel is more famous. As Ambrosius fought the Saxons in the south, so the famous Arthur was a mobile defender of Solway and the north-west. Most of our information about Arthur comes from Geoffrey of Monmouth, that most unreliable historian, but when the myth and legend have been cleared away, we seem to see a British general, Romanised in equipment and cavalry tactics, being rushed from place to place to meet recurring threats from Saxons and recalcitrant Britons alike. He is associated in legend with "Merry Carlisle", and I think in fact it might have served as his temporary head-quarters. It would be the logical base for his last battle at Camlann, the site of the Roman fort Camboglanna near Gilsland in Cumberland.* Here he would be defending the eastern arm of the crossroads into Solway, the arm pointing through the Tyne gap to Newcastle and the east coast, the route along which Agricola had planted his Stanegate and Hadrian had followed with his Wall.

After Arthur's death, the English threat from the east was consolidated when Ida founded the kingdom of Bernicia in 547, but the renewed threat met reorganised defence. In south-west Scotland, the House of Coel had either divided into smaller states or ruled through various sub-princes. Two very great ones appear in the region. In one part, which I call Strathclyde for convenience (though its boundaries are vague at this date), was Rhydderch, whose name may be perpetuated in Carruthers near Birrens. He was allied with another great ruler, Urien of Rheged, the region south of Strathclyde which embraced the Solway from its capital at Dunragit in Galloway, passed Carlisle and reached as far as Rochdale in Lancashire. Urien and Rhydderch were allies at the Battle of Arthuret in 573. We have already met the mysterious mound of Armterid as a glacial esker marking the presumed site of this battle on the north-east flats of Solway. It seems likely that this famous battle gave Celtic Christianity a decisive victory over pagan forces. One of the contestants was Gwendolow, whose name perhaps persists in the neighbouring Carwhinley. Tradition says that the famous St Kentigern (or Mungo) was a descendant of Urien, and an even stronger tradition makes Rhydderch his patron. There are certainly a number of churches around the Solway with very early dedications to Kentigern and his association with Dumfriesshire is generally accepted. Another tradition associates Merlin with the battle, but I think we might forget this one. Urien has been called "Lord (or Shepherd) of the Solway" by a late source, and the Solway equated with the Merin Rheged, the Sea of Rheged. Perhaps this was the Solway's early British title, although an Irish source later called it "Tracht Romra"—shore of the strong

* For Arthur I am following suggestions made by O. G. S. Crawford in *Antiquity*, 1935.

tide. A poem of Taliesin describing a Pictish raid on Urien's territory gives a description well fitting the estuary, and his title for the site, "Gwen Ystrad", the white strath, would fit any of the seething fords that provided fields for battle.

By this time we find that the princes of Rheged are allied with the latest invaders of the south-west of Scotland, the Scots from Ireland. It was one of these, Aedan, who led the defence of the west against the greatest leader the English had so far thrown up. Ethelfrith won his battle at Degsestan—Dawston in Liddesdale— in 603, driving a wedge into Dumfriesshire. Apparently Ethelfrith was fond of wedges, for he soon split the northern British from the Welsh Cymry at Chester in 616. As there is no story of any great battle by which the English became Lords of Rheged (i.e. Solway), it was probably achieved by treaty after the marriage between Ethelfrith's grandson, Oswy, and a descendant of Urien.

Quietly Galloway, Dumfriesshire and Carlisle slipped into the realm of England. We find towards the end of the seventh century the Anglian lands of Northumbria stretched to their greatest extent as far as Galloway. We find a new English church created by the Synod of Whitby maintaining the best elements of both Celtic and Roman traditions. Its organisation and links with the Continent were Roman, but its love of learning and missionary zeal were derived directly from Celtic tradition. The great schools of Anglo-Saxon England as well as the energy which carried its ideals over much of the Continent were an extension of the spirit that began in a Solway isle with Ninian. The climax of this unique combination was reached in the greatest school of carving that Britain has ever known.

The greatest works of this school were two related crosses. One stands at Bewcastle in the wild northern fells of Cumberland, and the other on the low saltings of the Solway in the Dumfriesshire church of Ruthwell. Some may admire the Bewcastle cross more than that at Ruthwell, and its setting outside the church and against the fells is certainly the more impressive, but Ruthwell cross, preserved with taste in the church, is infinitely lovely when it gleams and shadows its carvings in the light of an early Solway evening.

I confess elsewhere to a partiality for the traditions of the Celtic west, but the Anglian off-comers to Solway also had a virile culture, and I must try to be fair to them here. Regarding these crosses, about which many opinions are held, I choose to suggest that they are symbolic of the blending of the best influences of these two branches of our heritage, Anglo-Saxon and Celtic, like the Church which gave them life. This is a personal opinion and to some will seem quite wrong, but at least I have eased my conscience by indicating that there are differences of opinion. Everyone must agree on the fundamental aspect that will appeal mostly to the pilgrims who visit them, and I would urge a visit, as the plaster casts that exist in London and elsewhere are but a mockery of the true work. Their beauty and uniqueness are almost miraculous. When one has studied other crosses in the same line, it is as though a struggling art form suddenly skipped the years of apprenticeship and adolescence and arrived at full maturity. These two crosses have many similarities and but few differences. They are invariably discussed together to facilitate comparison and chronological and artistic argument. In a book like this it is quite hopeless for me to give any summary of the mass of detail that has been poured from the pens of many scholars whose lifetimes have been devoted to the study of these cross shafts, and I shall content myself with a few generalisations.

There is a photograph (number 6) of the Ruthwell cross, taken from a viewpoint chosen to show several of the most interesting aspects. The figure carving from the Gospels is the main part and is on the south face shown and the north one at the back. Next there is the pattern or decorative carving on the east and west faces. The camera shows the gracefully proportioned interlacing vine scrolls enlivened by fantastic animals popping in and out of the loops to nibble the grapes. All the panels have wide margins on which there is carved lettering. Around the figure sculptures is the story of the events portrayed in each panel written in Latin in the language of the Vulgate. On the margins of the decorative panels is carved a story in runes.

The Ruthwell runes are Anglo-Saxon. When the cross was first set up after various adventures during which it was broken, thrown out and finally rescued, the minister asked various Scandinavian scholars to translate the runes. Runes are a form of writing which can trace its ancestry from the Greek alphabet, modified for use on stone and wood, through eastern Europe into Germany and thence north to Scandinavia, where many examples exist. However, a distinct set of runes lingered in Germany and crossed the North Sea with our Saxon ancestors. It was possible some years ago to confuse Scandinavian and Anglian runes, and Dr Duncan's consultants, world famous in their own Scandinavian runic language, achieved nothing but ridiculous results from their work at Ruthwell. It was a famous Anglo-Saxon scholar, J. M. Kemble, who at last deciphered the runes with almost perfect exactitude. His work was tested and the story of this check is truly amazing. After Kemble had found that the runes represented a sacred Anglo-Saxon poem, he discovered that there had just been made a translation of a medieval document known as the Vercelli codex which he was amazed to find contained the same poem, *The Dream of the Rood*. It is a tribute to his work that only three words were found to be different in the two versions. This poem is not only one of our very earliest treasures of literature but can stand as a powerful piece of writing for any age. From the long poem, I quote here the three extracts, carved in the seventh century, that can be traced on the Ruthwell cross:

The cross "a gallows-tree, but not of shame"; is made to speak:

"Then the young warrior prepared himself—'twas God Almighty, resolute and strong; brave, in the sight of many, He went up upon the lofty cross, to save mankind. I trembled in His clasp, yet dared not bow, or fall to earth; I had to stand there firm. A cross they stood me there; I uplifted the great King, the Lord of Heaven, and yet I dared not stoop. They pierced me with dark nails: you see the wounds, the open gashes; I durst harm none of them. They scorned us both together. Stained was I with the blood that streamed. . . .

. . . Christ was on the Cross. Then men came thither, hastening from afar unto their noble Prince. All this saw I. Sore pained, I bowed me . . .

. . . wounded with shafts. Him they laid down, limb-weary; stood by His head; they looked upon the Lord of Heaven. . . "

Story sculpture, the decorative pattern, Latin and runic inscriptions make a unity of literature and art, and I think it is certain that all the work on the cross was done at one period and by the same sculptor or the same small group working under an inspired

master. The runes were Anglo-Saxon and *The Dream of the Rood*
is generally considered to be the work of a Saxon, possibly
Cædmon of Whitby. However, much of the work has a flavour
that implies its link with earlier Celtic art, and I personally believe
that such a sudden flowering of Anglo-Saxon art could only have
taken place with a leaven of Celtic inspiration. Here difficulties
arise. The Saxon invaders were not altogether the dull and stolid
typical Teutons that some writers have made them out to be. In
carving and writing and most especially in fine personal orna-
ment, revealed at its best at Sutton Hoo, they had a tradition that
could be traced, if with difficulty, back to Classical times. It has
been suggested that some of the Irish art forms on crosses quite
definitely Celtic had distant origins in the pagan work of continental Saxons, and the Irish carvings have been linked by skilled
argument with similar ones at Hartlepool. Personally I remain
unconvinced that we must thank the Saxons for too much in the
artistic field. Christianity, crosses and carved monograms were
certainly early in Celtic Galloway, and it is begging the question
to chase their origins too far back. Even the most fervent Celtic
enthusiast would not, to go to a ridiculous extreme, claim that
either stone carving or Christianity began in his region.

When I look at these crosses, it seems most important to
remember that *if* they were erected soon after 675, the previous
twenty-five years had seen the Northumbrian church steeped in
Celtic usage. From the second conversion of the Angles by Aiden
from Iona to the Synod of Whitby must have been a period vital
to the north and ripe for creative expression. Add to this the sup-
position that the English who came to Solway may have employed British craftsmen with Celtic traditions going back to the
La Tène age who had remained in the south-east during the
periods of invasion to mix or marry and eventually become
absorbed, and it would be indeed remarkable if the crosses in this
north-west zone did not have more than a flavour of the philosophy and skill of the Celts. So much for the artistic background
of the "Anglian" crosses.

The dating of these monuments has filled the lifetime of
scholars. I have suggested, so far without reserve, a late-seventh-
century date, largely on a basis of inscriptions at Bewcastle,
though there is plenty of artistic evidence to support this theory.
From an archæological point of view and a consideration of the

related cross at Hexham raised to Bishop Acca, W. G. Colling-wood, who knew more than most people about pre-Reformation crosses, suggested the eighth century. Other scholars, here and in America, have given excellent reasons for dates in the tenth and even twelfth centuries. I think that at the moment the earliest date finds the most favour amongst the experts, but I suggest that the general reader who is interested tackles as many books as possible on the subject, remembering all the while that learned scholars other than the one he happens to be reading may have arguments for a different date which appear quite strong in isolation. This study of the literature can be recommended to any adventurous reader. One book will lead to another; he will learn to understand runes and be taken in imaginary travel to the Greek sculptures, the wonderful ivories of the Ravenna chair as well as through a pleasant survey of Britain's other crosses. The reader who has found enough in my far too brief survey will be content to seek and find the beauty in this worshipping sandstone.

The presence of the Ruthwell cross implies Anglian command over the Solway during a period of some prosperity, and similar conditions are made manifest during the visit of St Cuthbert to the city of Carlisle. Bede's information about this visit gives a reliable and pleasant picture of conditions in the city during the eighth century, but before I discuss it, let us spend a few minutes in the present-day city.

In 1953 the Mayor of Carlisle went to see a Roman well that had just been revealed in Scotch Street in the course of preparations for the rebuilding of a shop front. Carlisle is like that. It is so full of history that whenever a hole is dug on a new housing estate, in an old shopping centre, in the course of building a new school playground and even in a sewage works, something from its ancient past is revealed. Each of these instances relates to a definite example. Carlisle's leading citizens seem always to have been proud of the city's antiquities, for St Cuthbert in 685 was then shown by the mayor (perhaps town reeve would be more accurate) the Roman buildings and a rather special Roman fountain. I am not suggesting, although it would be a happy coincidence, that the well discovered in 1953 was St Cuthbert's fountain. It is not impossible, but other wells have been discovered in the town, some Roman and others more recent.

Carlisle castle's well, drained a year or two ago, was rather disappointing as the finds were both recent and domestic.

Cuthbert had just become the spiritual lord of monasteries under Lindisfarne. King Egfrith's pious sister, Elfled, was extending her work to the west, and centred her activities on Carlisle. Egfrith's queen was staying with her in the city when Cuthbert visited it, and Bede tells with deep intensity how Cuthbert, his mind not on antiquities, saw in a trance, whilst he was being shown the well, the death of Egfrith in battle. The battle was that of Nectansmere (near Forfar), and although it was a turning-point in the struggle between English and British and the beginning of an English decline, the Solway must have stayed in the Anglian territory, for there were bishops at Whithorn for over a hundred years to follow, and even in the ninth century the dead body of Cuthbert, which now lies in Durham Cathedral, was borne in the direction of Whithorn to escape the fury of the Danes. Tradition has it that the body was embarked from Workington. Other biographers of Cuthbert allow him two previous voyages in the Solway, but both are extremely legendary in the worst sense, one telling of a cruise in a stone boat.

With the coming of the Vikings, whose boats first struck Lindisfarne in 793, my crossroads simile truly serves. The Viking raiders are usually divided into two sections and to the Solway they both came, Danes from the east and Norsemen from the west. The Danes reached Carlisle about 875, whilst their Swedish counterparts were pressing across Europe to Constantinople. Carlisle is fortunate in having an archæological adviser to its Council, and in 1953 that adviser, Mr F. G. Simpson, a leading authority on the Roman occupation of the north of England, obtained permission to dig in the Cathedral Close. His hole was only about eight feet square, but it revealed an amazing section of the history of the city. Visitors to Carlisle see only half the Norman cathedral. About two feet down Mr Simpson exposed the foundations of the other half. The present truncated nave is a mere remnant of the full nave that was destroyed and robbed by Leslie's men to strengthen the city walls during the Civil War. Under these foundations, Mr Simpson's workmen found themselves among a mass of bones and skulls, and much interest was aroused because of the possibilities of interpretation. Here was a story of many bodies thrown into a pit in a most unchristianlike manner. They might represent a re-interment to make room for new burials, and such is, in fact, the probability. Alternative suggestions envisaged a mass burial after some plague or even the results of a massacre. It seems unlikely that the last interpretation is correct, but the discovery certainly reminded the inhabitants of Carlisle that Halfden, the Dane, had destroyed Carlisle and massacred its inhabitants in 875.* To finish the story of this hole, between fourteen and twenty feet down were found timber and stonework representing three distinct periods of Roman history from Agricola's first fort, Luguvallium, to the Roman town's decline.

The other sea raiders, the Norsemen, seemed to have arrived more quietly in Solway, but they came steadily over a long period, and the study of their settlement areas—using the evidence of place-names—shows a dense Norse immigration throughout the region. The imprint of these sailors on our traditions and even on the modern map is greater than that made by any other single people who came to these crossroads since the Iron Age. Adventuring from the rock-bound fiords of a Norway suffering from a strange over-population in economic prosperity (as it did again in the nineteenth century), they came with the spring winds across the North Sea to other craggy inlets in Orkneys, Shetlands and the Hebrides. Further journeyings brought some to Ireland and thence to Galloway, west of Criffell, but possibly the greatest incursions were to Dumfriesshire and the Cumberland coast when King Harald Fairhair of Norway invaded the Hebrides and Man to punish tax-evading emigrants. One attraction of the modern Isle of Man seems to have had an ancient precedent.

Refugees from Harald colonised the districts mentioned, and the traces of their settlements are seen everywhere, though they seldom built in permanent stone. They built on hill and promontory, in vale and meadow, and the "brows" and "nesses", "dales" and "thwaites" are their memorial. They fished in the channels where men "haaf" today, and their ceremony as well as Iron Age economy is revealed impressively in the broken swords and giant pins in our Solway museums. In monument they follow Ruthwell, in age if not in style, and in small churches founded

* This massacre is not proven, but I believe it to be a fair assumption from combining the Anglo-Saxon Chronicle entry, year 875, and Florence of Worcester, year 1092.

early on these shores are remnants of the Viking art. The most famous in the country is near to Solway and is the slender shaft at Gosforth. It is a sad thought that many of their boat burials, being on good Solway flats, have no doubt been ploughed and scattered like the one that existed at Gretna until the last century. They are easy to destroy and tricky to excavate properly. As an Irish archæologist said, "If you are seeking something that can't be seen you have got to know exactly what to look for", and the wood of these ancient boats is too often just a different coloured earth. Some other burials have revealed their treasures, and Beacon Hill, Aspatria, with its lovely view across the Solway, produced the skeleton and weapons of a magnificent Viking seven feet tall; a man I would like to meet, but not in battle.

The Solway visitor may see signs of other earthworks that may be Viking but await the trained mind and skilled trowel before proof is forthcoming. Two in particular intrigue me personally. One in England is a small mound in front of the policeman's house half a mile east of Bowness village. The other, a hundred times as big, is on the Scottish side on the shore of Milton Loch, nine miles from Dumfries. Should the visitor go to see if low water still reveals Mrs Piggott's excavation of the crannog which disgorged perhaps the earliest British plough, he will see across the loch a mound, boat-shaped with accuracy, but in size like a veritable liner. It is again a thing to query, not showing results to study, but the local farmer has noted some buried structure of wood within the "prows".

In literature, too, there is evidence of Viking settlements, and I select just seven words to quote. They give a foresight of a political decision that was long in the balance. A paragraph from the Orkneying Saga ends with the words ". . . in Galloway where England and Scotland meet".

The Norse loved fighting, so we are told, but I think that we may have over-emphasised this to judge from a contemporary quotation. Let us say they could fight magnificently when it suited them, and let us add that they maintained a great respect for law and were capable of first-class administration, as can be seen from the Domesday Book of their descendants. The now common conception that the decision of the majority is binding on all who vote was first practised in these islands under the Danelaw. It is a long step from this early tenet of what we call democracy to the year 1838, but in the study of the democratic tradition, it is more than interesting that the small town of Maryport, on a coast so thoroughly occupied by the Vikings, was the first town in Britain and perhaps in the world to elect municipal officers by secret ballot.★

We can now leave the Dark Ages. Different authorities each have their own views about the most convenient terminus for this period. In the south, the year of King Alfred's accession, 871, is usually taken, and in Scotland, the union of the Picts and Scots under Kenneth mac Alpin between 843 and 850 marks a suitable division. For my own district, I find it convenient to end with the period of the Viking adventurers.

It doesn't really matter, anyway. The term "Dark Ages" is purely artificial, and it is also very misleading. The darkness is in the lack of reliable material and in the minds of a past generation of scholars and teachers, and there are still many adults for whom history begins in the year 1066. How can ages be dark which saw the advance of the Church from Ninian, Patrick and Columba through many great developments to the Synod of Whitby, and which embodied a world of art in the two great crosses we have studied? The literature of the period too, from Beowulf to Bede, is treasure ever valued, and an age that produced the Book of Kells and the Gospels of Lindisfarne certainly does not merit its usual title.

The Church of the Middle Ages grew naturally out of the foundations we have been studying, and therefore in this chapter I am going to include without a break a survey of the medieval Solway church.

The stones of Solway from the grey ruins of Whithorn to the red bones of Carlisle Cathedral's famous east window and on to the Romanesque door of St Bees are the heritage, sometimes still alive, of the medieval Church. Life in Solway during the Middle Ages, as throughout Europe, was dominated by the Church at every turn. The monks between their prayer bells furthered the cause of learning and taught western Europe how to farm. Men of every class were made generous under the fear of hell, and bishops and kings strove for temporal dominion. We left the Church at its point of highest supremacy in the Dark Ages, and perhaps its later leaders thought that when Europe was

★ The first "secret" vote was in 1833—not 1838—but it was too badly managed to be truly secret.

Christianised, missionary fervour had finished its task and its members could withdraw from the world. Some had even become worldly; but when ideals tarnish and old faults return disguised, there are always men who take their place in the line of history; men who in themselves and by their preaching offer a new ideal appropriate to the later age.

St Benedict of Nursia was one of these men. His austere reforms, first associated in England with St Dunstan, at length spread over the British Isles, and the three vows of his followers were finally heard on the shores of the Solway.

I shall tell how St Bees lost a coalfield to a later squireachy, but now if we can sift facts from legend, we may learn how they got it. The earliest church at St Bees may have been founded in the seventh century by an early Irish missionary, St Bega, who came seeking by sea a place to build her church. She was offered by a sardonic landowner as much land as the snow would cover on midsummer day. It would be kinder to Cumberland to credit the vast area of St Bees church-lands to a miracle rather than our normal weather. A pleasant story but entirely legendary.* There may have been a St Bega but her story cannot be disentangled from a mass of miracles, legends and place-names, and an alternative suggestion that the name comes from "sancta bega", a hybrid translation of "holy ring", seems more probable. Certainly the church was reported to have a Norse arm-ring, already ancient in the thirteenth century, which had all the functions of a famous relic. There may have been remains of an earlier church when the Benedictine priory was founded in the twelfth century as a cell of St Mary's, York. The priory was burnt by the Scots in 1315, but like other Cumbrian houses which suffered that fate, it recovered and prospered until the dissolution. Its new owner spared the church, which was restored in the early seventeenth century, and since then it has been used, again restored and slightly altered, as the parish church.

There is another Benedictine house, also founded from York, at Wetheral, east of Carlisle. It is really outside my limits, and I mention it for the sake of visitors to the city. Wetheral is not far away, and it is the loveliest of the city's retreats. The inn provides

---

* I am kinder than Daniel Defoe who visited St Bees in the eighteenth century. About these tales he wrote: "I leave them where I found them, (viz.) among the rubbish of the old women and the Romish priests."

a good dinner, and the red sandstone of the gorge through which the Eden flows has caves and Roman-quarried inscriptions.

In the twelfth century the Cistercians came to Solway. This Order rejuvenated declining Benedictine austerity when a few monks from Burgundy formed at Citeaux an order which revived the forgotten precept "that they are truly monks if they live by manual labour, as our Brothers the Apostles did". The Cistercian Order spread throughout western Europe, emphasising again the medieval unity of Church and language. One of its founders and an early abbot of Citeaux was an Englishman, Stephen Harding, and St Bernard was one of its greatest members. The rules of this Order directed the monasteries away from the soft rich lands into the far valleys and deserted mountains where there was nothing but wood, water and stone to supply their simple needs. It was perhaps coincidence that sheep thrived well in the wilderness. Another reason for their choice, less frequently mentioned, was that much of the richer lowland was already in the hands of other Orders.

From Citeaux, monks came to Yorkshire, to Rievaulx and Fountains. Rievaulx, founded in 1132, had several daughters, but the two that concern us are Dundrennan (1142), because it is near the Solway shore, and Melrose (1136), because it is the parent of Holm Cultram (1150). Dundrennan itself branched out with Glenluce in 1190 and Sweetheart in 1273 as the last of the Cistercian foundations in Scotland. The lives of these last four abbeys with the sweet-sounding names were bound up for many centuries with the landscape of Solway and the livelihood of the men who worked their lands. We shall visit these abbeys in a later chapter, but here I shall choose an element of each to illustrate the pattern of the times. Dundrennan to me is the most beautiful, though badly ruinous, and to all Scots its symbolises one great poignant moment in their history when Edward Maxwell, the last abbot, welcomed Mary Stuart to spend what proved to be her last night ever in her kingdom.* She sailed from Abbey Burnfoot, where the monks had built a harbour for their thriving exports, to Workington across the Solway. From there she moved slowly by Cockermouth and Carlisle to imprisonment and ultimate death.

* The Abbot welcomed Queen Mary, but she may have spent the night at Lord Herries' house, "Terregles".

The remains of Holm Cultram at Abbeytown across the estuary cannot compare in the sightseer's eye with those of Dundrennan. Holm Cultram is still working as a Parish Church and is much smaller than it was in its greatest days when it was bigger than Carlisle Cathedral. Its outbuildings, however, were restored to house an attractive Arts Centre which was formally opened in 1973, but which is now, in 1982, sadly affected by a shortage of cash. The records of Holm Cultram are wonderfully preserved and translated, and I shall use this great source of history many times throughout this book.

Holm Cultram suffered during the Solway struggles. Bruce pillaged the abbey although his father was buried there, the "Hammer of the Scots" made it his headquarters and the Earl of Douglas blackmailed its monks. In troubled times it was like a shuttlecock, but the years of its founding represent an age of peace and unity across the Solway Firth. Its lands were given by Alan fitz Waldave, a Cumberland Norman, but its foundation charter was confirmed by Prince Henry, son of David I of Scotland. Even when Henry II of England took the abbey under his protection at a later date, it was still ecclesiastically under the rule of Scottish Melrose. The unity of the early medieval Solway would be emphasised still further if the lands of the Holm were drawn on a map. In Cumberland they stretched as far as Workington, and in Scotland, though less continuously, far into Galloway. The only friction recorded was when Dundrennan became slightly jealous, but eventually an agreement was made about the division between the two abbeys of the lands round the Nith.

The Cistercians had another abbey further west in Galloway on the fringe of our region. May I simply commend it to the visitor to whom its name, Glenluce, might hint at its attractive setting in the Vale of Light? Glenluce interests those who like to add practical to æsthetic appreciation, for there they can see the original plumbing, handle lead pipes made six centuries ago and note in passing the monastery's brewery as well as some charming rock-plants which a recent custodian has introduced to break the harsh edge of the ruined walls.

There is plenty of romance in the Solway, and around our last Cistercian abbey, which watches the estuary from the foot of Criffell, is woven one of the world's great love stories. I have a belief that generalisations, like political slogans, are always wrong,

88

and so in spite of the fact that "everyone knows the story of Sweetheart Abbey", I am going to tell it again. It is a lovely story and a true one. John Balliol married Devorgilla when she was fifteen, and they were happy together for forty years. Their families separately were fabulously rich, and after John's death, Devorgilla became the greatest heiress in Britain. They had lived at Fotheringay, at Barnard Castle, at Buittle in the Stewartry as well as at John's home in Picardy, and all the happiness of this beautiful woman had consisted in the presence of her husband. When he died, they were not divided; his body was embalmed and his heart, enclosed in a golden casket, accompanied her for the rest of her life and at her death, when it was buried with her in the abbey she had caused to be erected on Solway in memory of her husband. Every lover's talk preserves her memory.

Many of the Normans sought blessing hereafter by endowing monastic orders, and not only Sweetheart, but Wigtown, Dundee and Dumfries all benefited from the munificence of Devorgilla, as Whithorn, Kirkcudbright, the abbey we have already visited at Dundrennan, Glenluce, Lincluden near Dumfries, Whithorn Priory and Tongland Abbey owed their existence to the patronage of her ancestors, the Lords of Galloway. Devorgilla also built for the present traveller in Solway—you will see her lovely bridge photographed above the weirs at Dumfries (photo number 7)—and she built for the scholarship of the future in Balliol College, Oxford. It was another John Balliol, her son, not husband, who was to figure so poorly in the struggles yet to come. We shall leave for a later chapter that other aspect of the Cistercian Order, that fabulous wool trade that was a mainstay of greatness in the Middle Ages, and move on to consider the less conservative religious Orders of the twelfth century.

The regular canons who built by these shores were the Augustinians and Premonstratensians. The black-robed Augustinian canons who arrived early in the twelfth century were never a large or very wealthy order, and of their several fine churches, one only rose to the dignity of a cathedral, the cathedral of Carlisle. Their rule was based on the writings of St Augustine, and each centre had twelve or fifteen canons under a prior. You can see the Prior's houses at Carlisle and Linstock, and one at nearby Lanercost. Edward I stayed at Linstock and Lanercost, taxing the resources of the latter to the limit. These canons reversed the

Cistercian motto; *their* work was to pray, and the "observances" preserved from another of their priories, Barnwell, Cambridge, gives a remarkable picture of the pattern of their days and nights.

Two Premonstratensian priories flourished in Scottish Solway. Holywood is one translation of *sacrum nemus*, and the *sacred grove* not far from the present parish church of Holywood is associated with standing stones. This gives us, beyond the medieval abbey, a link with Dark Age traditions and goes back to earlier cults stretching into the Bronze Age. Nearby, another religious settlement, the cell of St Congal the hermit, has named Dercongal Wood. The other Premonstratensian abbey was built at Whithorn over the foundations we have thought were St Ninian's. This abbey is made more worth a visit by the wonderful collection of early Christian inscribed stones in the nearby museum. Space and light as well as stone are utilised in this museum, and when I was there last, there was an interested and therefore interesting custodian.

Too much emphasis on the monks and the canons is apt to give a false impression of the religion of the Middle Ages. The Church had two other stems which looked less at themselves and more at the common man. In "common man" I include the uncommon landowner. It was often the latter who kept and subsidised the parish priest. Interesting though a study of this aspect is, we must leave the parishes and wander the towns amidst the poor and the sick in the steps of the preaching orders or, in that more descriptive phrase, the Mendicant Friars. Dark Age preaching and teaching lived in the monasteries, but in the Middle Ages congregations were found in the market place. Economic circumstances, as they did a century or more ago, brought poverty disguised as prosperity in the form of overcrowded, growing urban populations. The badly needed missionary fervour which the monks would not and the parish priests could not give was found in the lives of the black and grey friars. The black friars were Dominicans, and one thinks of them as one buys second-hand books in a back street in modern Carlisle. As in many other towns, the only tangible surviving memory is in the name of a street, Blackfriars. When the Dominicans first came, they were lodged outside the small, walled triangle that was Carlisle, but later they were lucky and built a convent on the left just inside the

English gate. The Wigtown convent of Black Friars was incidentally another foundation of the noble lady, Devorgilla.

The friars who have most touched the heart of succeeding
generations were the Grey Friars or Franciscans, often called the
Little Brothers. They arrived in England after the Black Friars,
but settled in Solway first. In the words of their rule they lived to
preach and begged to live, but like the Black Friars they soon
developed pleasant convents—sanctuaries of kindliness and learning. Throughout the ages, remnants of their lawns and orchards
existed in Carlisle's changing city until during the last century or
so the sites of the friars' houses sprouted hotels and banks.

One of the most valuable source treasures for the history of the
Solway between 1201 and 1346 was written by two nameless
Franciscans who probably belonged to Carlisle. Lanercost canons
may have revised and extended the text, and the document,
known as the Chronicle of Lanercost, is now in the British
Museum. One must admire the Little Brothers. Although
scholars—Roger Bacon was of their Order—they refused to
isolate themselves from the people, and I like the old description
of their churches as large, plain, without aisle and simply for
preaching. When they had not churches of their own they had
licence from the Pope to use the local parish church. I have said
they were learned; we cannot doubt that many of them were
also sincere and effective in the pulpit. They were not always
popular with local parish priests.

Dumfries was given a bridge by the Lady Devorgilla, and as
if she had not stored up enough grace in heaven, she built a convent for the Little Brothers beside the bridge. It was founded
about 1262 and lasted close on three hundred years. It provided
a stage on which the spotlight of history burnt fiercely for a
short time in a drama of murder which altered Scotland's destiny
when Comyn was killed by Bruce. No trace of the chapel now
remains, though its whereabouts are known and excavation has
revealed some details of it. Its foundations lie beneath shops and
buildings in the right angle between Friars' Vennel and Castle
Street, but there are elements of uncertainty about the details of
the altar that was stained by Comyn's blood. For the visitor, a
plaque on a wine-store gives the story, but the archæologists of
half a century ago found a possible altar, and out of many
skeletons just two so placed as to cause them to support Fordun's

record that Comyn and his uncle were laid by the friars *behind* the altar after that desperate day in 1306. The church was not pulled down after this, as is sometimes suggested—but on the contrary was supported by the penitent King.

We cannot doubt that the Franciscans in Dumfries obeyed their rule and begged to live, but we know, too, that the upkeep of their house was assisted by tolls levied at the bridge. Perhaps Devorgilla's influence at Court was behind the £5 17s. 6d., the £7 16s. 0d. and so on that were granted yearly by Alexander III. The way in which the conscience of Britain worked in the Middle Ages is revealed in a charter that tells how the Pope in 1431 and 1432 granted indulgences to those who helped in repair work on the bridge. More than a hundred years after this, at a time of English supremacy, the Warden and two friars were summoned from Dumfries to Carlisle to surrender the Friary. The English plans misfired, but the Warden was detained as a hostage and, I am sorry to say, later hanged. The friars were living in this house in 1549, but anticipating dissolution, they gradually disposed of their lands to tenants in feu, setting an example to many Scottish houses. Friars' Vennel is not, as often thought, a vestige of the oldest part of the town, but has, in fact, been extended to obliterate Newton Street, once the heart of the "new town". At least it was new in the thirteenth century when old Dumfries was to the south around St Michael's. Whilst the Grey Friars in Carlisle had settled in the town, their Little Brothers over the Border had preferred a site outside. Charles Hume, the last Warden of Grey Friars and probably the last friar in Scotland, had been pensioned, paid and left the town in 1574. His pension was £20 a year, and after settling for a lump sum of £110, he lived another fourteen years. Evidently he was not an optimist. Kirkcudbright had two smaller friaries of the Order called Franciscan Observant. One was on St Mary's Isle and the other is but a memory where now the castle stands.

The friaries followed the monasteries to oblivion. They represented perhaps the last outcry of the medieval conscience, a phenomenon strange to us. These islands were finding new interests and prosperous trading; the lords had looked into their consciences and the monasteries had benefited, but the merchants were beginning to look out across the seas.

CHAPTER VI

FRONTIER AND BORDER

WHEN we turned aside to look at the development of the Church in Solway, we left the district a prey to the attacks of the Vikings as well as to the efforts of the British and Scots to prevent English expansion. I could sum up this position in one battle that involved them all if I were convinced that it had taken place in the Solway area, but as I am not, I am just going to mention it here by name for the sake of chronology and leave other details until the last chapter. It was the Battle of Brunanburh, and it may have been fought at the Burnswark I have earlier described as intriguing.

We saw the fortunes of the English ebbing after Nectansmere, and they reached their lowest point in the second half of the ninth century with the extension of the British kingdom of Strathclyde to embrace the two shores of the Solway. However, the reconquest of England under Alfred and his successors approached from the south the newly united kingdom of Scotland under Kenneth mac Alpin. Solway stood between these forces and from this time the lands around the Firth might be likened to a shuttlecock.

In 945 it seemed as though the game would go to England, for the Anglo-Saxon Chronicle records: "In this year Edmund harried all Cumbria", but it goes on to say that he "let it all to Malcolm, King of the Scots, on the condition that he be his helper both on sea and on land". Presumably Edmund required the services of the Scots against the Viking raiders, and the Scots saw the wisdom of an alliance with England. This view was confirmed when a later king of the English, Edgar, met eight under-kings on the Dee at Chester, amongst whom was Kenneth, King of the Scots. These under-kings "swore that they would stand by him and be faithful to him". This treaty was one of the earliest quoted in support of Edward I's claim to sovereignty over Scotland. For practical purposes, it encouraged the Scottish kings to incorporate the whole of Solway in their administrative sphere. The southern border of the Scottish "annex" may have been close by Penrith. Kings often met on their frontiers, and in 926 after Athelstan had "subjugated all the kings who were in the Island" —including Constantine of the Scots—". . . they confirmed peace in the place which is called Eamot,* on the fourth day before the Ides of July".

I have likened the events of these years to a game, and the game was not yet over, for Siward, the English Earl of Northumbria, took Cumbria in the reign of Scottish Macbeth and the later efforts of Malcolm Canmore to recover it brought Scotland up against the formidable power of the Norman conquerors of England.

The Solway part of Cumbria remained outside the England of William the Conqueror, and it was left to his son, Rufus, to complete the Conquest and give the north-west a defensible frontier. Once again the Solway was chosen to divide the two realms, as it had been under the Romans. In 1092 William Rufus came north with a great army, took Carlisle "and restored the town and built the castle". Carlisle had never recovered from its sack by the Danes. Some life had continued, but the amenities of the Roman city and the civic pride of the Anglian had both disappeared. The Anglo-Saxon Chronicle tells us that Rufus "thereafter came south hither and sent thither a great multitude of churlish folk with women and cattle, there to dwell and to till the land". These "churlish folk" were English peasants, perhaps some of those who had been turned off the land to provide the King with his great game reserve in the New Forest, for William "loved the red deer as if it were his son", and they apparently brought new life to a town in which adversity had bred only apathy. On the promontory looking north and girt around with rivers, Rufus built a strong tower of wood, and this first Carlisle Castle marks the beginning of the city's new life as a frontier town.

During the reign of Henry I of England, relations between England and Scotland were friendly, but Henry took an important step to bind these newly won territories more closely to England in the creation of the bishopric of Carlisle. This broke the control that the Bishop of Glasgow had over the area, and

---

* Eamont. Another source gives nearby Dacor (Dacre), and the castle here is traditionally connected with the meeting though, in fact, it was built four centuries later.

added Norman ecclesiastical jurisdiction to political domination. The civil war which broke out on Henry's death once more swung the fortunes of the Solway. Scottish forces intervened on the side of Matilda, who was the niece of their king, David I, and the southern shore of Solway fell under Scottish rule once more. Carlisle, again a thriving city, was more than once the seat of Scotland's Parliament, and no doubt was the scene of great rejoicing as David himself knighted Prince Henry, Matilda's son, in the old Castle Hall (finally removed by nineteenth-century "improvers"). It was on this occasion that Henry promised to confirm Scotland's possession of the lands around Solway when he became king of England. This book would have been very different had he kept his promise.

This period was important for the Solway, for it saw the establishment in Galloway and Dumfriesshire of certain great families round whom the history of two kingdoms was to revolve. David was a great king, a noble builder, but no true Scot. He had spent his youth in exile at the Court of England, and his outlook, friends and sympathies were Norman. When he regained his kingdom, he granted the Norman barons who followed him much of the land of Scotland.

We have already met the Balliol family of Barnard Castle who later gained lands in Galloway. To be really accurate, I should say they were Picard not Norman, but they built typical motte-and-bailey castles at Buittle and Kenmure in the Stewartry. David gave Robert de Brus from Yorkshire the Lordship of Annandale, and his main fortresses were at Annan and Lochmaben. There is still a castle at Lochmaben, but I think the only stone from the Brus's Annan castle is the one now preserved in the Annan Council Chamber. The first of the Comyns, important later in Galloway, was David's Chancellor, and with David, too, came the Maxwells of Caerlaverock, who loom large in the story of the West Marches, the de Soulis family of Liddesdale and the Herries and the Stewarts, who both settled in Nithsdale. Richard Walensis or Wallace gained lands in Ayrshire, but his descendant struck the first blow for Scottish independence and brought the armies of Edward I to the Solway.

From this time on, Scotland, like England, followed the normal feudal pattern, but with two differences. For feudalism to be effective a strong king was essential, and Scotland was at times unlucky in this respect. Secondly, feudal barons must make themselves the masters of their region and place it at the service of the king. In Galloway, however, a vigorous and independent native aristocracy on the one hand and the new barons on the other not only were strong enough to act independently of or even against their king, but as time went on quarrelled amongst each other. The warfare against England was therefore accompanied by very little national feeling, and at first with no enthusiasm, for most of the Scottish lords remembered their English possessions. The situation was aggravated by a genuine hostility of the native Scots to their Norman rulers, and Walter of Coventry summed up the situation when he said:

> "the more recent kings of Scots profess themselves to be rather Frenchmen, both in race and in manners, language and culture; and after reducing the Scots to utter servitude, they admit only Frenchmen to their friendship and service."

At this phase of its history the Solway is a frontier, sometimes bloody, but more often overlaid by supra-national interests. The lords on the north owed allegiance to two kings and thought more of themselves than either, and the great monastic houses with their lands and rights served two countries but acknowledged ultimate allegiance to a power that was neither English nor Scots.

David of Scotland was strong and held the reins until he died in his capital, Carlisle, in 1153. His grandson, Malcolm, who followed was hardly, at the age of thirteen, able to oppose King Henry II, who apparently had forgotten his oath and forced Malcolm to give up his lands in the north of England, though his rights in Huntingdon were continued. Henry gave orders for Carlisle Castle to be strengthened, and to David's stone keep and inner bailey he added the outer bailey and built walls to connect the castle with the town. From this time, exactly eight hundred years ago, Carlisle has remained an English city in spite of attacks and destruction. It has guarded the southern shores of the Solway Firth for England and has been the key to the defensive system of the west.

Carlisle suffered a siege by William the Lion though the English captured him later, and there was warfare across the Border during the troubles in the reign of John—it is interesting to see Alan of Galloway among the barons who forced John to sign Magna Carta—but in 1237 an agreement was made which legally settled the vexed question of the northern counties of England, including the southern shore of Solway. Alexander II abandoned his claim to these counties and received in compensation "200 librates of land within the said counties". This land comprised the manors of Penrith, Sowerby, Langwathby, Salkeld, Carleton and Scotby, all within Cumberland and all strategically south of Carlisle and away from the Border. For these manors, Alexander rendered "annually one red falcon (a goshawk) to the king of England and his heirs at Carlisle through the hands of the constable of the Castle".

During its shuttlecock existence, the Solway and the Border had become the scene of endemic disorder. Lacking any sure authority to whom they could refer their grievances, people had begun to take the law into their own hands. The sturdy, independent and not particularly honest spirit of the Border had begun its long adventures. Following the settlement with Alexander, an attempt was made to deal with the peculiar problems that had grown up, and in 1249 twelve knights were appointed from each kingdom to study the situation and draw up regulations to deal with it. These first Border laws were to be enforced by the magistrates in the towns along the Border. This proved too difficult and dangerous a task for them, and at a later date the holding of the March Courts was put into the hands of Wardens, royal officials of considerable consequence themselves and backed by the power of the central government.

Before we meet the Wardens of the West Marches, we must turn back to look at the man whose policy towards Scotland transformed the whole atmosphere of the borders and infused it with a bitterness and violence far exceeding any that had gone before. Gaunt Edward Longshanks was brilliant, hard and legalistic, and it was unfortunate for Scotland and especially Solway that his reign coincided with the succession of a young girl to the Scottish throne and, at her death, with a dispute amongst the nobles of Scotland. Edward I's earlier activities in Wales were a pointer to his wider policy of uniting all Britain under one rule. His first move was peaceful, and he planned, with the blessing and approval of most of the Scottish leaders, to marry the little Margaret of Norway, Queen of Scots, to his son.

Her death in 1290 on the voyage to Britain put an end to this
scheme, but not to Edward's opportunities. Thirteen men claimed
the kingship, and an independent arbiter was chosen to avoid civil
war. Edward of England was the obvious if unfortunate choice.
Most of the "competitors" were Norman and three, whom we
have already noted, had an interest in Solway: de Brus (or Bruce),
Balliol and Comyn.

Edward was advised by a Council of Scottish and English
barons. His law was just, and John Balliol, the son of the Lady
Devorgilla, was his choice. The choice turned out to be convenient for him and tragic for Scotland. Before judgment was
given, nine of the claimants swore to accept Edward as overlord
of Scotland, and after the choice they were not allowed to forget
this promise. Without doubt, he treated Balliol badly, summon-
ing him to England on the slightest pretext and finally demanding
Scottish troops and money for his campaigns in France. By
October 1295 even Balliol had had too much. He formally
renounced his homage and in league with France against the
common enemy—the beginning of the "Auld Alliance"—prepared to attack England in the north whilst the French hoped to
intensify their war against Edward in France.

Curiously enough, the first blows in the Wars of Independence
were struck by the English, who seized the manors of Inglewood
in case they harboured a fifth column. The man who struck this
blow was the Constable of Carlisle, Robert Bruce, son of the
"competitor" and father of Edward's greatest adversary.

On 26th March, 1296, the army of Balliol invaded Cumberland
over the river waths and the suburbs of Carlisle were once again
in flames. Four years earlier the city had been destroyed by fire,
the common enemy of the Middle Ages, and on that occasion
the choir of the Cathedral, temporarily roofed in wood as money
had run out, was seriously damaged. The Chroniclers of Lanercost probably exaggerate the viciousness of Balliol's attack in
order to justify Edward's retaliation in the sack of Berwick.
Edward now saw the opportunity to realise his ambitions, and
led his army far into Scotland. Balliol was deposed and Edward
enlisted on the famous Ragman Roll the names of two thousand
Scottish nobles who swore fealty on the Gospels and renounced
all connection with the Franco-Scottish league. I should point out
that some of the Scottish nobles, including Bruce, who had land

in both countries, held aloof from Balliol's rebellion, national feeling not yet having triumphed over personal greed.

Some Scots fought on, and found a leader, skilled in guerilla warfare, in William Wallace, whose campaigns, fought at first in the name of King John Balliol, brought Solway into the forefront of events. Carlisle was invested for twenty-eight days, but Wallace retired after ravaging Lanercost, and Lord Clifford retaliated violently against Annandale. Edward used Carlisle as one of the bases for his next operations, and on 22nd July, 1298, he defeated Wallace at Falkirk.

I have little to say about Wallace and the Solway. Our local source, the Chronicle of Lanercost, is unduly bitter and vindictive throughout this period and very pro-English. Blind Harry's stories from across the Border, whether they are all true or not, at least indicate the regard of the Scots of the time for their great hero.

In spite of Edward's victories, the position of the English around Solway went from bad to worse. The garrisons of Dumfries and Lochmaben were running short of supplies, and little ships hurried across the estuary and up the Nith and Annan to revictual them, but greater events were afoot. Edward was tired of small battles and annual skirmishings, and in 1299 prepared an all-out effort to dig out Wallace from the warrens of the south-west. In the months that followed, stores began to build up on the Solway's southern shore around the little port of Skinburness.

Today Skinburness is a tiny hamlet of whitewashed cottages alongside a couple of hotels. It is protected by the shingle spit of Grune, and the inlet which once served as a harbour for half a hundred ships is now marsh, mud and sand. There is no scene more typical of the wild loneliness of Solway and the texture of its surface. You can see this in photograph number 8. Some abandoned harbours like those of the old Cinque Ports retain a flavour of their past, but in this inlet there is no hint of the glory of the days when it sheltered the fleet of England. In previous campaigns, Edward's commissariat had broken down and he knew that the Scots' scorched-earth policy would never let him live off the country. This time he planned to make no mistake. His fleet would follow the line of march and supply the army at points along the northern Solway coast. We have details of the victuals, and I have already mentioned one of several wrecks, the *Holy Cross* of Lyme, which had to be specially guarded at Silloth because it was carrying a cargo of wine. The core of fighting vessels in the fleet came from the Cinque Ports, but craft from Whitehaven, Workington and Allonby were recruited to swell their number. More than fifty ships were reported in the estuary in the year 1300. A typical fighting ship would have a master paid sixpence a day, two constables with the same rate of pay although a lower rank, and perhaps forty seamen who each got threepence a day. The whole fleet was commanded by four captains under the Admiral, Gervase Alard of Winchelsea, who received two shillings a day and was given a black *horse* on which to return home after the campaign was over.

Stores were built up at Skinburness, and Edward arranged to meet his land army in Carlisle on 24th June, 1300. They marched north across the Sulwath, six thousand strong, a few days later. From Dumfries—already in English hands—he turned aside to receive the surrender of Caerlaverock Castle. The interior view (photo number 9 that follows the Skinburness photograph) is of more recent period. Even had it existed in 1300, Edward would not at first have seen it. The curtain walls of Caerlaverock are grim and bare and its gate was shut against him. Edward was not prepared for a siege, and the tiny garrison at Caerlaverock held up his mighty army until the engineer, Friar Robert of Ulm, could bring up siege engines. Some came from Lochmaben and others across the Solway, damaging a ship on their way. A contemporary poem, "Le Siege de Caerlaverock" describes the scene, and credits Edward with gallantly pardoning the heroic defenders when at last they capitulated under the attack of the catapults. The Chronicle of Lanercost perhaps reports more accurately when it tells that "he caused many of those found within the castle to be hanged".

From Caerlaverock, Edward pushed west and made contact with his main fleet at Kirkcudbright on 23rd July, and later by the Waters of Fleet and the Cree. As in the case of Skinburness, the imagination is strained trying to visualise a fleet in these quiet waters, but at least there are still ships in Creetown and Kirkcudbright, though the harbour at the latter is now a bus station. The Scottish armies were skilled in guerilla warfare. Edward could not make contact with any large force, and the only casualty recorded was his cook, while further back his lines of communication were threatened by the Scots and a supply wagon was ambushed and captured at the Sulwath. He began to retreat, and was back at Sweetheart Abbey on August 23rd and Caerlaverock on the 29th. It is not absolutely certain at which of these places Archbishop Robert of Winchelsea delivered the famous letter that we met in an earlier chapter, but in any case it suited Edward to continue the retreat, especially as Pope Boniface might have stirred up trouble for him in France. Edward again crossed the Solway back into England, and lingered around the English shores, staying at Linstock, Rose and Holm Cultram. When he went back to Dumfries in the autumn to strengthen the castle—with wood floated from England across the Firth—he came to terms with the Scots. A truce was made and the area lapsed into uneasy quiet.

Edward was away from Solway for six years, though his son made a pilgrimage to Whithorn in 1301 and Skinburness and Kirkcudbright continued to be maintained as naval bases. The capture and execution of Wallace seemed to presage a quieter period, but in 1306 Edward was suddenly faced with a menacing situation.

There are two distinct Robert Bruces. Up till now we have seen only the powerful Norman baron, unwilling to commit himself to any action which would jeopardise his English possessions. Possibly he still entertained hopes of gaining the throne through Edward's favour. It soon became clear to Bruce, however, that compromise with Edward was impossible and that Scotland's future depended on driving the English from the land, but his plan to win the throne was betrayed to Edward by the Red Comyn, who paid the price of his treachery in the Friary Church at Dumfries. Bruce was crowned at Scone—though Edward had removed the Stone and Balliol the crown—but all did not go easily for him at first. From this time we see Bruce the hero, the single-minded Scot of a hundred thrilling stories and sacrifices. He was forced to retire for a time to Rathlin Island, but at length news reached England that he had landed in Ayrshire, and the Cumberland ports of Whitehaven, Workington and Skinburness were ordered to fit out an expedition to capture him. Edward was old and ill, but he nerved himself to go north again. It is difficult to imagine his feelings. Perhaps they were tinged with bitterness, not merely because he felt the prize slipping from his grasp, but because of the change in Bruce, Bruce who had been a good Norman, whose father had been Edward's constable, and who himself had sworn fealty to Edward on at least five occasions. Edward remained some time at Lanercost hoping for a return of health, while the busy preparations went on in Carlisle and Skinburness. From Lanercost he moved slowly and painfully in his litter to Carlisle, and there Parliament met. For a brief moment, Carlisle's streets were busy and bright with their throngs of rich and noble visitors, including Peter of Spain, the Papal Legate. Edward again delayed here, but delay did his cause no good, and Carlisle was alive with rumours that he was already dead, so he moved on towards the fords that had witnessed his unfinished enterprise seven years before. Solway was to stand again as the symbol of his doomed hopes, for there near Burgh, in sight of the estuary, he died. The only reminder of his presence is a slender stone pillar standing on the deserted expanses of the marsh.

It was not to be hoped that his feckless son, now Edward II, would continue the campaign, and Cumberland was left to defend itself as best it could against the Scottish king, growing daily stronger. Invasion came in 1311; Lanercost was severely damaged and the northern counties, seeing that they could look for no help from the King of England, bought off the Scots, but Cumberland was so impoverished that it had to give hostages instead of money. When Edward did at last bestir himself, the result was Bannockburn, and the Scottish raids became more frequent and destructive. Carlisle suffered many times, Holm Cultram was ravished though it housed the remains of Bruce's father, and the Scottish armies encompassed Cumberland and reached into Lancashire.

The most stirring event of these years was the great defence of Carlisle Castle by its constable, Andrew de Harcla, against Bruce himself.* De Harcla is one of the most interesting figures on the English side of the border at this time. He was largely responsible for the defeat of the malcontent nobles at Boroughbridge, and was created Earl of Carlisle for his services, but so great was the destruction caused by the Scottish raids in Cumberland that at last he opened up negotiations with Bruce in an effort to save the

* Described in vivid detail in the Chronicle of Lanercost.

county from complete devastation. Legally this was treason, though Edward was forced to accept similar terms later. As a traitor, de Harcla was executed on the gallows hill at Harraby outside the city walls, but he was a rare man who combined bravery with good sense, and no true Cumbrian will hear a word against him. The illuminations around the initial "E" of Edward II's charter to Carlisle show de Harcla defending the city walls against the kilted Scots. They also show a type of siege engine used by the Scots, the operator of which has two noteworthy features. The first is a woebegone expression and the second a spear which skewers him from chest to back.

The war dragged on into the reign of Edward III, who revived his grandfather's policy of trying to place a puppet king on Scotland's throne, and I have told how Edward Balliol, surprised by Lord Archibald Douglas, now the rising power in Galloway, fled from Annan across the Solway sands to the protection of Lord Dacre in Carlisle, but let us now leave this tale of war and raid and see what changes it had wrought along the Border.

There is no doubt that the ambitions of Edward I had changed the whole atmosphere, for now the peoples on the two sides of the Firth were divided by their awareness of nationality, while the breakdown of the ordinary processes of law and order made every man his own avenger, and introduced the feud to bedevil human relations. It bred a sturdy independence and affected even the tenure of land. Tenants in so insecure a position recognised little obligation but that of defending it. This latter fact came in time to be recognised officially. The "Rules for the Defence of the Borders", drawn up at the end of the sixteenth century, lay it down that:

> "tenantes be well and sufficientlie horst and gerde, as by the tenure of their holdes landes and fermes, which they have verrie good, and at verry small or litle or no rentes, they are for defence of that contrye bounde to be."

The problem of law and order was further complicated in the west by the existence of a strip of land north of Carlisle between Esk and Sark which belonged to neither country and was known as the Debatable Land. Its inhabitants were described in a report to Elizabeth's Council as "a people that wilbe Scottische when they will, and English at their pleasure". They were organised strongly on a clan basis, and their names, Armstrong and Elliot and Graham, figure again and again in the reports on Border lawlessness. Violence bred violence:

"they are grown so to seke bloode, for they will make a quarrel for the death of theire grandfather, and they will kyll any of the name they are in feade with."

They could snap their fingers at ordinary justice because

"hardly deare anie gentleman of the cuntrey be of any jury of lyfe and death yf anie of them be indyted."

There was probably more order on the English side of Solway than on the Scottish, for in the Scottish March the influence of family was as strong as it was in the Debatable Land, and the Scottish kings could not control the families who rose to power in Galloway and Dumfriesshire. Cumberland had no real counter-part of the Douglases whose power reached its climax in the fifteenth century, or of the Scotts whose representative, the "bauld Buccleuch", so discomfited the English Warden, Lord Scrope, in the sixteenth. Apart from these magnates, however, there were dozens of smaller families whose enmities made the problem of enforcing order infinitely more difficult. Crichtons, Maxwells and Johnstones all had their personal quarrels, and in addition the King tossed the Wardenship of the Scottish West March backwards and forwards among them, and each refused redress for injuries inflicted under the previous regime. No region can live entirely without law, however, and in course of time the borderers worked out a rough system of justice which mitigated the worst effects of the conditions under which they lived. In the first place, they recognised and accepted the conditions as they were, and then set up a code of rules to deal with them.

The key to the whole system was the Warden, who was appointed by the Crown and had very wide powers. He had power to levy forces from the local people, who, as we have seen, owed this service as a condition of their tenure, and in times of official peace it was his business to arrange meetings with the Warden of the opposite March at which grievances could be settled. There were certain customary places at which these meetings were held. Those between the two West Wardens were held at the Lochmabenstane, and between the Wardens of West and Middle Marches at Kershopefoot at the point where the Kershope Burn joins the Liddel. For these meetings, a day of truce was proclaimed, which lasted from sunrise on the day of the meeting to sunrise on the following day.

On the appointed day, the Wardens left for the meeting well supported with lords and knights, mounted and fully armed. Both sides gave assurance that they would respect the day of truce, and then got down to business. Before the meeting, bills giving the details of each complaint were delivered to the opposite Warden, and it was his duty to see that the accused was present to answer the charges against him. These bills could be dealt with in three ways: the Warden himself might declare that of his own knowledge he knew the defendant to be innocent; secondly, the case might be tried by a jury of six men from the defendant's own country; thirdly, as the Scots in particular were not too ready to convict on the sole testimony of witnesses from the other country, they might demand the testimony of an "avower", who was someone from their own country willing to swear, either openly, or secretly to the Warden, that the complaints were justified. If a true bill was found, it was filed and marked "Foul"; if the defendant was acquitted, it was marked "Clear".

While these cases were going on, the Wardens were settling the claims on bills filed at the previous meeting. One of the difficulties in settling these claims arose from the very human habit of claiming far more than the real value of the stolen property, so that it was at last decided to draw up a scale of values for the more usual goods, generally animals, that figured in these bills. Sometimes, when a lot of bills had been filed, a sense of desperation seems to have come upon the proceedings, and the Wardens totted up the totals on either side and cancelled them out one against the other.

These meetings did not always go according to plan. Lord Scrope's reports to the Council contain numerous complaints of abortive meetings, particularly with Cessford, the Warden of the Middle March. Cessford was also Keeper of Liddesdale, which lay hard by the isolated region of Bewcastle, and was as lawless as the Debatable Land. In this area, affrays did not always stop at robbery, and Scrope insisted that cases of murder should be settled before other matters were discussed. Cessford asserted that such cases were not within his competence, and a good deal of acrimonious correspondence passed between the Wardens before the dispute was settled at "the highest level".

A violation of the day of truce led to one of the most famous incidents in the story of the Solway. One of the most notorious reivers of the west was an Armstrong, immortalised in the Border ballads as Kinmont Willie. Reiving was in his blood and he had been a thorn in the side of Lord Scrope for several years. Like many of the reivers, he had a foot in both camps. He was secretly aided in many of his exploits by Lord Maxwell, and his daughter had married an Englishman, Thomas Carleton, who was hand in glove with the Lowthers, and they at that time had their own personal quarrel with Scrope. It was not surprising that Kinmont had come through his adventures unscathed, and that Scrope would have sacrificed many successes to lay hands on him.

The opportunity came at last. Kinmont was present at one of the March meetings, and so too, on the English side, were members of the Salkeld and Musgrave families, who had suffered on many occasions from Kinmont's raids. It is probable that Kinmont flaunted his immunity on the day of truce before his enemies, and angered them so much that they lay in wait for him as he returned unsuspecting to his home and delivered him captive to Lord Scrope. This was a flagrant violation of the day of truce, but Scrope was not going to give him up now that fortune had delivered him into his hands. Angry letters demanding Kinmont's release were sent to Scrope by Sir Walter Scott of Buccleuch, then Keeper of Liddesdale, but Scrope passed the question to the Council, and King James made no more headway with Elizabeth than his deputy had done with Scrope.

Buccleuch was not the man to let the matter drop. He gathered a band of men at Morton Tower in the Debatable Land, and armed and equipped with scaling ladders, they rode south to Carlisle. In silence under cover of a mist, they forded the Eden and came up under the castle wall. Their scaling ladders were too short, so they broke down the postern gate. The sentries gave the alarm, but the attackers made so great a commotion with shouts and braying trumpets that the garrison thought a whole army was upon them and retired to the keep.

> They thought King James and a' his men
> Had won the house wi' bow and spear:
> It was but twenty Scots and ten
> That put a thousand in sic a stear.

Buccleuch had been told by spies in what part of the castle Kinmont lay, and soon he was freed and borne out to safety. The ballad tells the story with triumphant gusto.

> Wi coulters and wi' fore hammers
> We garr'd the bars bang merrilie,
> Until we came to the inner prison
> Where Willie o' Kinmont he did lie.

> Then Red Rowan has hente him up,
> The starkest man in Teviotdale;
> "Abide, abide now, Red Rowan,
> Till of my Lord Scrope I take farewell."

> Then shoulder-high with shout and cry
> We bore him down the ladder lang;
> At every stride Red Rowan made
> I wot the Kinmont's chains play'd clang.*

> "Oh, many a time," quo' Kinmont Willie,
> "I have ridden horse baith wild and wood
> But a rougher beast than Red Rowan
> I ween my legs have ne'er bestrode."

There is no more dramatic adventure in our Border history. No damage was done, no property stolen, no prisoners were freed except Kinmont himself; the whole operation was carried through to vindicate the peculiar code of honour of the Border. There is another side to the question, however, which shows the equivocal position of many of the local people. Kinmont could not have been rescued so efficiently if Buccleuch had not been told in what part of the castle he was held, and the whole force passed twice under the walls of the Graham's tower at Netherby without

* Poetic licence—Armstrong was not chained, but at least one smithy is pointed out near Longtown where his fetters were struck off!

any attempt being made to challenge them. This is remarkable in an area subject to constant raid where every home was on the alert against attack. One can only presume that the Grahams had prior knowledge of the affair and chose not to intervene.

This was a common feature of the times. In spite of the ban on intercourse between English and Scottish borderers, there was a considerable amount of trade between the two, often it is feared in stolen goods. Carlisle did a thriving trade in hides, and leather seems to have been the staple of the town's industrial economy, for four of the eight craft guilds which played so great a part in the development of its municipal life were concerned in some way or other with this commodity. There were constant complaints about the sale of horses over the Border, and reports to the English Council again and again mention this as a cause of the unsatisfactory state of the Border musters. We have seen, too, in the Kinmont adventure that marriage between the various Border families seriously complicated the business of bringing offenders to justice. Love and the hope of profit play ducks-and-drakes with the pious regulations of governments.

We have taken a leap forward in considering the special code of justice which grew up out of the extraordinary conditions of the region. Let us now pick up the thread of events at the beginning of the fifteenth century. I have mentioned that one of the difficulties in the way of establishing order in our region was the fact that the Scottish kings could not control their over-mighty subjects, and this fact applies too in England during the period when Yorkist and Lancastrians fought for supremacy.

The power of the Douglas family in south-west Scotland had continued to grow during this period, and I turn from the smaller raids to look at a more regular engagement in which that family took part. In 1449 the Douglases were matched against the Percys of Northumberland, and Annandale and Cumberland suffered severely from raid and counter-raid led by these men. The culmination of these was the Battle of the Sark, when in spite of the powerful English longbow, the Scots triumphed over the English, largely it seems through the obstinacy of Wallace of Craigie, a descendant of the great Wallace, who refused to accept defeat and broke the English right-wing when all seemed lost. The English soldiers were forced into panic flight, and many who escaped the sword perished in the swollen waters of the Esk.

A Douglas had been in command at the Battle of the Sark, but James II determined to put an end to the pretensions of this family, and his aim was supported by many smaller families, who were jealous of the Douglas power and perhaps coveted their lands. William, the eighth earl, was murdered by James himself, but when his brothers gathered their forces to avenge him, Maxwells and Johnstones, Scotts, Beatties and Carlyles rallied to the side of the Crown, and in May 1455 met the Douglases in a pitched battle at Langholm on the Esk and defeated them. A good deal of their land was taken by the Crown, but the men who had helped were not forgotten. The Douglases' island stronghold of Threave became a royal castle and Annandale with Lochmaben Castle was granted to the King's second son. The Douglases fled to England, their power broken, but their intrigues helped to increase the bad blood between the two countries. The removal of the Douglases left the way open for the rise of the Crichtons and Maxwells, who were unfortunately divided by a feud. The Crichtons were Lords of Sanquher and Sheriffs of Nithsdale, while the Maxwells were Stewards of Annandale. It is an indication of the conditions of Scotland at this time that in 1508 Maxwell attacked Crichton in Dumfries and forced him to flee to his castle. This left Maxwell victorious in the town that Crichton as sheriff was supposed to hold in the King's name.

The sixteenth century brought peace and strong government to England, but a chapter of disasters to Scotland. That country, true to the "Auld Alliance", attacked England when Henry VIII went to war with France, and her king and most of her nobility were killed or taken prisoner at Flodden. This disaster was not followed by a general invasion of Scotland, but marauding parties under Lord Dacre crossed the Border into the Scottish West March, and it was reported that Lower Annandale and Eskdale were "now clearly wasted, and no man dwelling in any of them this day, save only in the towns of Annan, Stepel and Wauchope."

Throughout the early part of the century, the depredations of the dwellers of the Debatable Land grew more daring under Johnnie Armstrong, and the lands of Lord Maxwell suffered in particular. As he could not suppress Armstrong by force, Maxwell tried to buy him off, and made him a grant of land at Langholm. James V did not approve of this policy of appeasement, and came in person determined to teach the Armstrongs a lesson that would not be lost on others in the district. The arrest and summary execution of that surprised and affronted reiver gave the ballad-makers another subject for their songs.

The ambition of England to extend her power into Scotland came to the fore again in the middle of the century, and the situation was complicated by the religious differences produced by the English Reformation. Warfare flared up again and our region saw the complete rout of the Scots at Solway Moss in the neighbourhood of Longtown. There was complete confusion in the Scottish army, and the English commander, Wharton, dashed in when he saw the situation and put the Scots to flight. Many blundered into the treacherous "quaking bog" and perished—as Bronze Age man might have done when he lost the axe (see page 56). Lord Maxwell was among those taken prisoner, and gave up his castle to Henry, so that once more the English ruled in Caerlaverock. Thomas Carleton, who held it for England, was hard pressed at first by the Scots, and there is an interesting description of the roads in Dumfriesshire from Wharton, who relieved him, which sounds very much like an extract from one of the more harassing parts of *Pilgrim's Progress*. It was Lord Maxwell, incidentally, who was behind the Act authorising the first use in Scotland of a Bible written "in the vulgar toung in Inglis or Scottis of ane gude and trew translatioun". Thomas Carleton continued to wander about the area almost unchecked for a year, "Kirkobree" being the only town to offer much opposition.

Although warfare blazed up again in Edward VI's reign, the end of strife was near at hand. England was ready for peace, and a truce was signed in 1551 which was to be the basis of a perpetual peace. It was followed by a settlement of the question of the Debatable Land. This tiny parcel of land—it was only about ten by three miles—had an influence on the whole of the region far out of proportion to its size. It was first described as "debatable" about the middle of the fifteenth century, but as an Englishman I must confess that in previous centuries there had been little debate; it was admittedly Scottish. At one desperate stage in its history, neither country would own it, and both Wardens issued a proclamation which allowed Englishmen and Scotsmen to "rob, burn, spoil, slay, murder and destroy" anyone who dwelt therein, and no one was allowed to build there.

However, the settlement of 1552 ended this policy of despair. Commissioners from both countries, together with the French Ambassador as arbiter, finally agreed on a line from the Sark to a point on the Esk "opposite the house of Feargus Greme". The "western" part was awarded to England and the "eastern" to Scotland. The lack of compasses in these times is indicated by the last description; the Scots Dyke runs east–west so it was the northern half, equivalent to the parish of Canonbie, which went to Scotland, and the southern half, or Kirkandrews parish, which went to England. The adjoining parish of Morton was split by this division which makes plain why Dumfriesshire has a parish called Half Morton.

It was one thing to draw a definite frontier, but quite another to turn the people of the Border into law-abiding citizens, especially as reiving could sometimes be a useful instrument of policy. A raid over the Border, which Elizabeth could disavow, was as useful on occasions in dealing with Scotland as were the activities of the privateers against Spain. Generally speaking, however, Elizabeth's policy was to try to bring order to the frontier, especially when Mary Stuart was in England and the attitude of the north was uncertain, but how difficult that was has been shown by earlier mention of the problems of Lord Scrope. The whole system of defence in the West March was tightened up, a survey was made of the castles in the district, and recommendations made for their improvement, and the arrangements for keeping watch and ward were restated. Rockcliffe Castle was a key fortress in the system of defence for it commanded the fords near the mouth of the Eden, and the rules laid it down that the Warden should have a hundred or two hundred men "nightlie with him, especiallie at the ebbinges of the water, some to watche at the fords for the keepinge out of the Scottishe theves of Greteney, Redhawll, Stilehill and others of the Batable Landes". Clearly the officials in the north knew their Elizabeth, for they go on to say "and all this maie be done without anie chardges or expences to her Majestie".

In some places soldiers were necessary, especially in Bewcastle where local conditions made it difficult to employ the men on the spot

> "by reason that the chiefest and ableste borderers and tenantes thereof are herede and slaine by the Scottishe theeves of

Liddesdale, and can skarselie now in anie good time be broughte
to the former estate and savetie thereof againe, as yt hathe bene
chiefly by reason of the deadlie foode and great hatrede between
the Greimes and the Musgraves."

That a little low cunning was sometimes as useful as force is
shown by the report of a conference between Lord Scrope and
Walsingham on an occasion when the system of Wardens'
meetings had broken down:

"That it is thought convenient to bind with such of the loose
men as have not committed murthers and spoiles upon her
Majesties subjects, whereby it is hoped . . . the loose men that
now spoyle England, may be drawn to commit their spoyles
upon Scotland, being assisted underhand by some loose men of
England; as also such to be winked at as shalbe receavers of
such goodes as by them shall be stollen in Scotland. Those at
the amity of England to be spared. This course being held for
two or three months, it is hoped the Scots will be forced to
make redress, and also to sue for return to the old custom of
warden meetings."

Better, to my mind, than low cunning was kindly common sense,
and the vigorous personality of cheerful Sir Robert Carey shines
solitary in those days. After complaining of raids to his Scottish
opposite number and getting no satisfaction, he sent a big party
to capture approaching thieves as painlessly as possible. He took
a dozen of the ring-leaders and entertained them with his best
fare for a few days and then sent them home when they promised
not to repeat their offence. Being borderers, they kept their
promise.

The gradual improvement of conditions on the Border made
possible the development of municipal life in Carlisle, and the
city's most treasured possession, the Dormont Book, dates from
the early days of Elizabeth. The method by which it was com-
piled shows that municipal affairs were now in the hands of the
eight craft guilds as well as the Merchant Guild which had formerly monopolised them. The by-laws in the Dormont Book
show a growing pride in the appearance and order of the city,
though when one notes that refuse was not to lie before the doors
for more than eight days, it is not surprising that the city had a

dreadful visitation of the plague in 1597, which carried off many of the inhabitants as well as the bishop. Other regulations remind us that the shadow of disorder still lay over the city and that Carlisle was still a Border fortress always watchful against attack. Watchmen were on duty on the walls day and night, and as dusk fell, the gates were closed and a heavy chain drawn across the road between the city and the Eden bridges. No Scots were allowed to live within the city, and no apprentices were engaged who lived north of Blackford and Irthing. Carlisle men were still afraid of the enemy in their midst. Carlisle produced a number of leading citizens at this time of whom she continues to be proud. One of the most honoured was Edward Aglionby, Member of Parliament and many times mayor. He was a man who did his duty without fear or favour, and paid for it with his life at the hands of the Carletons.

The three centuries of acute disorder which followed Edward I's interference in Scottish affairs had an interesting effect on domestic architecture in our region. The reivers came to rob, and what they could not carry away they usually burnt. The obvious reply to this was to build in stone and to build so strongly that a few defenders could keep an attacking force at bay. There was no need to build to withstand a siege; these attacks came swiftly out of the night, and the reivers were back again over the Border before light dawned. A place of refuge was the prime need, though many of the stone towers, called peles, which sprang up all over the district were homes as well as fortresses. They are a characteristic feature of the borders, and form the core of most of the older mansions and farms, especially on the English side of the Solway. They are to be found scattered over the whole region, but the greatest concentration is in Cumberland and Dumfriesshire.

The towers on both sides of the Firth were built to a similar pattern. They are rectangular in shape with the ground-floor room vaulted in stone so that if the outer door was forced, the tower could not be burnt. The walls vary in thickness from four and a half to ten feet, and the upper stories were gained by a newel stair within these walls. The narrow entrance into the basement was protected by a heavy door of cross-barred iron set so close to the jamb that it could not be lifted off its hinges. When peace came at last to the Border with the union of the crowns, James ordered that "the haill of the Irone yettis * in the houssis on the Bordouris to be removit and turnit in plew ironis or other necessar work", surely a Solway variant of beating swords into ploughshares. The roof of the tower was either flat or had a flat walk around and a low-pitched roof so that watch could be kept and the defenders could retaliate. There was usually a small turret at one corner, and on this was an iron basket in which a beacon fire could be lit to spread the alarm throughout the neighbourhood.

There was a complete system of communication by means of beacons in both Scotland and England. Any castle or tower which commanded a wide area of the countryside had provision for these "bayle-fires", and some of the iron baskets can still be seen. There is one on the roof of what remains of Hoddom Castle, but there will soon be no castle under it. In England the system seems to have been wider in its scope, and the news of an impending attack could be flashed back as far as Lancaster via Penrith and down the coast. This reflects existing fact. We know that the bigger Scottish raids did penetrate well into Westmorland and, for instance, to Furness Abbey. North of the estuary there were two lines of beacons up Annandale and Nithsdale linked at Pantath between Mouswald and Ruthwell, and stretching north past Moffat in Annandale and up Nithsdale to the Ayrshire boundary. The wild mountainous country at the head of these valleys would make longer raids most unlikely.

In some places, perhaps where there was no local family of enough consequence to build a pele which would serve the immediate area as a refuge, churches were fortified in the same way. Two of these are still in existence in Cumberland near to the Solway at Burgh and Newton Arlosh. At Burgh the "irone yett" still survives, as does the one in the pele tower under whose shadow I live. Churches as such were no protection, and their pele towers are as strong as the domestic ones. Solway men might trust in God, but they took the precaution of keeping their powder dry.

Scottish peles are in some respects different from those in England though the principle is the same. Like much of Scottish architecture of this period, they show the influence of French ideas. This is most marked in the roofs of some of the peles,

---

* The words "yatt" and "yett" are still used locally for gate, and a noisy kiss is likened to the sound of "the sneck (catch) of a Pardshaw yatt".

which were often high pitched and had a stepped gable. The Scottish pele had two doors, an outer one of oak and an inner grill of iron. In England, wooden and iron gates were combined by boarding in the spaces between the crossing bars. In Scotland the door was often, though not always, on the first floor and was approached by a flight of steps. An unusual round tower can be seen at Orchardton; it is unique in Scotland and has been likened to a Danish "rath".

One Scottish tower deserves special mention, for mystery surrounds its name. This is Repentance Tower on Trailtrow Hill, north of Annan. It is primarily a watch tower, for it has no living-quarters. It has an unrivalled view of the Solway, and was a key position in the beacon system of the north as it is visible from both Wardlaw and Burnswark. It was built in the middle of the sixteenth century by John Maxwell, who became Lord Herries, and over the door he carved the single word "Repentence".* John broke faith with the English to gain the hand of Agnes Herries and the broad lands of Hoddom to which she was heiress. Lord Wharton, the English Warden, had fourteen of his hostages hanged on Harraby Hill, and bid John ask God's mercy for sacrificing them. Was this tower, built to help the countryside, his act of repentance? It seems rather out of character; more likely it was an act of defiance.

Away from the Solway fords and the land border, the castle excites more interest than the pele, and innumerable mottes indicate the coming of feudalism to the region. Of the early examples, all that can be seen today are the mounds of motte and bailey both protected by deep ditches, though recent excavations have indicated that the motte at Mote of Urr, near Dalbeattie, was crowned with a massive wooden keep. This imposing motte and bailey castle, probably built by a vassal of Roland of Gallo-way, guards a still-used ford and its ditches even now defy the intruder. Its mounds are largely artificial though they possibly incorporated Dark Age earthworks as at the Mote of Mark.

In Cumberland, splendidly sited Liddel Strength watches the northern approach to Carlisle and shows a more complex arrangement of baileys, but in England generally, these castles were replaced by stone ones earlier than in Scotland.

The earliest stone type—a single keep and surrounding curtain

* Herries' spelling.

wall—is rare in south-west Scotland for Bruce destroyed many of them, but the *old* castle at Kirkcudbright was a good example. McClellan's imposing castle near the centre of the town is a late-sixteenth-century structure built on the site of the old priory of the Grey Friars. Stone from this priory and from the old castle were used in its construction.

Threave Castle, just west of Castle Douglas, the stronghold of the Douglases, is of simple construction though it was built much later. In many ways it is like a very large and elaborate pele. Perhaps it did not need the refinements of fortification that the other castles of the same period had, for its position is immensely strong. It lies on an island in the Dee and the river can only be forded at one point, though there is a boatman-guide for the modern visitor.

Castle building in Scotland did not pass through all the same stages as it did in England, but some show a certain family likeness to the concentric castle of the thirteenth century. Buittle was one of these. It was probably built by John Balliol when he married Devorgilla and became Lord of Galloway east of the Cree, but this castle is now in such a ruined condition that it is difficult to trace its exact form. Some of the stones from it are in the nearby pele. Edward I never introduced into Scotland the magnificent concentric castles he built in Wales; money had become too short.

South of the Solway there are relatively few real castles, but many buildings called castles which were, it fact, fortified manor houses. The main system of defence used the imposing castles of Carlisle, Penrith and Cockermouth which came under royal control. Of the many fortified manor houses, three have a close link with the Solway. Wolsty, described later, watched over the Silloth coast for Holm Cultram; we have already seen Drumburgh as the terminus of an important Solway ford; and the castle at Burgh, whose outline was recently discovered by excavation, has an obvious strategic link with the Eden fords through the death nearby of Edward I. These fords were also guarded by Rockcliffe Castle on the north bank of Eden, another known by excavation only.

A number of later Scottish castles show the influence of changing military conditions on castle building. War was becoming a skilled business, and mercenaries began to replace the part-time soldier. Unfortunately, you could never be quite sure of the loyalty of mercenaries, and it became the practice for the private quarters of the lord to be quite separate from the rest of the castle and to be concentrated around the gate so that the lord had control of this weak link in his defences. Morton and Caerlaverock were built like this, and certain structural changes at the latter indicate the introduction of gunpowder. The later addition of a Renaissance dwelling-house inside the grim curtain walls of Caerlaverock rather obscures the original plan, but gives the most delightful and sudden architectural contrast in all Solway.

CHAPTER VII

FARMING

BETWEEN the geography, the economics and the prejudices of each age, a compromise is reached and the farming landscape achieves a temporary integration. The present pattern of the Solway lowlands with their small irregular fields, high hedges, long windbreaks, massive walls and scattered farms (the last more especially on the Scottish side) is only about two hundred years old. Before then other pressures and other ideas shaped the scene within the limits imposed by soil and sky, and even today the brown of cattle in the scene is being replaced by black and white.

We can only guess the importance in prehistoric and Roman times of the grazing of horses, cattle and sheep, and it is not until the medieval days of the Cistercian abbeys that the agricultural picture becomes easy to comprehend. For years after the monks had gone, one could look back and say that the highest peak in Solway farming had gone with them. They had two advantages: one was their skill and single-mindedness, and the other the condition of their tenure, which, being in free and perpetual gift, represented the highest ideals of any farmer. An important chapter in the story of Britain's greatness is the story of the woolsack, in which the monasteries feature large. The Cistercians believed that "to work is to pray", and their sheep farming, coinciding with rising population and prices, led to great prosperity. Theirs was an age of wholesale contracts. To build their abbeys, they often mortgaged their wool for years to come in spite of ecclesiastical bans on this practice, but they introduced into the north a system of agriculture that produced wealth from wild land beyond the dreams of the original owner. I suspect that the lords occasionally compromised with their conscience to give their poorest land to the Church. But it all raised sheep. When Edward I was in these parts, Holm Cultram exported to Flemish and Italian merchants more than thirty sacks of wool a year, good-quality wool worth between ten and twenty marks a sack. A sack contained about two hundred fleeces, so one can estimate that the flock of the abbey comprised at least six thousand sheep.

A similar picture could be painted for Dundrennan, Sweetheart and Glenluce. The monks worked hard and with their hands, but I should be giving a wrong picture of the period if I did not tell how the work was carried out under the delegated responsibility of lay brothers and agents by a host of small people. Even in those glorious days, the latter often had the position of serfs. They could be bought and sold with the land as Herdwicks are in Cumberland today. The Herdwick is loth to leave his native heaf; the serf dared not. They were outlawed if found outside their owner's boundaries. The abbey was the centre of a well-ordered community, but had granges and tofts and houses, widespread to control its business. Holm Cultram had a prior's house in Carlisle, an exporter living on the Tyne, several tofts in Dumfries, a barn at Silloth, and granges all over the area, of which Rabycote is for me the most interesting. Rabycote is near Cardurnock Marsh, and I mention it because of its monastic origin, because it is a marsh farm and because it is still beautiful with its original fifteenth-century barn, decorated by the rebus of Abbot Chambers, whose family lived there, and set with its garden in a misty bank of trees watching over the Waver.

The abbeys decayed, and until the effects of the Improvers were felt, rather late up here in the north, there followed an undistinguished period. In many cases the farmers were little more than crofters, producing food for themselves and the laird or lord under an antiquated system, in-field-out-field, which lasted here as late as anywhere in the British Isles and incidentally is called around the Solway "rig and rean".

Farming was most backward on the Scottish side. Until the Union, there was no English market, and poverty was aggravated by the sufferings caused, especially in Galloway, by reactions to the Covenanting movement. The Scottish farmer in the seventeenth century had much less security of tenure than his English counterpart—either the yeoman of the south-east or the independent statesman of Cumberland. In Galloway a few families grouped together in a township would work the in-field in strips, intensively if not scientifically, and have one or two Galloway cattle on the out-field, half for themselves and half for the laird. Both laird and tenant were miserably poor. This phase in Scotland was ended by enclosure when the union of the Parliaments in 1707 opened England to black cattle. The Union incidentally was economic as much as political. Agricultural poverty had been brought to such a depth by famine between 1696 and 1703 that about a quarter of the population were beggars, and the other three-quarters could not afford to help them. To the lairds, enclosure was the obvious answer. Dykes were built, fewer herdsmen needed, and lands, traditionally open, restricted to the cattle of the laird. The tenants' struggles slowly changed from respectful protests to desperate action. Whit-Sunday, 1723, is a day still remembered in Galloway. About half the cottars, herds and small tenants got notice to quit. Several emigrated at once, but others brooded, met and planned defiance—Kelton Hill Fair in Kirkcudbrightshire was their rendezvous. A popular ballad of the time, written by James Charters of Dalry, described the common mood. I give half a verse of the lyric:

> The lords and lairds, they drive us out
> From mailings where we dwell.
> The poor man says "Where shall we go?"
> The rich says "Go to hell!"

The bitterness was not quite unrelieved; Captain Johnson, a laird near Castle Douglas, met a thousand rioters with ale, bread and cheese, and a promise that no one would be turned out as long as he lived, and the day ended with rejoicing. (Captain Johnson's civilised methods remind one of that earlier exception, Sir Robert Carey of the English West March.)

Levelling the dykes was almost the only action possible, and in 1724 the stones began to tumble. The movement spread and sympathy and boldness soon allowed levelling in daylight hours. The levellers published a manifesto which affirmed their loyalty whilst defending their actions, and it was widely circulated, but in the end they were beaten, and the next phase of Galloway agriculture had begun.

This was the phase of cattle-droving, and the black cattle came through Dumfries and down to the English markets in their thousands. They were especially in demand on the fattening pastures of Norfolk. Cattle from Ulster, via Portpatrick, joined the stream of those from Wigtown, and there was quick prosperity for dealers and agents as well as for the lairds. Cattle might change hands several times before reaching market, and failure and bankruptcy jostled with fortune on those dusty roads. In ten days, twenty thousand cattle might pass through Dumfries toll-gate on the way to England. The road was studded with smiths who had to shoe them for their long walk. The drovers were wise and highly-skilled, and it is said that they knew more ways of avoiding paying tolls than any travellers of any other age. One way of avoiding the toll at Gretna that covered the river crossings of the Esk, was to drive the cattle across the estuary fords. Samuel Smiles has vividly described a crossing by the Bowness wath in which the cattle were caught by the tide and many were lost.

Whilst the droving was going on in the years after enclosure, the land around the Solway saw much agricultural improvement, in common with that of much of Scotland. The union of the Parliaments not only allowed Scottish agriculture to catch up a serious lag behind that of England, but in some ways to surpass it within the space of a century. A few weeks after the Levellers of Kirkcudbrightshire had risen, a meeting was held in Edinburgh (8th June, 1723), and some three hundred gentlemen from all over the country formed themselves into the "Honourable Society of Improvers in the Knowledge of Agriculture in Scotland", a society which gave valuable service, mostly advisory, until brought to an untimely end in 1745, many of its members having supported the unlucky Stuarts.

The first secretary of this society, Robert Maxwell of Arkland, came from Kirkcudbrightshire, and he was probably a driving force behind its formation. Robert Maxwell was very much like England's Arthur Young; although not a great farmer, he was, by his work of publicising, preaching and teaching, a notable servant of Scottish agriculture.

There were local as well as national Improvers' Societies, and a neighbour and contemporary of Maxwell became in his later years the first president of the "Society for the Improvement of Agriculture" in the south-west of Scotland. This was William Craik of Arbigland, near Kirkbean, a good practical farmer and a leader in the application of the new ideas. He was probably one of the first to use the English plough in place of the cumbersome Scottish one, although his own procession with two oxen behind two horses would look rather antiquated to the modern tractor-farmer.

The Craik family has an interest to us in more ways than agricultural. His mother was one of the well-known Aglionby family of Cumberland, and they had many associations with Flimby on the English Solway. But it is his daughter who interests us more.

Helen Craik had three claims to our attention, each one worthy of more than a mention. In her own right, she was a promising poet, although little known outside the Solway area. Secondly, her poetic work brought her into contact with Robert Burns, who took her work seriously and continued a long and friendly association.

The third aspect of Helen Craik is more intriguing, but less well documented. It is fairly certain that she became infatuated by one of her father's grooms. It is also certain that this man died suddenly soon after. A verdict of suicide was returned, but the Craik family, in spite of its influence, was not able to quell local suspicions that one of its members had a hand in his death. It is certain that the poetry of Helen Craik changed from a happy, cheerful style into a gloomy, even morbid, one somewhere about this time, and soon she left the district for ever. She evidently put the Solway between herself and her memories, for she died in Flimby at the age of seventy-four.

Whilst this improvement was going on north of the Solway, the agricultural revolution was affecting Cumberland, which shared with Scotland the dubious distinction of being well behind the times, although Philip Howard of Corby introduced turnips to Cumberland in 1745 and clover in 1752, some years after they had been pioneered in East Anglia by Townshend.

Although Philip Howard was the earliest of the new farmers, John Christian Curwen of Workington was the greatest. Born John Christian, he married his cousin, Isabella, the heiress of Henry Curwen of Workington, and took the family name and estates, which he proceeded to farm on the new lines. He introduced shorthorns into Cumberland as well as other animals, some of which, such as the merino, failed, and pioneered the penning of sheep on turnip land. His enthusiasm and vision have their memorial today in the country-known show of the Workington Agricultural Society, which he founded in 1805.

The improvement of the land by drainage, always important on the Solway soils, was stressed by Dr Robert Graham of

Netherby, grandfather of the great Sir James of political distinction in the Home Office and the Admiralty.

The nineteenth century saw a confusing pattern in the agriculture of both sides of the Solway. The Napoleonic Wars stimulated production of cattle on the north in Galloway, and cropping on the south when for a period sufficient wheat was grown in Cumberland to provide a surplus for export. The end of the war brought falling prices for cattle, the lack of a market for wheat, and a general period of poverty and instability made worse in Cumberland by the beginning of local industrial urbanisation. The introduction of the spinning jenny and factory weaving took away from the cottages and small towns many profitable side-lines, and even in the towns themselves, paper mills, glassworks, bobbin mills and suchlike soon collapsed under economic depression. On a lesser scale, this was applying to south-west Scotland as well, and in Annandale are traces of old flax vats or "lint-holes" which represent the days when every farmer grew his own flax and scratched and spun it in his own kitchen.

Violent aspects of this early "rural depopulation" and urban depression could be seen on both sides of the Solway about this period. In 1826 a memorable drought had strained the situation to breaking-point, and the price of oatmeal rose to an exorbitant figure. A meal-monger of Maxwelltown known as "Three-shilling Rab" quarrelled in the market about his prices. After being examined and committed to prison, he was released on bail. He was foolish enough to increase his price by twopence a stone "on account of his trouble". This roused the wrath of the crowd, which soon became a violent mob, and the houses of other meal-dealers suffered great damage before the violence abated.

Three years later the citizens of Dumfries saw a similar riot, but one with an entirely different cause. It was due to the halt in transit at the King's Arms Hotel of William Hare, who was being escorted out of the country after turning King's Evidence in the notorious trial of Burke and Hare. This second riot was of course far less destructive of property than the earlier one about the people's food, but apparently the mob got out of control, and it was long remembered by those who were present.

English Solway had already met the meal mob in the winter of

1817, a year of great distress in consequence of bad harvests. The Corn Laws then in operation had caused all breadstuffs to rise to famine price, and bad weather had long detained vessels in the harbour (up to fourteen weeks), producing a shortage locally of food and work, which added to the sufferings of the poor. Word went round that a Mr Lawson of Bowness was preparing to ship flour from a barn at Allonby to Liverpool, and a gang of men and women, wild and hungry, with faces blackened, raided the store. There was only one constable at the time, and he, David Beck, had only one arm, so the raid was successful, but the following day troops were brought in and a conclave of magistrates took and examined witnesses. The doggerel rhymes which celebrated this occasion have a strange echo of the Levellers' lyric that we met a century earlier,* as can be seen from this fragment of a popular song:

> The poor, half-hungered and half-dead
> For want of meal, for want of bread
> While rich men are luxuriously fed
> With mutton, beef and veal, Man.

> They little care how miserably
> The poor may live, or, doomed to die,
> They point and in derision cry—
> "You stole young Lawson's meal, Man."

I digress a little now to describe a common type of house of the agricultural and village worker of the Solway in this period. The house would be built of mud or clay with a thatched roof, and Hutchinson, in his *History of Cumberland*, tells how neighbours assisted to build one in a few days. He suggested that a house built this way on a low stone foundation was expected to last a hundred and fifty to two hundred years. Whoever told Hutchinson that (he wrote in 1794) had faith that modern visitors to Solway will find justified in the little village of Burgh-by-Sands. He will find thatch and mud cottages, known as Clay Dobbins (the original word was "daubings") although the roof is now often covered with neat red-painted corrugated iron. These cottages look charming and some are still lived in, though much altered inside (one half is no longer reserved for the animals). Once the weather gets into the walls, destruction proceeds rapidly,

---

* See page 120.

but the curious observer can even be grateful for this, for one that is now decayed shows clearly the timber cruk construction that is a building style inherited from the time of the Dark Ages.

A similar example can be seen at Torthorwald in Dumfriesshire, and its companion, dismantled a few years ago, was well known as the boyhood home of Dr T. G. Paton, a notable missionary of the last century. Probably they were quite comfortable in the early nineteenth century, but we can see from Celia Fiennes how one near Gretna had appeared in the bad days of famine a century earlier.

"They have no chimneys, their smoke comes out all over the house and there are great holes in the sides of their houses which letts out the smoake when they have been well smoaked in it; there is no roome in their houses but is up to the thatch and in which are 2 or 3 beds even to their parlours and buttery; and notwithstanding the cleaning of their parlour for me, I was not able to beare the roome; the smell of the hay was a perfume and what I rather chose to stay and see my horses eate their provender in the stable than to stand in that roome, for I could not bring myself to sit down."

Miss Fiennes seems to have been unlucky in her hosts, and I must admit that even in Carlisle, she found

"tho' I was in the biggest house in town, I was in the worst accommodation, and so found it, and a young giddy landlady that could only dress fine and entertain the soldiers."

In the agricultural upheavals at the end of the last century, the lands around the Solway suffered less in their comparative isolation than many other counties, although the century saw big changes in the farming landscape, especially in south-west Scotland. The main factors were the coming of the railway, the steamship and the general improvement in road transport. North of the estuary, the changes could be seen more dramatically than to the south.

In the days of cattle droving, the black Galloway cattle were almost the sole pride of the south-west, and reports for the Statistical Accounts of the three counties published in 1795 show their importance. In Dumfries, for example, "the true Galloway breed of cattle, in proportion to their size, is the handsomest and best in Britain and draws the best price in every market in the kingdom." One of the Galloways, bred by William Craik, is said to have weighed more than ninety stone, and was too big to hang in the shambles of Dumfries.

With the coming of the steamship and the railway, two things happened. The first was that droving ended; the second, that dairying came to replace it. The steam packets from Belfast to Liverpool short-circuited the original droving through Port Patrick, and this trade became negligible by 1840. Even the Galloways were finding competition on home ground from better feeding stores like the Shorthorn and Angus, though some fat stock were dispatched for some years direct by steamer from Carsethorn to Liverpool.

There had been hardly any dairying in Galloway, just a little cheese-making based on black cattle in the west, but eventually Ayrshires began to filter into Galloway despite local prejudice, and with the Ayrshires, the age of dairying began, an age in which we still live.

We have considered some of the economic and historical background to Solway farming, and it will not be out of place to look at the physical background before we talk about the present day. In earlier chapters we have seen how the lands around Solway are geologically more akin to the lowlands of Britain than to the highlands in which they are set. The sea and river soils and the boulder clays largely derived from soft younger sandstones give a low and gentle environment that is confirmed and supported by that other agricultural determinant, the weather. The division between highland and lowland Britain has been noted in relation to rocks and cultures, and it is equally marked when weather is considered. From this point of view, Solway is again an exception. Most of highland Britain is wet compared with the south-east lowlands, and inland from Solway, north and south, are regions with mean annual rainfalls ranging around a hundred inches. Snow quite normally lies on the hills for up to one hundred days, and I have found patches in north-facing gullies in mid-Cumberland well into July. Close to the Solway, however, there is less than forty inches of rain a year, and a small patch near Rockcliffe Marsh averages less than thirty, although I am sure that residents will find it hard to believe. This gives a truly lowland atmosphere, and off-comers, who strike a wet spell in the Lake District, might with advantage take an hour's journey to the coast where they will often escape the dark mountain clouds.

Solway is not quite so lucky when it comes to temperature. There is quite a long growing season—when the average monthly temperature is above 42° F.—from early March to late November, but there are rarely very high temperatures and there is not enough dry sunny heat for summer harvests. August is, of course, one of the wettest months of the year; September the loveliest and often most equable.

Although the worst problems of rain and snow and the consequent difficulty in improving land can be forgotten around the Solway, it would be wrong to give an impression too near perfect. Although certain areas, especially in Galloway, are gentle and mild and, in fact, are known for rare and delicate plants, the Solway can suffer from cold winds and sharp frosts. The drumlin-sculptured land that lies slightly inland affords many hollows into which frost sneaks often and lies easily. The waters around the Solway do generally keep the coastal lands warm. Close by the water, there is a little growth all year and snow rarely lies for more than a few days. As if to mark the contrast with moorland not far distant, one Solway farmer is proud that his lambs are born around Christmas. To temper my generalisations, however, I must report that in this last cold February (1954) the sandbanks of the Solway were covered with frozen snow for more than a week, and the floating snow and ice, looking very like an arctic pack, caused locally many pounds' worth of damage to salmon nets. The year 1881, incidentally, saw ice-floes up to ten feet thick in the Solway. It is worth mentioning that salmon suffer directly from ice in this and no doubt other estuaries. They take in small fragments of ice which clog the gills and suffocate the fish, and shore dwellers have been known to be guided by gulls—especially the greedy great black-back—to an easy catch of nice fresh-run Solway salmon killed in this way and left by the ebbing tide.

The cruellest manifestation of the elements is often a visitor to Solway. On either shore can be seen the seaward fringe of trees, leaning drunkenly to the north-east, each tree shorn by gales of half its western symmetry. There have been historic storms in the Solway, and when the gales sweep across the water, there are no dykes midst the waves for shelter. Having lived on this shore and lost windows and gates and seen the roof of a fifty-foot hall lifted and dropped a hundred yards away, I speak with deep feeling when I say that the wind *can* blow, but in spite of the work, the danger and the anxiety, I love the exhilaration of the fast winds and the short seas—when I am on the land!

The present pattern of agriculture in the region is based on a compromise between what these natural factors will allow, the developments of the past, the practical needs of the present and what can be foreseen of the possible trends of the future. This is not the place for a study of the detailed facets of Solway agriculture, but a broad survey is possible if local divergences may be neglected.

Both sides of Solway are similar in that animals predominate over crops. This is not to say that there is *no* good arable land— we have seen how wheat-growing was stimulated at one period— but I shall omit detail concerning arable farming as it is less particular to the region. As far as cattle are concerned, it will be easiest to consider the two sides of Solway separately.

Considering Scotland first, we saw how the replacement of black Galloways by Ayrshires marked the end of a notable phase, and provided the basis of a dairying economy, an economy which still exists. Having said this, I must mention two present-day trends. One is the return to the breeding of good beef, an aspect of farming that nearly disappeared under the emphasis, almost the exclusiveness, of wartime dairying. One or two farmers persevered with their pedigree herds, and as no beast is more symbolic of the Solway than the Belted Galloway, farmers like Faed Sproat and James Brown in Scotland, and James Westoll in England (only just—his farm is on land once Debatable), call for a special mention in my story. They have persevered with this very ancient and distinguished polled breed (one can be seen in photograph 12), and the present position with a free market and a growing demand for good beef cattle is no doubt doing something to justify their faith. Although it is good to see the neat Ayrshire, and it has brought much prosperity, there is no sight in Galloway finer than the fields of belted cattle on the long road down to Borness in Borgue.

Thousands of visitors to Galloway will have seen Faed Sproat's Belties on Monument Hill, near Gatehouse, but he left this farm last Martinmas to run the old family farm at Borness. In many ways, Mr Sproat personifies Galloway. His father composed the song, *Bonnie Gallowa'*, and his own name has associations with two distinct periods. "Sproat" is Scandinavian, and "Faed" celebrates the renowned Gatehouse and Solway painter, John Faed, R.S.A. Faed Sproat has died since these paragraphs were first written but his son, George, still maintains a herd of Belted Galloways in addition to other more recently popular breeds. Another Belted Galloway enthusiast is Jack Graham of Redcastle. Long may they prosper.

To return to the more general aspects, the second trend is a tendency in many areas, though by no means all, to replace Ayrshire cattle by Friesians. This is an aspect which is more marked on the Cumberland side and one to which I shall return.

For many decades, when farmers talked of cattle in Cumberland, they thought only of the Dairy Shorthorn—the Ayrshire was "the poor man's cow". The lowland pastures around English Solway have won fame through their suitability for this dual-purpose Shorthorn, and the Shorthorn is still highly regarded, particularly just inland and up the Eden Valley. With the growing demand for milk, however, the Ayrshire became the basis of dairying in the lowlands of Cumberland though it did not replace the Shorthorn, and Cumberland is now classed as a dairying county more than a breeding one. The continued increase in the price of milk is today bringing the Friesian in great numbers to Cumberland, and this in one way is an extension of the old practice of breeding dual-purpose cattle, for not only has the Friesian an enormous milk yield, but its big frame can carry plenty of meat which seems to thrive on Cumberland feeding.

This picture is slightly complicated by other factors about which there are differences of opinion. Some farmers dislike the idea of dual-purpose cattle and prefer to rear exclusively for meat or for milk and their herds still differentiate parts of the Solway landscape. Others are faithful to the Shorthorn as a dual-purpose animal and regard the Friesian as almost a temporary intruder. Then, for those who are going over to the Friesian, there is the problem of milk quality, but this problem seems to be increasingly met by keeping a few Jerseys to augment the fat content when the milk is mixed.

To round off this brief section on cattle, I should mention that, besides the normal dairy herds and Galloways, other breeds are sometimes kept, often for fattening. Blue Greys (Shorthorn bulls and Galloway cows), for example, can often be seen on the moss-lands and round the river estuaries, and there are one or two herds of Jerseys, for example that of the Grahams of Netherby. Before I leave this subject, I ought to mention milk processing. The Carnation Milk Company, Nestlé's and, of course, the Milk Marketing Board all have factories around the Solway, and the chief collecting-centres are at Dalbeattie, Kirkcudbright, Max-welltown, Carlisle and Aspatria. The importance of dairying generally in the region is indicated by the fact that Dumfriesshire was the first Scottish county to have none but attested cattle, and Cumberland became in 1955 the first county in England to achieve this same standard.

The mountains and moorlands around the Solway support the usual breeds of hill sheep such as Herdwicks, Swaledales and Black-faced, but there are plenty of sheep, too, on the Solway lowlands. Some of these are of special interest to us as they are pastured on those marshes we have called the heart of Solway. The most popular sheep are generally cross-bred ewes, of which Suffolk cross and Half-bred (Leicester-Cheviot) and Grey-faced (also a Border Leicester cross) can be seen in many parts of the region. One or two of the marshes on the English side, especially Rockcliffe, provide extensive grazing and have often been quoted as the winter home of yearlings, especially Herdwicks, from the Cumberland fells, but the tough little Herdwick is seen less often than formerly. One reason for this is that the Herdwick, and I am very sorry to see this, is slowly disappearing from many Lakeland fell farms. Another factor might be the threat and danger of flood-ing. In spite of protective works, this threat sometimes becomes a reality, as it did in November, 1938, when a twenty-four-foot tide was backed by a great south-westerly gale and about a thousand sheep were drowned.

Solway has two interesting associations with the breeding of horses. The first concerns the "Galloway Nag", a tough little beast now mainly historical, but one which once was popular, to judge from many literary references from Shakespeare to the Brontës. Secondly, the Solway plain, particularly around Wigton, has a happy tradition—though one which is slowly dying with the times—of breeding the famous Cumberland Clydesdale horses.

One or two industries associated with the farming lands of the coast are extractive rather than agricultural. Forestry is extensive on the Scottish side of Solway, and its growing importance I shall mention in a later chapter. Closer I think to farming is a traditional Solway activity. Along the living coast and on the farmlands round Solway we have come across great areas of moss and flow, and these have for centuries provided peat. For years peat has been cut on both sides of the Solway by farmers and cottagers, mainly as a household fuel. And what a fine fuel it is! I sometimes burn it in my caravan, and its aroma is finer than the incense and the lotus of any Eastern temple. Peat is still cut in this small way all around the Solway, but it has in the modern age a wider significance. It can be mined by modern methods or ripped up by special tractors to form a foundation for new forests, and recent experiments have been made with turbo-jet designs to make peat-burning gas turbines which will eventually supplement hydro-electric power in times of water scarcity. There is great opportunity in south-west Scotland for these last two applications of peat, but I fear that in the more obvious development of this resource, the English side of Solway is leading the way. The mosses around Kirkbride are worked in a very scientific and large-scale way, and acres of neatly cut moss and stacked peat (it is matured for two years before processing) can be seen on, for example, Wedholme Flow. This Cumberland peat has a variety of uses: in its granulated form it is used for many horticultural purposes, while block peat is used in orchards and still is a popular fuel. Tailings and litter make good bedding for animals, and the fine ground dust is used as a dressing for lawns and bowling-greens. Amongst this variety of uses, we can come back to farming with peat meal which is produced specially for cattle-cake manufacturers.

Finally, let me mention Solway salt. Salt-works were important in past centuries and are mentioned in many old charters. The salt of Ruthwell in particular was famed as the best in the north. The remains of the kinches or pits used in the manufacture of Ruthwell salt can even now be traced on the merse of Priestside, and some of the "salt-pans" across the estuary will last much longer, for they are cut into the solid rock. The true salt-pans, which were used after the solution of brine in the kinch had become concentrated enough to float an egg, were made of metal, and were heated by great fires of peat. It used to surprise me that, despite the obvious importance of salt-making in the region during the Middle Ages, Solway used to import salt from Cheshire—often as ballast in ships returning from Liverpool—and it was brought into other parts of Scotland from the Baltic. Large amounts of salt were needed, however, in the days before artificial feeding of stock, when meat for the whole winter had to be laid down at Martinmas. Excellent though Ruthwell salt might be, rock salt was better for preserving.

Taxation made salt an expensive commodity, and so, in spite of the limited uses of the distilled variety, Solway salt continued to be made along our coasts, and even smuggled from them, until the tax was discontinued in 1825.

Salt-making is now a dead industry in Solway, but I have mentioned it because it lingers in place-names all around our coast. Southerness—until recently Satterness and once Salterness —Saltcotes of Ruthwell and Abbeytown, Saltpans, near Allonby, Saltom Bay, near Whitehaven, and others link the land to the waters once again.

CHAPTER VIII

FISHING

IF I had to name some symbol for the Solway Firth, I should pass by the fords, the geese, the frontiers and the ships and choose the Solway salmon. Whether it costs two pounds a pound, as it does today, or "ninepence for two pieces of Salmon, halfe a one neer a yard long and a very large Trout of an amber coullour",* this king of fish occupies both the heart of the estuary and the hearts of the men who seek it.

The fishermen who divide the Solway and may meet in the middle at the Altar stone have much in common with each other, but before we meet them, let me get one or two differences out of the way. Broadly speaking, salmon fishing in English waters is a public right vested in the River Boards which issue licences, whilst on the Scottish side, such rights are private ones granted under Crown Charter. In both cases, there are local permissions to obtain, fees to pay and regulations to keep, and quite a few amateur fishermen have found that the law in Scotland, though different, is quite effective.

Another main difference concerns fishing by means of "fixed engines", as stake-nets, poke-nets and similar devices are legally termed. The fact that Solway comprises both *English waters* where such engines are generally illegal and *Scottish estuaries* which are treated specially leads to an obvious inequality which at times proximity has made to appear injustice. The present situation is based on regulations made after tremendous discussion in the 1860's when it was decided to "throw down" fixed engines on the English side. Wandering near Bowness at low tide, I have often come across rotted stumps—perhaps the last of these ancient stakes. Scottish fixed engines escaped destruction mainly as the result of a Scottish Act of 1563, the exact interpretation of which is still in doubt. This Act was designed at a time of Border stress so as *not* to protect fish which the English might take. An Englishman today might possibly be able to erect stake nets if he

* Miss Celia Fiennes paid this in 1698.

could show a right by grant, charter or immemorial practice, and if such a net was in use in one of certain years. If anyone could do this, he might be lucky, for the salmon seem to be running to the south in the present years, but he would be unpopular with a great many individual fishermen.

Fishermen are grand characters, but they are apt to enjoy a bit of litigation. Alan Fairford, in Scott's *Redgauntlet*, advises his friend, Darsie (professionally), to keep out of any fishing quarrels . . .

> "The legality of the mode of fishing practised by your friend, Joshua, is greatly doubted by our best lawyers, and if the stake nets be considered as actually an unlawful obstruction raised in the channel of the estuary, an assembly of persons who shall proceed, via facti, to pull down and destroy them, would not in the eyes of the law be esteemed guilty of a riot."

I shall take Alan's advice and mind where I tread in these waters. If I happen to write the words "standing in the middle of the estuary", I mean, of course, just south of the boundary line or just north depending on whether I happen to be standing fishing with an Englishman or a Scot. I do not want to start the Border Wars all over again.

Sir James Graham of Netherby almost did that in the eighteenth century, and Scott used this true incident as the basis for the fictional riots over stake-net fishing described in *Redgauntlet*. He tells in his notes how Sir James built a cauld or dam dyke across the Esk. The local Scots considered that this stopped salmon coming into their country, but there seemed to be no court in those days competent to give judgment. The Scots therefore, armed with fowling-pieces and fish-spears, on a pre-arranged signal of rocket lights, assembled in numbers on the banks of the river to give their own verdict. Sir James armed many of his own people and was able to get military aid from Carlisle to defend his property. Fortunately, prudence on both sides won the day, and Sir James agreed that a breach should be made in his dam, sufficient for the passage of fish. The river finally had the last word when it swept away the dam dyke altogether.

Scott does not mention in this note that the English and Scots respectively had been putting up and pulling down a fish-garth on this stretch of the river for something like six centuries. When

James IV challenged the Earl of Surrey to a duel, the two main points of contention concerned Berwick-on-Tweed and the fish-garth on the Esk.

If my words about the action of the river might be thought to put an end to this story, I should go on to say that in 1951 the matter was again in the news. An Act of Parliament in 1948 allowed an English River Board to levy charges on fishing in that part of the Esk that is in Scotland. In the present enlightened age, a public enquiry held in Carlisle was sufficient to convince White-hall of the error of its ways—without direct action from the Scottish Borderers. As a matter of antiquarian interest, there is an ancient building close to the site of the garth known as the Coop-house which was an ancillary to the salmon trap.

Scott's use of a similar incident allowed him to put into the mouth of Joshua, the Quaker, a piece of dubious philosophy which *still* does not convince the river fishermen.* When Joshua is accused of stopping fish from going up the river by putting up tide nets, he answers:

> "Thou killest the fish with spear, line and cobble net, and we with sinkers and with nets which work with the ebb and flow of the tide. Each doth what seemest best in his eyes to secure a share of the blessing which Providence hath bestowed on the river and that within his own bounds."

For many locals the haaf net seems the best way to secure a share in the blessing. Great skill is required to use this net properly. It may *look* easy, but then so does any skill when done well. Almost any fool can stand with a haaf net for as long as he likes, or as long as the tide will let him, without fishing. To do the job properly requires a good constitution and strong wrists, a quick mind, an X-ray eye and an intimate knowledge of the Solway shores. A haaf net is a rectangular frame with wood on three sides to which is fixed a billowing net stretched tight to make the fourth side. An extra piece of wood sticks out from the middle of the long side at right angles for the fisherman to hold. The frame is about sixteen feet by five feet and even though a light kind of wood is used, you can imagine that carrying and swinging a haaf net is not a job for weaklings. From the mouth of the rectangle,

* *Redgauntlet.*

135

the fine flax net is trailed out by the water like a long tail divided more often than not into two parts as it splays on each side of the fisherman's body. The haafers sometimes fish in teams, and in parts of the Solway still use the old traditional method of casting the mell (or drawing lots) for position, a custom said to date from Viking times. I should imagine that the haaf-net man without much height, or one unable to run fast, would watch this ceremony anxiously. There is a story that in one district the positions of the team were marked landwards from a fixed iron stake that had long survived in the water, and that in one particularly dry season the poor man who drew the last position was condemned by his luck to fish for salmon from February to September on an excellent piece of dry land. . . .

I think Bill Lawson* is the only full-time salmon fisherman left on the English side, and great credit is due to him for continuing this traditional, if difficult way of life. The community life of any village is held together by a few people, and in Bowness Bill Lawson is one of these. I find elsewhere in Solway that the fishermen, whatever his technique, usually provides stability in a rapidly changing community, as we shall see at the other end of the Solway when we call on Adam Birrell. As a fisherman, Bill Lawson has that sort of instinct that allows him to measure the weight of an extra ripple on the surface of the Solway fifty yards away even in the dusk and tell you what is underneath it, a shallow or a deep, fresh or salt, salmon or fluke. Like Adam Birrell across the water, he has more than a practical interest in his quarry, and I have found that many of our fishermen are good naturalists and great readers, as are these two.

I remember standing talking with Bill Lawson one beautiful September evening as the dusk rose from the water, and we were standing in a strange place, near the middle of the Solway. It can be very pleasant standing in this estuary perhaps a mile from land, as long as you do not sleep or even dream, for "he who dreams on the bed of the Solway make wake in the next world", especially if, as Scott continues, "the sky threatens a blast that will bring in the waves three feet abreast". We were standing, as I said, talking or listening to the birds as they came in for the evening. The Firth was at its loveliest. The water pushed against our legs and its ripples glinted golden in the light of the sun, which hung like a red ball low over Criffell. We had to lean to keep our balance

136

against the currents, constantly shifting our position to find firmer foothold on the drifting sand. This is an action which in time becomes automatic; you always seem to be stepping up a few inches, but you never get any higher. It is like being on a slow descending escalator. Quite suddenly, Bill was off with that peculiar high-stepping run that moving in two feet of water entails. He had seen a familiar ripple which tells of the presence of a salmon, and he was after it, shoaling the fish, not waiting for it. This one got away, probably because I had been claiming too much of his attention, or because the fish had been warned by the presence of us both. A swimming salmon can feel at a distance the pull of water round the waiting fisherman. I did, however, learn something more of the habits of salmon on this occasion by watching its escape. They tend to move into the streams and eddies of the fresher water going down from the river. Perhaps temperature as well as saltiness controls their movements and helps to explain the mechanism whereby from the open sea they manage to find the estuary of the river in which they were born. In the Firth they like the fairly shallow water and seldom dive deep, but they can take evasive action into a deeper channel when pursued. The fisherman has to know a good deal about the normal habits and the special tricks of his quarry, and he gets to know intimately a stretch of water whose surface and colour and depth—particularly the last—are ever-changing. The bed of the Solway is never the same for two days running, and sometimes quite drastic changes can happen to the course of the channel overnight. The fishermen on both shores anxiously watch the swing of the main channels, for they may decide which country will have the largest catch of Solway salmon in a given season. This is really important; a bad season, in these critical times, will often tempt a man to seek some more profitable employment. When the viaduct that crossed from Bowness to Annan was taken down, there was much interest in the submarine course of channel and bank, and tremendous changes were reported over a short period. Talking of channels, I have not mentioned that the word "haaf" is Old Norse for "channel" or "stream", so it seems probable that haafing goes back almost a thousand years. I wonder how far forward it will go! It may at least be preserved by the growing number of amateurs and part-timers, who find in this strenuous way of fishing both a wonderful recreation after the daily grind as well as an addition to the larder of one of nature's tastiest dishes. Of course, even the amateurs sell as well as eat, and I know of one small boy who may have a bicycle this summer if his father's week-end hauls are big enough.

Stake-net fishing may be even older than haafing. Both forms of "sand" fishing, as the old chronicles call them, are well attested in medieval times, and in several of the mouths of rivers running into the estuary, particularly the Cree, are very ancient foundations of fish-traps made with timber stakes and brushwood in days when nets were not available.* But nets go back a good long time. One of the earliest fishing concessions was made by Hugh de Morville at Sollebrough, and allowed "one entire net" with adequate space on the shore for drying it. I have written earlier about the farming interests of the Cistercians, and most of their abbeys were also concerned with fisheries. There are many charters granting fishing rights to the monks, and a further series of grants handing on the rights to various tenants who sometimes paid their rent in kind. Many extracts from the old charters are given in Neilson's *Annals of the Solway*, but I just want to mention one or two that seem to have a specific point of interest.

First is the system of tenure. A grant by Thomas de Multon to Holm Cultram of "the full fishery in the water of Eden, pertaining to the freehold in the vill of Burgh; that is, two nets to each carucate of land" seems to imply that the fisheries were held in a similar way to medieval rights of pasturage. In passing, we may note that the water near Burgh is called the Eden in this early charter although the end of Rockcliffe Marsh, limiting the mouth of the river, would be further inland than it is today. In the Middle Ages the Solway was more than once called "the waters of Eden". Holm Cultram charters refer to the types of fishing practised. One mentions "both sea and sand fishing" at the mouth of the Wampool; another gives the right "to have and to hold a fishing boat with pertinents at the mouth of the Alne". The Alne became Ellen, and Ellenfoot later changed to Maryport, and this early charter is the first mention of the site of this town, which still has its "fishing boats with pertinents". The most tolerant grant seems to have been that beside Redkirk Point, given to the monks of Melrose Abbey by William de Brus, who specified that they could practise whatever kind of fishing they chose. With

---

* Modern equivalents sometimes still use brushwood for cheapness.

Redkirk Point we can come straight back to modern times, and visit the range of stake-nets there fished by David Graham, and by his father before him. It is not stretching things too far to name Mr Graham's nets as the descendant of the original fishery granted by Robert Bruce's father.

Stake-nets are rather complicated things, and as few people venture into them, I will try to give a brief description. Look first at the photograph facing page 166, which shows a range in Auchencairn Bay. You will see a net about sixteen feet high stretching well into the water fixed to a row of stakes. The poles are about seven feet apart, driven well into the sand with a pile-driver, and in a low Solway sun each pole is a beautiful story of the sea from its dark-green limpet-covered base to its sun-bleached top. This "cross arm" is guyed with thick nylon rope, and leads the fish into the first pocket. From this, another arm, the flood arm, stretches first parallel with the coast and then turns at right angles into deeper waters towards the second pocket. This echelon process is repeated four or five times. The range in the photograph has four pockets and each is a large and maze-like structure. To over-simplify the description, I could say that there is one box inside another, and a system of narrowing entrances, which tempts the fish into a long corridor where he waits to be collected when the tides run out. The last of the entrances, about a foot across, and known as the "straight mouth", is liable to catch any fisherman who feeds too well on his own salmon. The pockets are some forty-five by twenty feet, and really have a more complicated pattern than I have told. They are roofed with net as well and can fish the salmon on both the ebb and the flood.

The laws governing salmon-fishing are many and involved. Some in particular specify the size of mesh for different sections of cross-arm, pocket and ebb-and-flood arm. They are kind to the fish on Sundays, for the pocket must have "a hole" at least four feet six inches wide between 6 p.m. on Saturday and 6 a.m. on Monday to allow the fish to proceed "without let or hindrance". This is also kind to fishermen. Twice a day the tide runs out, and as ebb-time varies as the season moves, you can imagine the feelings of the men of the stake-nets as they tramp perhaps a couple of miles across the sands at dawn or dusk, wet or fine, hot or icy-cold, only to find at the end, as so many of us do nowadays, empty pockets.

Stake-net fishing is not only difficult but can be dangerous and there is often a long walk to the nets. If I take you on a morning's trip with a fisherman, you might appreciate more the salmon so delicately served in a London hotel. It is a cold morning, and it takes quite a few minutes for him to get ready. He puts on thigh-waders, or chest waders if the water demands it, and gets ready for a long, chilly walk. He will take a compass, for the Solway, always a lonely place, becomes eerie and dangerous a mile from shore in a sudden mist. Our mists are not dirty, but you tend to walk in circles—footprints in wet sand soon disappear—trying to guess from the sounds in the air and the shape of the ripples on the sand which way lies land until the flood-tide sneaks behind you, or comes roaring like an express train. A whistle is useful, too, in these circumstances as in mountaineering, and he usually slips his watch (as fishermen do the whole world over) inside the fold of his cap; he hopes to keep his head dry, if nothing else. He won't forget pipe, matches and tobacco, and a knife to cut it, especially the knife—it might save his life as well as cut his smoke. If the currents do happen to sweep a man off his feet, and he is wearing chest-waders, he is soon held down or even turned upside-down by the weight of water in his boots. A little quick-thinking, and a few cuts with a knife in the right places, might make all the difference. On the whole, these Solway fishermen, at least the full-timers, are not likely to get caught. They combine sense and experience too well for that, though they may get into trouble trying to rescue amateurs. I have heard some rich vocabulary on this subject. Rather like sailors, they seem to dislike the one obvious precaution that you or I might take. I know of very few Solway salmon men who can swim. . . .

While I have been writing, he has gathered his creel and his little truncheon, and set out across the sands to see what his net has collected. One of the most interesting if economically useless aspects of stake-netting is the daily surprise at the oddments you can find in the pockets.

Even on normal days, the salmon is not alone in the net. Always around the bottom of the back net in the "gut" there will be, hiding under a mass of damp sand and left water, a dozen or more flat fish, usually flounders (or flukes as we call them up here). The bigger ones among these are quite useful, and many a small service has been repaid with a bunch of flukes. He must be prepared to extricate not only these pleasant little fellows, but over the years a mixed bag, including sharks, seals, sturgeons, rays of all kinds, the occasional drowned sea-bird, and the very occasional corpse, as well as other unmentionables. Further along the coast at Creetown, Adam Birrell has even reported a catch of roe-deer, and grey seals are fairly common. The fishermen kill these because of their bad influence on the salmon, and it seems rather a pity that the small, subsidiary industry which dealt with these seals has now died out because there is no one who can or *will* tan the skins. That royal fish, the sturgeon, used to be caught in most seasons, but for some reason seems to be getting scarcer. I think the record sturgeon caught in a stake-net weighed twenty-five stones, but it is dangerous to put this in print, as someone will be sure to have heard of a bigger one.

When fish are talked about in Solway pubs, the conversation can often turn to whales. Whales and sharks are quite common, and sometimes small ones get tangled in nets or big ones get washed up, dead or dying. There was some fuss, panic and pub-licity around Workington a year ago, when a school of sharks was seen and hunted, but any of the Solway fishermen who cruise that part of the estuary could have told almost the life-history of this family from its first appearance, a single shark, some years ago. Sharks and whales provide a great spectacle for the landsman, and in a photograph I have, a bottle-nosed whale, washed ashore near Maryport in 1937, looks almost as big as the gasometer behind it, which is equally unsightly and more permanently smelly. Whales also provide entertainment and exercise for lawyers, and in their treatment there is a slight difference on each side of the Solway. In England, whales are the property of the Crown, and the coastal revenue officers have written instructions on how to treat their charges and where to send the jawbone for identification in special cases. An old law says that the whale is royal, like the sturgeon, but whereas the king gets all the latter, the whale must be divided and the head offered to the king, and the tail to the queen. The interesting, if surprising, reason for this, given by an old writer on English law, was that the queen required a stock of whalebone for her wardrobe!

"A quhail fundyn on the see cost" was treated differently in Scotland, according to ancient acts of Parliament. It was a royal escheat which the king usually passed to the Church, and both

Holyrood Abbey and Dunfermline benefited under this tradition. Neilson quotes a dubious fragment of old Scots regulations
which bases the right of escheat on the weight of the fish (they
used the popular word to describe this mammal). If it did not break
down a six-ox cart before high-water-mark was reached, the fish
went to the adjacent landowner. Otherwise, it was the king's.

I can imagine the torments and legal intricacies that would
ensue when a whale drifted on to the shore of one landowner,
was washed on to the land of another before its weight could be
guessed in relation to the ox-cart, and at the same time was in
danger of being rapidly manufactured into oil by the local
peasantry while the landowner who claimed it was sending to
Carlisle for barrels, knives and cutlasses. All this actually happened in 1719 about a point on the Scottish shore of Solway,
Lougan, and Dr R. C. Reid published the main documents
relating to this whale in a most entertaining paper in the *D. & G.
Transactions*.

Here are just three short extracts from the mass of accounting
that was done when the matter had finally been sorted out:

	£	s.	d.
July 7. For 24 men and six women imployed in cutting up the fish and carrying the fatt and gathering the oyle, the men att 1 shilling and women at 10*d*.	1	0	0
July 13. For 13 pints of brandy given to the workers the time of cutting doun the fish it being absolutely necessary the smell being so noisome and the weather hott.............................	1	6	0
July 13. For a stranger seaman who understood the manner of boiling te same att five groats per day	0	10	0

A total of £94 5s. 3d. was spent on this whale when all the
items were totalled (although the contemporary accountant
strangely enough made the total £87 15s. 3d.), and even if the
profit was small, a great deal of fun was no doubt had by all.

One man involved, the Earl of Rothes, certainly had great
expectations. His predecessor in the office of Vice-Admiral for
Scotland had obtained two whales at a cost of £90, and made
above £700 sterling apiece from them!

This adventure with the Lougan whale has led me away from

stake-nets, but as it has involved a note about the expenses associated with "fishing", I would like to go back and consider the costs of fishing by "fixed engines", as stake-nets are legally called. Ivo, who founded the Kirkpatrick family, had a fishery in 1190 "between the fishery of Blawad" (a ford near Torduff Point, now called Blaatwood) "and the water of Hesch" (Esk). Ivo's land included a place to stretch his nets, and the annual rent was one pound of pepper, or six pennies. I do not know how much is the rent of a modern fishery, but the cost of erecting stake-nets, with netting at roughly £1 a pound, and yards of thick nylon rope (I can hardly afford a hundred feet of thin stuff for climbing) plus labour costs and the uncertainty of storms * and the wiles of the fish, make it obvious why you can only have Scotch salmon at a price. If you are one of those fabulous people who like salmon at Christmas (there is a close season from 9th September to February 25th), you will have to pay even more, for only a very few of the best fish are held back for the special refrigeration process. The majority caught in Solway stake-nets go straight into the warehouse on the shore to be weighed—25 to 30 lb. makes good eating—packed in ice and dispatched to Billingsgate. The Solway salmon is usually killed in the water, and with water in it; it is not bruised in the nets, and, I think, can be said to be the finest eating of any in the world.

There is another form of fishing with "fixed engines", which I ought to mention briefly. This is by poke-nets and is restricted to the parish of Annan. Poke-nets are let in clouts by Annan Town Council under Crown Charter. Each licensee must reside in the parish and may not hold more than fifteen clouts, each of which has four bags or pokes which are usually together in long rows or banks. At the time of writing, there are about seventeen rows on each side of the Scottish stump of the old viaduct. Iron stakes are driven, about four feet apart, deep into the sand, with about five feet showing at the ebb: The top of a long net is fixed to the top of the stakes and at the bottom to iron rings, which can slide up and down the stakes. The currents push this net into a long bag, say from knee to chest height, except at week-ends, when the ringed edge is raised to the top to close the mouth. The bottom of the bag swings just above the bed of the sea as the tide

* Floating ice is most dangerous, and has this year (1954) badly damaged stake-nets.

bulges it out. When a salmon enters the bag, its own weight carries it below the bottom rope, and it is captured. Pokes fish both the ebb and the flood, but as the fish may be bruised and knocked about, they are not always best quality.

Two other forms of fishing are associated with the Solway, either in modern times or during the past. These are what is called "boat fishing" and fishing from horseback. I will leave the latter for the moment and concentrate on the boats. First of all, there is the whammel boat, which is designed specially for salmon-fishing, and to be used with particular nets. In Scotland, whammelling (what a nice word!) is limited to an area bounded by the eastern side of the parish of Ruthwell. In England, things are slightly different, and, as far as I know, anyone can use whammel boats, though the licence costs more, but at the present I do not think anyone *is* doing. Even in Scotland, hardly any are used for their original form of fishing because a lot of expensive net, a crew of two or three, and, of course, a costly boat, are all involved. Two boats only specialised in this way last season, and it says a lot for the co-operative spirit of Annan fishermen that all the other local boat-owners shared the licensing expenses through their Association. The skipper of a whammel boat explained his economics in these words, "Every fish has to be divided into three—a third for the boat, a third for my partner, and a third for me." Nets vary from four to seven hundred yards long, although shorter ones of about three hundred yards are used in England. The boats which were built at Annan are grand little craft. They are about eighteen to twenty feet, with a five-foot-nine beam, half-decked and with lug and mainsail. They are built with air-chambers—frequently removed to give more room —and a half-keel, and make excellent and unsinkable sea-going boats. A friend in Silloth managed to get hold of one when the fishing declined which proved most suitable for pleasure purposes. This was a rare case, surely, of a blacksmith at sea. When the boats are working, the fine flax net is twice-folded and skilfully arranged in the stern of the boat with one end attached to a pole near the shore, floating vertically under the influence of cork at the top and lead at the foot. The boat sails out across the tide, and the net is paid out so that it is kept vertical by a combination of floats and lead sinkers. The net is hauled several times in each tide, with a rhythmic action splendid to watch. The weather should not be too good for whammel fishing, and each boat is equipped with sets of net of different mesh for use under different conditions.

Another small boat, or rather a number of them, is even better known in the Solway, and with them we leave our noble salmon for another delicacy, for I shall next describe the Annan fleet of shrimp boats. I am sorry that I have to report that this dignified little fleet is much smaller today than it once was. The boats are similar in size to the whammel boats. Most of them are powered by a great variety of home-fitted engines, and are petrol or oil-driven, although you might think from a superficial glance at the fleet in the estuary that they were small editions of the old coal-burning trawlers. The flames and smoke that belch from their assorted stacks belong not to the works, however, but to the shrimp boiler. These tough little boats almost scrape out of the estuary of the Annan after an hour or two of ebb, and after about six hours of ebb (the Solway is said to ebb until the next high tide) they come rushing back, racing with the water, scrambling for position. This is a tricky business, and a dangerous one. If the incoming tide catches the boat with its rudder set too far over, tremendous strength is required to keep control and guide the little boat between banks that only leave inches to spare.

The crews of these shrimpers—usually there are two men to a boat—spend all their time in the shallow waters of the estuary, and as the haafer knows his channels, so must they know the banks to avoid getting hanked (or run aground), especially when they are trawling. The Solway shrimp trawl is a long, flattened cone of a net, looking burnished on shore from its soaking in red lead. The wide entrance to the net is literally a mouth, curving backwards from the ends of an eighteen-foot wooden beam, which is kept about eighteen inches above the bed of the sea by two skids, triangular iron hoops at right angles to the beam and at each end of it. The lower lip of the net mouth scrapes along the sand in the form of a thick and weighted rope and the upper lip floats a foot or two higher under the lift of corks. The shrimps lying on the sand have to be disturbed so that they jump over the lower lip, and their life is without doubt rudely disturbed, for a loop of chain fixed to the ends of the beam drags its semicircle a few inches in front of what I have called the lower lip of the trawling-net.

After each trawl the long net (it may be twenty feet) is hauled, untied at the tail, and emptied into the hold. From the foot-wide deck this operation is most precarious, but the varied contents are soon selected, popped into the boiler and the unwanted and unpleasant catches, together with the shrimps not yet grown-up, are thrown back into the sea. The work goes on, and when the next lot is hauled and ready for boiling, the first batch is hung over the side to cool in the water until the crew are ready for the next trawl. Solway-shrimping is a business that combines short periods of strenuous exertion—especially when the net gets full of sand—with very delicate navigation. The fleet works as one team, and the boats keep in touch with each other with few signals and fewer words.

The richest banks are not always found in the same place, and the fleet wheels as one ship to extend its search or follow the hopeful signs. The waters off the Blackshaw Bank are often most rewarding, but there is sometimes a good catch waiting on the banks off the English shore near Allonby Bay. Although the shrimps—they are actually pink shrimps or prawns—command a good price in the market, this form of fishing has become less profitable over recent years. One English merchant at the beginning of the century used to send his shrimps all over the country, labelled with the words "The Shrimp King", but these labels are now souvenirs. In more recent years, shrimping from Annan has declined as well, and it has been suggested that the beds have been over-fished in the last decade, as the universal use of power in place of sail has enabled faster and more extensive trawling. Whatever is the true cause, it is a sad fact that this gallant little fleet now musters only fourteen regular boats, where once fifty or sixty were a common and splendid sight in the Firth.

Most of us associate shrimps with crabs and lobsters, and although the lobster pot is not so familiar a sight in the Solway as elsewhere around these islands, I want to say a little about this industry, both because it seems to be decreasing today, and even in the past the Solway grounds have not received anything like the attention they deserve. Those who know both crabs and lobsters from the Solway are unanimous about their quality, and, as for numbers, a decade or two ago it was possible for four men, working two boats, to take twenty-five thousand marketable lobsters in a single season. Both crabs and lobsters abound, especially from Luce Bay to Wigtown Bay around the main spawning ground off Burrow Head. The hen lobsters come in from the deeper water, beginning in March and reaching the main run of three to four-year-olds (averaging two pounds) about the middle of August. They leave about October. The local people say that they arrive with a storm and leave with a storm. I feel sure that in this season there is opportunity for some of the younger generation to get back into an occupation of their fathers that can be both satisfying and very profitable. The crabs are present in the same season and I am told they are about their best in April.

I have not exhausted all the forms of boat-fishing. We shall see later how many of the harbours of the Solway have become silted up and deserted generally during this century, but even today these harbours often shelter the one or two boats that carry on the traditions of fishing and sneak out through the winding channels when the water gets high enough to lift them off their mud. A lot of these boats are owned by part-timers, but there are a number of men from Creetown to Annan who still get their livelihood from the waters. These fishermen regard all the estuary as their home, and go in different seasons to different parts for a variety of catch. They may shrimp in the spring, rejoice in the herring when it pays one of its now rare visits, and prosper from the plaice, which often follows the tracks of the shrimp, and is found off the southern shore, at its best, between August and October, and in really great numbers, in recent seasons, in the Scottish seas off Southerness. I have mentioned the herring and the plaice, and in some years there is a sufficient number of these present to merit the invasion of the bigger Solway ports, especially in West Cumberland, by boats and trawlers from Ireland, Scotland, Man, the Lancashire coast and even, in recent seasons, from as far away as Denmark. Although these bigger boats are not allowed to fish the shallows of the estuary, their crews make a colourful addition to the inns that crowd the harbours of the ports of West Cumberland.

So much for modern fishing. From the point of view of the picturesque, it is a pity that the most intriguing technique the Solway has ever seen has now disappeared. Azilian man, in prehistoric times, left his spear-heads and harpoons as the earliest evidence of a craft now practised only in the tropic seas. In the sixteenth century Camden was amazed to see how fishermen on horseback rode up and down these shallow waters, spearing the fish with their long leisters. His amazement was repeated by Darsie Latimer in *Redgauntlet*, and Scott's notes on the affair at Netherby indicate that fish-spears could be used for more than one purpose in the later eighteenth century. The typical fish-spear of the Middle Ages seems to have had two prongs, the inner edge of each being serrated to grasp the fish firmly, rather like a goosander's beak. Two techniques were popular; they were known as "sunning" and "burning the water", the difference being that burning was done at night under the light of hand-torches; also, different types of leister were used. There are many references to spearing throughout history, and most of the authorities differ, perhaps because they often write about different periods, in their description of the spears and the number and form of the prongs. For the most vivid description I would recommend the one in *Guy Mannering*. This art appears to me to have required great skill, especially when the leisters were thrown rather than thrust (but not when the salmon were spawning). Today spearing is merely one of many illegal methods of fishing.

I cannot end this chapter without a mention of modern river fishing, although I have no space to go into details. The rivers that come into Solway provide good enough fishing to bring many holiday-makers—I know one who travels weekly from Liverpool to his Sunday cottage in Galloway—but the fisherman will know where to find more detailed information than I could give here, and the historian will be able to find many references to fishing rights—in the Eden, for example—in the charters of old abbeys such as Wetheral. I shall say nothing at all about the less legal forms of fishing that I am afraid are only too common around the Solway. The last time I spoke in a mixed company about this subject, I discovered at the end that I had a water-bailiff in my audience.

We began with the noble salmon; let me end with the valuable herring. Imagine yourself in a little boat somewhere in the darkening estuary at the end of a summer day when all is so still that the crests of the hills, and even the silence that covers them, are reflected in the water. At first there is no sound from the gleaming shoals that slide beneath the surface, but they are there, alive and in their millions. It is no exaggeration to say that you could catch them, you could not help it, with a bucket and a rope. You are not watching the sea; suddenly there comes the sound of hail, but it is not hail; you turn round, with elbows on the little deck, and are held, entranced, by the sight of thousands of herring imitating the salmon (perhaps they, too, have their parasites!), leaping out and smacking back into the water. The spell is broken after a few minutes. Some unknown voice gives the word of command; the leaping stops in one half-second, and the shoal is away.

CHAPTER IX

INDUSTRY AND THE SPECIAL AREA*

THE main drama of industrial Solway has been staged on a wedge of land based on the coast from Whitehaven to Maryport thrusting inland to Wigton and out under the waves. This is the West Cumberland coalfield.

Cumberland as a whole might be likened to a Lakeland farm with an attractive and welcoming parlour for visitors and a small back kitchen where no attempt is made to disguise the work that must be done. The National Park is the parlour to West Cumberland's kitchen. For most of this chapter, we shall be kitchen visitors.

The story of West Cumberland is the story of three towns, Whitehaven, Maryport and Workington—the order is purely historical. Whitehaven developed early, became the first port in Cumberland and the third in Britain, and today memories of prosperity and failure linger in the well-planned streets with their rather shabby Georgian houses. Workington has had more variety and less suffering than the other two, and its reward is in its busy bigness which straggles along the coast. Maryport, neat and compactly built, the last to be developed but the second to achieve prosperity, suffered worst of all, and its picturesque docks are today almost empty of ships.

There is a happier sequel to the story of each of these towns, but we must go back in history to see the beginnings and the developments that made them what they are today. Those who associate the industrial revolution with the development of coal-mining will be surprised to learn that Whitehaven was exporting coal to Ireland in the very early days of the seventeenth century. In an earlier chapter I wrote about the legendary ways in which the monks of St Bees obtained their lands. What matters more to us now is the way they lost them. After the dissolution, these lands were granted by the Crown in 1560 to Sir Thomas Challoner and were later sold by his son to two partners for £2,000. Very soon afterwards, one of these partners, Gerard Lowther, bought out

---

*Various minor revisions have been made to this chapter since it was first written in 1955. The present position (in 1982) is summed up in a special note on page 168.

13. Salmon fishing. Stake-nets in Auchencairn Bay

14. Maryport Harbour. The town has turned its face from the sea

15. The Eden Bridge, Carlisle, pivot of Solway routes

16. The symmetrical slag of Risehow Colliery. ". . . coal from under the sea"

17. Hydro-electric Station, Tongland, Kirkcudbrightshire. ". . . the cleaner power of a later age"

18. Queen Mary of Scotland came to Solway through the gates of Dundrennan Abbey

19. ". . . to Fisher's Cross, just east of Bowness, which became glorified by the name of Port Carlisle"

20. The Solway Viaduct. ". . . a gallant monument to an age of reckless enterprise"

21. Workington. ". . . through quiet Portland Square with its cobbled roadway and dignified houses"

22. "Kirkcudbright . . . is light and open, brightly painted and has a flavour of history"

23. "Dumfries . . . retains a special atmosphere as the town of Robert Burns"

24. St Bees Head. "...so I turned back along the Solway and walked up over Tomlin"

the other. This land included the Whitehaven coalfield. In due course, the Lowther family rented a stretch of coastline of about 150 acres for £1 per annum. This became the port of Whitehaven. The character of the Lowthers has had a lot to do with the history of West Cumberland, and at our first meeting we can see that they knew how to snap up a bargain. That this aspect of their character could be extended, as far as Gerard was concerned, into the political field is shown in a comment made by the contemporary Lord Warden of the West March, Lord Scrope of Bolton, who called him "Old Belzebub".

Other squires in the district followed with similar ideas. The Fletchers of Moresby were rivals of the Lowthers, and wanted to develop Parton as a harbour by building a pier to take coal boats (you can see Parton on photograph number 4), but the then lord, Sir John Lowther, the true founder of the Lowther fortunes, won the day with a combination of wealth, skill and influence, and delayed the Act required by the Fletchers. The unimportant port of Parton which was finally built had an ancestor no doubt in an earlier harbour protected by Roman Moresby.

Workington developed later. At first it was just an outport of Whitehaven and even in the coal rush the Curwen family, as lords of Workington, seemed to have a more balanced approach which culminated in John Christian Curwen's attention to agriculture. It was not until the 1740s that the Senhouse family followed the general trend and, beginning to mine the coal on their land, added a harbour for its export. Thus was Maryport born. Before 1748 only one house had been built on the site. Although the timing is different, and the Lowthers certainly led the way, the pattern of growth of these three towns is very similar.

West Cumberland has no hinterland, but its coal was exported so successfully that Whitehaven gained the complete monopoly of the trade to Ireland. Exporting requires boats. Wooden ships were fairly easily made in these little harbours, and slowly a great tradition of shipbuilding joined the rapidly growing exploitation of coal. The Lowthers of Whitehaven were interested in and encouraged shipbuilding because it concerned their coal, but as the years went on, the ships carried other goods. Traders and merchants settled in the town and established businesses, and in the eighteenth century there was great prosperity on all sides which hid for a time a slowly developing rift. Liverpool, Glasgow and other great ports of today all lagged behind Whitehaven in the colonial trade, and the visitor will find it hard to recall that Whitehaven was once one of the two greatest ports concerned in the tobacco trade. I have mentioned a certain shabby elegance that lingers in the plan of the town, and this elegance dates from the days of prosperity when Sir John, as a member of the Royal Society, would no doubt converse with Britain's greatest planner. Sir John may easily have given information about the new mining inventions of his great engineer, Spedding, for the Whitehaven pits were famed in those days as the most efficient and the deepest in the world, and Sir Christopher Wren for his part might in exchange have offered advice on the planning of the town. Whitehaven for long was master of the Irish coal trade in spite of the angry polemics of the great Dean Swift against its monopoly, but gradually in the eighteenth century it lost its position in the general world of trade, although shipbuilding remained fairly strong. Two things were happening. Firstly, the industrial revolution was giving ports like Glasgow and Liverpool a rich and well-populated hinterland supplying a growing quantity of manufactured goods and importing foodstuffs and raw materials from abroad, while the hinterland of Whitehaven still contained a similar number of sheep to that in the seventeenth century and very little else. Secondly, the deterioration of the port was certainly speeded up by the conflict which had gradually arisen between Town and Castle, which was the popular way of defining the trade and shipping interests of the merchants and the coal interests of the Lowthers. The merchants and the shippers were finding great difficulty in keeping up an efficient flow of goods and a satisfactory production of ships in a small and antiquated harbour which was, of course, still on Lowther land, and the lord of the manor did not encourage any expansion of the shipyards which might interfere with his plans for coal. Men saw the beginning of the end when the firm of Brocklebank, now known all over the world, left West Cumberland and took its shipbuilding to Liverpool. The "Castle" had progressed far, but only in coal, from the days when the first baskets were hauled up a sloping ramp, but I want to pause for a moment when I mention progress. The first mining accident recorded in Whitehaven was in 1737, when "fire-damp killed twenty-two at 4 o'clock in ye M". They are learning to use fire-damp in Whitehaven today and it is fed into the gas grid, but even in this scientific age one's ideas of progress are marred by the memories of recent disasters.

Though the development of the pits went on, we cannot afford to disregard the short-sightedness of the hindrance to shipping and trade. Even more surprisingly, the Lowthers made little attempt to develop the rich deposits of hæmatite iron ore in the district and, in fact, hindered its exploitation by others. The Fletchers of Parton got a little of their own back in this quarrel by allowing a Frizington man to store and ship his ore from their port when the Lowthers refused to handle it. I think, too, that something in the autocratic behaviour of members of the family (although a common symbol of the times) was partly responsible for future happenings. When a householder at Whitehaven claimed compensation for damage by subsidence to his property and took the case to law in Carlisle, Lord Lonsdale * locked out every one of his miners and refused to open the pits until the citizens of the town had signed a promise not to claim compensation for damage or injury. This was in 1791. Whilst Whitehaven was slowly going down hill with quarrels and shipping troubles, the other two towns were on the upgrade, and we can end the story of Whitehaven's great days at a public ceremony in Maryport in 1857 when with great jubilation—over twenty toasts were drunk—the new wet dock, called the Elizabeth Dock after the squire's wife, was opened. This dock, the first non-tidal (or wet) dock on the Solway—later joined by another, the Senhouse Dock—could handle coal as well as other goods, and killed the trade of Whitehaven, so ending a chapter, rich though marred, in the history of that port.

The nineteenth century saw the days of Maryport's prosperity. The Senhouse family seem to have been less quarrelsome than the Lowthers, though they probably made very much less money. They built Maryport neatly; until recently there was only one curved street in the town and this gives an air of compactness that is still striking. The fact that the town stops suddenly and the countryside starts without any straggling enhances its approaches and is pleasing to visitors as well as residents. Some of the latter are apt to be cynical about the square form of the streets. It certainly is the best way to crowd as many houses as possible into a small area. However, the high open square in the town cannot

* As the Lowthers had now become.

be accused of squalidness. It is where the wealthier elements lived and even its name, Fleming Square, adds respectability. The second Humphrey Senhouse, founder of the town, had married Mary Fleming, whose father was Bishop of Carlisle. He gave her name to the town, and Maryport has only been known as such for 205 years. It might be as well here to try once and for all to correct the popular misconception that the town was so called because Mary, Queen of Scots, arrived there after her escape from Langside. This is in quite modern guide-books and I heard it repeated in Kirkcudbright last year by an official custodian of the Ministry of Works. His face expressed disbelief when I suggested that Queen Mary had landed at Workington many years before Mary Fleming had become Mary Senhouse and Ellenfoot changed to Maryport in her honour.

The founding of the town was preceded by the publication of a remarkable piece of propaganda which managed to suggest on the same page (a) that Whitehaven had so much coal that a port at Maryport would assist its disposal, and (b) that as the coal of Whitehaven would not last long, it would be advisable to develop the seams at Maryport. However, Maryport got its harbour and we have seen how its later improvements affected Whitehaven.

Maryport was not obsessed by coal, and shipbuilding grew to a very satisfactory level, especially when one considers the general age of wooden ships. Incidentally, Thomas Henry Ismay, who founded the White Star Line, was born in Maryport. Photograph number 14 shows an almost deserted harbour, but I have old photographs taken from a similar spot on which you can count forty or fifty masts of vessels in the harbour and docks and others waiting in the roads. Other photographs look down from the same little hill to record the launchings in the narrow River Ellen of vessels like the *Netherby*, a beautiful three-master of fourteen hundred tons. Ships up to two thousand tons were launched into this river, bringing a now forgotten fame and a half-holiday for the school children. The only way to get such a ship into the narrow river was to launch it broadside, a thing elsewhere unheard of in those days, but invariably accomplished with no more damage than a few hundred sets of wet clothes from the enormous splash. There is sadness in these photographs, fot now the harbour is empty and the dock gates silted * and the

* See footnote on page 15.

mansions of shipbuilders split into flats. The last broadside launch was in 1914, and they took away the lifeboat in 1949. It could only be used for the few hours of deepest water each day, but the town felt the loss and so did Bob Fisher as he steered it out of the harbour. His father before him had served in the crew and both had taken part in many memorable rescues. It is now based on Workington, the port which also inherited the commercial prosperity that once belonged to Maryport.

I have not space to tell of the many fine ships that were built on this Solway coast, but one at least is of interest to a much wider field. The *Lycidas* was launched in 1902 and became a transport vessel of the Siamese navy, renamed *Chang*, according to *Jane's Fighting Ships*.

The Senhouse Dock had killed the Lowthers' port of Whitehaven, and retribution followed in 1927. The instrument of death was similar. Workington opened a new dock that would take really big ships, the Prince of Wales Dock. With the steelworks behind it, it was a dock that could be and has been kept open and free from silt. Maryport's two docks, opened with such ceremony, soon took on a derelict look. Until the emergency of the Second World War, they were useful as swimming pools for children and very little else. This year (1954) the wash-out of a coal-seam at Risehow by some prehistoric river has again emptied these docks of shipping.

I have left the story of Workington until the end and it is the happiest story of the three. It began with coal, continued with shipping and flourished with iron and steel. The second half of the nineteenth century saw feverish activity in the little towns from Egremont to Cleator Moor a few miles inland from the Solway coast. Long, bleak streets grew up, iron-miners were imported from Ireland, County Durham and the Isle of Man—my grandfather was one from Man—as coal-miners had been attracted to Whitehaven in the seventeenth century. The fulfilment of the iron rush was in 1861 when the firm of Cammell moved from Derbyshire to Workington and laid the foundations of a steel industry which enabled that town to keep going with some sort of balance even in the black days of the coal depression. Today the United Steel Company, although not the only heavy industry in the region, is a symbol of work although in 1973 its future is threatened. Were there no signposts, you could travel at night from Carlisle by pointing your nose at the red glare that fills the sky as molten slag is tipped on the banks.

Workington suffered perhaps least of all the ports and Maryport the most, and I halt this dismal record in the blackest days of 1935 with over eighty per cent of the working population of Maryport unemployed. I shall soon describe the years of recovery, but it is worth stopping for a moment to see if any major causes of slump can be isolated.

Taking the district as a whole, two things stand out clearly and immediately. The first is that lack of a populated hinterland that I have already mentioned, and the second is the isolation of West Cumberland accentuated by an inadequate transport system that has cut the region off from other main centres of population. The two problems are of course related. Cumberland could never have had the equivalent of the English Midlands in close association, but it could have served many other districts had transport been better, and although the die was cast many years ago, it is worth recalling that George Stephenson himself suggested that the main north–south railway in the west of Britain should take the coast road around Cumberland instead of climbing over Shap. However, he was overruled and West Cumberland is still waiting for a good coast route and is still isolated, economically and culturally, from the main stream of events which flows through Carlisle.

There is another factor which is shared by all three ports. Not one of them was based on a first-class natural harbour. The harbours of Whitehaven and Maryport, especially the latter, have been severely damaged by gales on more than one occasion, and it is expensive to keep all three harbours clear of silt. An economic stimulus, more powerful than any we have found in this region, is required to go against nature, as we shall see in the case of Port Carlisle. Silt and storms have played a part in the Solway's recent economic history foreshadowed by the destruction of that once great port, Skinburness, on a day in February 1304.

So much for the general factors. Looking more closely at the history that I have told, it is noticeable that, of the three ports, the mantle of prosperity has seldom fallen on more than one in any period. The story has been of one up and two down, although the depth of the downs has varied with the character of the ports and the diversity of their industries. Briefly, three separate communities were built by three separate Lords of the Manor in competition rather than in co-operation. West Cumberland is not big enough in industrial potential and therefore in population to support three ports, especially with the pattern of communication that it developed. It is idle to speculate on what might have been, and yet, having a liking for idle speculation, I wonder if instead of cutting each others' throats the three towns—or the three Lords of the Manor—had got together and developed one major port to serve the whole coalfield and all the other local interests, the position in the thirties might have been very different. However, it is too easy to judge the past by the standards of the present, and regional co-operation is not so common even today that we can cast stones.* Without a doubt, the earlier Lowthers were ingenious and progressive as far as coal was concerned, and the later Curwens, as I have said, did much for the agriculture of the whole of the county. The Senhouse family not only built Maryport but had a great share in the construction of the earliest railway in West Cumberland, the Maryport and Carlisle, and the tradition of this separate company still lingers in Carlisle's Citadel station although the M. & C. Bay has now become Platform No. 2.

Turning to the years of recovery, we have to note two extraneous factors. The first was the influence on Government policy of the war between 1939 and 1945 and of the anticipation, towards the end of the thirties, of this war. Without this it is hard to estimate what would have happened to the coal mines of West Cumberland or to the people. The second extraneous factor was the political atmosphere of those years which dictated that certain humanitarian and palliative measures should be taken with regard to the depressed—later special—areas. Working with and often pushing these external factors was action within the coalfield itself. The district did not sit still and wait for help. The industrial population, and in particular the miners, had a long tradition of having to help themselves which showed itself in the work of rehabilitation and in whatever political action was possible, as, for example, in the Hunger Marches of the thirties. It also appeared in the energetic leadership of local citizens, who found an outstanding champion in Jack Adams, the miners' leader. The history of recovery, of pressure on governments and of the seizing

* Newspaper headlines still (May 1954) report competition between Maryport and Silloth about a plan to import Irish cattle.

of more than every opportunity available, is very largely tied up with the story of Lord Adams of Ennerdale. Jack Adams as he was always known and called by his friends is now dead but much of the prosperity of West Cumberland is his memorial.

The West Cumberland Development Company which grew up under his leadership was helped by the existence of a body of European refugees having skilled techniques but nowhere to practise them. The story of the setting up of new trading estates, the provision of factory space and capital facilities on easy terms, has often been told, and from 1938 the pattern in West Cumberland was one of rapid development. Whitehaven, Workington, Maryport, and in a lesser degree Aspatria each got its trading estate, and since then there has grown an air of prosperity in these towns enhanced by the renewed and urgent demand for coal that sent the men back to the pits.

It is worth noticing that the presence of new industries, employing in the main female labour, does not release the district from its dependence on coal and steel. At the time of writing, the future of steel seems assured, but the exploitation of coal in this field has aspects that are artificial. The field is not an economic one and should national demand be eased, West Cumberland would first see "rationalisation" (a stage we are very close to now) and then rapid decline. This might lead to a situation in which many women would still be able to find work, but many men would have no alternative to the dole. At poor best, regarding the family as a unit, each family would have some income and the worst effects of poverty would be avoided. Without wishing to overemphasise the more pessimistic aspects of the future, I should in addition make a point about the many and varied products of the light industries. Some of these, for example the ones connected with steel and engineering, and in this respect High Duty Alloys springs to mind, are no doubt stable enough to weather all but the most serious recessions. It is possible, however, that a number of those industries which cater for a more elastic or ephemeral market would soon suffer in a recession. Perhaps there was a warning of this during times of hardship round about the end of the eighteenth century when the lighter industries such as paper works, glass works and bobbin mills were the first to go and have never returned. Between the two extremes that I have mentioned, there is a great variety of products, the quality of which will enable them to stand against the best that any other part of the country can produce. Textiles would seem to be in a rather special position. There are in West Cumberland (and in Carlisle) many everyday textile products of a high standard and these have had a warning in the past few years that they will swing with the general prosperity of similar products elsewhere, but, as well as these, there are some superlative products whose quality is such that it would take a very great depression to influence their sales. To particularise, West Cumberland ought to be, and I think is, very proud of the fabrics that emerge from the West Cumberland Silk Mills of Miki Sekers.

It may be thought that in some ways these last few paragraphs concerning recent years are not much more cheerful than my earlier descriptions of the black days, but the West Cumberland people are not waiting for the worst to happen, and it is to the immediate future that we look for new developments which give rise to firm hopes.

The district has a tradition of what I call basic work which serves the needs of the age in which it exists. In the seventeenth century it was mining, in the eighteenth and nineteenth ship-building, joined later by the manufacture of steel. Things have gone wrong in the first half of our century, but with the help of light industries, a war, and an urgent demand for coal, the diffi-cult period seems to be passing, and the second half of the twentieth century might see the return in a new guise of the older pattern of production.

In the first place, West Cumberland is the home of Sellafield, a great centre for the development of Atomic Energy and the manufacture of plutonium. The building of Sellafield with its landmarking chimneys 415 feet high reproduced the old pattern of immigration from Ireland, and although this phase is now over, the running of the plant has brought in a permanent population of a high educational level without a background of isolation and depression that will in time produce at least a cultural stimulus exactly as the importation of new technicians for the trading estates has done further along the coast. I do not want to give the impression that all the technical posts in the new industrial centres are going to outsiders. The native West Cumbrian is taking his place in these modern industries, and this, together with the crea-tion of new Technical Colleges in Whitehaven and Workington, is destroying the conditions that previously forced many of the best brains to seek opportunity away from the district.

There are as many examples of the stimulating effects of outside ideas and people on West Cumberland industrial life as there are instances of contributions from the Cumbrians themselves. Another new idea, of the kind which I have called basic, has recently been introduced into the Whitehaven area. Here the expansion of an already established company has received local and—very practical—Government encouragement. This is a plant which produces sulphuric acid and cement from local anhydrite, a mineral which is in fact mined on the factory site itself. In abnormal conditions the products of this plant lessen the country's dependence on foreign supplies, and in normal times they serve the requirements of the parent company, and in addition compete favourably with similar products from anywhere in the world.

These two industries do not change the picture of West Cumberland by themselves, but I believe that they point the way. It is a pet dream of mine, and one which looks like coming true, that West Cumberland will have the first atomic power station* and perhaps the first household lamp to be lit by this new form of energy.

Scottish Solway has in some ways been lucky in having neither coal nor iron, and its granite-mining towns are cleaner and fresher than their coalfield opposites. In general terms, the lands to the north of Solway are agricultural and in consequence have a much smaller population than those to the south in spite of their greater area. Some idea of scale can perhaps be realised in the matter of shipbuilding, which is an industry common to both. Several ports on the northern shore are rightly proud of the grand ships they have built and sailed, but it is hardly any exaggeration to say that in general these ships have been about one-tenth of the size of their English counterparts.

There are parallels between the economic story of West Cumberland and that of the smaller Scottish ports. Both Dumfries and Kirkcudbright have many ancient records, and in the latter there is a complete set of Burgh Court Books developing into Town Council Minutes from 1576 up to the present day. These records give several indications of early rivalry between the ports. For example, Kirkcudbright enjoyed special customs rights along the

* Since this was written (1955) Annan on the Scottish side has the second; another Solway unity.

whole seaboard, and a quarrel arose in 1526 over a ship laden with wine which avoided the duties by going straight to Dumfries. As a result of this, two respected Dumfries burgesses, Herbert Maxwell and James Archibald, had to appear in court for dodging customs. The prizes of this competition were small, but there is no doubt that feelings ran high. I can find no mention of the West Cumberland squires ever coming to blows, but it is fairly certain that one dark night in the autumn of 1598 a party from Dumfries including the provost and bailies, all well armed, attempted to surprise Kirkcudbright and sack it "and to have slane and murdrist the complineris layand in their beddes". Apparently Kirkcudbright was not to be surprised and its citizens resisted, for the invaders "departit with schame and dishonnour" after damaging some barns. However, I must point out that far more old records indicate friendship, trade and co-operation between these towns than there would seem to have been from my single quotation.

Before I talk about the small ports, I ought to mention three larger ones to complete the picture, although they are outside my chosen Solway limits. They are all in the Rhinns of Galloway and have had or still have a great influence on south-west Scotland. Twenty-one miles from Ireland is Port Patrick, important as we saw in the days of cattle-droving. Though largely destroyed by gales in the nineteenth century, it is the only port in the north of the region still used by fishing trawlers. This is on account of its non-tidal, though difficult, approach. Stranraer, sheltered in Loch Ryan, is widely known as a live and busy rail-sea junction, the northern gateway to Ireland. Many readers, unless they know its bustle, will associate with it the tragedy of the *Princess Victoria*, lost in that great storm of January, 1953. Cairnryan, carved out of the solid rock on the eastern shore of the same loch, had a valiant history as a top secret port during the last war and parts of the Mulberry harbour were built there, but its future is apparently in the balance.

I have mentioned these three ports "for the record", and now let us come back to the Solway. Annan is perhaps the most promising of the small harbours, and I shall refer to it again, Smaller places like Glencaple and Carsethorn, which are the outports of Dumfries, Palnackie at the head of Rough Firth, Kirkcudbright, Wigtown and Isle of Whithorn are either silted up, in liquidation or derelict. Creetown is used by the Scottish Granite Company and as a local harbour is still functioning efficiently on the required scale.

There are hopes that some of these small ports might be cleaned up and used at least for local trade, but I think that with the very limited capital that the shipping interests in south-west Scotland seem to be able to attract, if Scottish Solway wants to develop harbour facilities, there might be a lesson from the death of Maryport and the dearth of Whitehaven with their bigger harbours and wet docks; that lesson is that any expenditure should be concentrated. A general opinion is that it would be best to develop Annan. Like the other ports, Annan has silted up, but it has been a thriving port in the past and it is getting ships in today with supplies for neighbouring chemical works and even for Dumfries. They sometimes come in rather precariously, and even with the water high, the Annan pilots have been known to ask the captain to shift his cargo to get the boat dead level for these pilots have to work in inches. It would benefit the growing industrial district if Annan were more used, although what the customs officer would say, I don't know. He has to travel more than seventy miles from Ayr to clear a foreign ship. The rest of the story of these ports is a small-scale story. Palnackie is occasionally used for timber and goods for a nearby depot, and goods are still coming in to Garliestown.

The biggest industries of Dumfries and Galloway are, of course, agriculture and the tourist trade. It is not part of my task to advertise the region, though I hope my descriptions have been accurate enough to indicate its attractions. These northern Solway shores could appeal to a wider range of tourist if public transport were good enough to enable the visitor without a car to see more than a tiny area in comfort. I have noticed, too, that the scarcity of Youth Hostels tends to discourage the youthful walkers that I meet in many other regions. These youngsters may not bring much money to a district, but they will both publicise its natural beauty and return themselves in later years. Agriculture has been dealt with in detail already and I hinted at associated industries when mentioning milk processing. Suffice it to say here that it is a highly efficient industry in south-west Scotland. The picture of Risehow Colliery (no. 16) is followed by a photograph which indicates that Scottish Solway makes use of the cleaner power of a later age. This hydro-electric station at Tongland, near Kirkcud-bright, is but one of a series which, under the South-West Scotland Electricity Board, serves both agriculture and industry and serves them well.

Then there is forestry. There are thousands of acres of State forest in south-west Scotland and a growing number of subsidiary industries, all of which help to stop the drift from the land. This is a tremendous subject and to do it justice is beyond both my scope and my capabilities, but its growing importance must at least be given a mention.

Dumfries, Annan and the Gretna district are the main areas of modern factory development. As a market town and trading centre, Dumfries has always been a pleasant and prosperous and busy place. It is the gateway to Galloway, and two modern firms have taken advantage of its situation and amenities and have built fine factories which are making a difference to the town, and which contrast in appearance at least with the older and smaller textile industry. One of the new ones is an I.C.I. centre, pleasant to look at and with a varied range of products embracing agriculture and the modern plastics industry. The other one is owned by the North British Rubber Company and makes a variety of goods from floor-coverings to golf balls. Down on the coast near Annan is another I.C.I. works that has raided a lightly populated agricultural area for its employees. In spite of its small size, Annan has another factory employing several hundred workers, the engineering firm of Cochrans, and there will soon be another working with timber. Since these words were first written the timber company has both been to Annan and (in 1981) has gone.

Finally, in this brief section I am going to bring together the agricultural interests and the industrial ones to consider what partners they make and what part they have to play in the life of the northern shore of Solway. I shall first introduce a group of people whose forward-looking action is a cheerful thing to see and one which is typical of a section of modern south-west Scotland. At the beginning of this chapter I talked about the West Cumberland Industrial Development Company, Ltd—to give it its full title. This is a company financed by the Treasury and concerned mainly in the building and rental of factory premises, and it has grown to be the most powerful instrument of recovery on the south of the Solway. There is across the Solway Firth a

Development Association too, but one with differences. In the first place, the Dumfries and Galloway Development Association is voluntary, without financial backing, and it owns no factories. On the other hand, it has the enthusiasm of a voluntary association of interested citizens. It runs a very good advisory service and publishes a useful and readable magazine. I am not saying it is the equivalent of the West Cumberland Association. It is not, and Dumfries and Galloway are to be congratulated that they have never had to face the problems that arose in West Cumberland, but the Dumfries and Galloway Association, under the energetic chairmanship of Colonel Robert Armstrong, provides a forum for a host of varied topics that affect the people of the south-west and well fulfils its smaller function. In a local way, it has had many successes, and I myself have to acknowledge the efficiency of its information service.

One of the problems which interests the Association is the rapid emigration from the agricultural areas of the three counties over the past few decades. The Association sees a solution in the encouragement of light industries and the promotion of local crafts and occupations on the one hand, and the bettering of housing, social and cultural amenities in the villages and small towns on the other. Very few will disagree with this policy and there is little doubt that new rural industries and improved amenities will at least stop whole families leaving the district because there is nothing for the girls and younger men. As in West Cumberland, however, new industries may bring new problems. Some light industries if not rooted in their environment might prove prone to depression. There is also the danger that should they offer too attractive an alternative to farm work, the agricultural labour problem might be intensified instead of alleviated. One of the answers to this last problem is for the farming interests in particular to improve amenities and housing. So far as Kirkcudbright is concerned, the position seems promising and rather better than in Wigtownshire. In Dumfries the new industrial development is encouraging new suburban housing, and the farmers are suffering from a shortage of young labour in consequence. As with many similar problems, the solution lies in that magical word balance, and we must look forward to the combined good sense of planners and local interests.

So far I have said little about industrial Carlisle, and to say nothing would be a mistake, for Carlisle is not a sleepy historical city but one that works hard for its living in a way that is insufficiently recognised. I shall be very brief about those things which are generally well known, from Carr's Biscuit Works, the remarkable development of Laings from a small business in a Cumberland village to a civil engineering firm with worldwide contracts in just one hundred years, confectionary, Metal Boxes, the cranes of Cowans, Sheldon, and the many fine textile works. One of these, Ferguson Bros, is now combining its old-established traditions with designs by Miki Sekers of West Cumberland Silk Mills. These and many other factories surround the ancient city and are not too smoky as yet. Their development has generally been smooth, for Carlisle is still the market of Cumberland, a great point on the routes of the west of Britain, and has a well-balanced economy. This is a great railway city too. You feel it in the station and round the goods yards and you guess it in the night hours when strings of peaked-capped railway men cycle from their sheds to the suburbs after shift-work. Less obvious is one of the military aspects. People see the Border Regiment and know that at present it is housed in the Castle, but they do not realise what a great percentage of the population earns its living in the widely scattered activities of a great R.A.F. Maintenance Unit which fringes the head of the Solway.

Most of Carlisle's industrial development has been dealt with elsewhere and is straightforward, but one aspect is a tangled story, although not an unduly depressing one as the city has been able to afford its experiments owing to its variety and balance. It is also a story that intimately concerns the Solway. It is the story of Carlisle's attempt to get to the sea. The earliest idea was an ambitious one. It belonged to the age of canal frenzy when it was easy to imagine ships sailing across England between the Solway and Newcastle. Even that generation, however, blanched at the thought of a hundred and seventeen locks over Agricola's Tyne gap at a cost of more than a million pounds. The western part of the canal was built and the advance publicity makes good reading; some of it can be found in Tullie House. It was not built to Maryport as had been originally proposed. This may have been a pity but is an historical fact. It went from the city to a spot called Fisher's Cross, just east of Bowness, which became glorified by the name of Port Carlisle, and it was opened on 12th March, 1823.

A nice touch for us is that the first ship to sail into Carlisle, with the committee on board, was the *Robert Burns*.★ In 1839 the railway from Newcastle to Carlisle was built and so this isthmus had yet another link from sea to sea, a hybrid on the line of Hadrian's Wall. The canal cost about ninety thousand pounds. It was eleven miles long and dropped sixty feet by eight locks and never paid its way. You can stand now on muddy merse between its gates where it once flowed into the Firth.

The death warrant of the canal was signed in 1845 when the M. & C. Railway, which we have already met, was completed. The M. & C. profited by the coal boom and the heyday of West Cumberland's iron and mild steel trade—Henry Bessemer had discovered that only West Cumberland iron-ore was suitable for his process—and the record dividends it payed indicate the monopoly of this railway over the trade from the Solway to the city. The railway war that followed is too complicated for me to detail—eight companies fought and not too honestly in this area; but the North British Railway took Carlisle to the sea in the city's second attempt. The canal was filled in and the railway track laid in its bed in 1854. Port Carlisle never flourished, and when the North British Railway got its extension from Drumburgh to Silloth, there was more hope of a good outlet to the sea. After a year or two, Carlisle was successful, in spite of opposition, in developing Silloth as its outport. A new dock was opened in 1861 in spite of the description applied to the railway a few years earlier that it was a line to nothing but a rabbit warren.

The M. & C. was soon challenged again, this time by the Solway Junction Railway, which incidentally finally killed Port Carlisle's remaining hopes, for even a fishing-boat had to lower its masts to get beneath the viaduct built by the Solway Junction Railway. For the first time in history, the Solway could be crossed dryshod. The line was opened in 1869 for goods and in the following year for passengers. It flourished with the freighting of iron ore to Lanarkshire until this was superseded by Spanish ore, and it was a serious rival to the M. & C. It shared their line from Brayton to West Cumberland but this was co-operation under threat, as the Solway Junction Railway had suggested building a

★ An even nicer touch is that on Robert Burns' personal visit to Carlisle he was fined for a "parking offence".

separate duplicate line. The viaduct across the Solway was a gallant monument to an age of reckless enterprise.

A comment on the lighter side gives a pleasant picture of the times. During the last years of the canal, passengers were taken on the last stretch to Port Carlisle in long horse-drawn boats, and at the beginning of this century the unused bit of railway line over the same ground from Drumburgh to Port Carlisle saw pleasure trips on the horse railway drawn by still-remembered Dandy. You can see what remains of the harbour of Port Carlisle in photograph number 19.

The railway no longer runs from Carlisle to Silloth, but road transport has been improved and Silloth is still the outport of the city, although not the busy one it was during the war years when Joe Wilson of Annan was its hard-worked pilot. There is an end to the story of the viaduct, and as it is particularly Solway, I can tell it to round off this main section of the book. It leaves us where we met in the waters of the estuary.

The Solway viaduct was 1,940 yards long without the embankments, 440 yards on the English side and 154 on the Scottish (you can see both these in photograph number 20), but it was an intruder in the Solway and the Solway took its revenge. It was damaged in the winter of 1875, when ice got into the hollow iron pillars and cracked them, but its greatest strain came in the dreadful winter of 1881. The Firth was full of ice blocks up to ten feet thick and many square yards in area and the tide and the wind piled them up at the head of the estuary. Danger was anticipated at the turn of the tide, and four brave men spent most of that cold night on the shuddering viaduct feeling the impact of the blocks of ice as they threatened to destroy the whole mighty structure which had withstood the waves of years. At last they had to retire with the news that the viaduct was going, and in the morning they found two gaps, one fifty yards and the other three hundred, through the viaduct.

The Solway viaduct was repaired in time, and regularly used until the First World War. From 1914 to 1920 no passengers were carried, though specially light trains continued to carry pig-iron to the Clyde. At the end of 1921 the bridge was considered unsafe and closed, and it was finally demolished in 1934 and 1935.

So ended a notable chapter in the story of Carlisle and its push towards the Solway and in the history of the viaduct that joined these shores together. No one was allowed across the viaduct after it was closed, but I have met several Solway men who managed to evade the watchman and walk the mile between Scotland and England. Some of them were caught and fined, but it was probably worth the risk, especially on Sundays. The decaying viaduct enabled the Scotsman to walk to Bowness for his pint. The unity of the Solway has been marked in many aspects of my story, but not in national licensing laws.

NOTES: 1982

This book was written in 1954/55 and revised in 1973 before recession hit the whole country and especially the north-west. Strangely enough few major corrections are called for in 1982. Even my less optimistic analyses are proving well-founded. West Cumbria is hardest hit, Dumfries next, while other towns are perhaps less affected though still suffering.

Although unemployment is high and Solway shares the slump the main contrast with the past is not with the 50s and 60s but with the 30s. Then West Cumbria was in despair and for long was depressed and delapidated. The fresh paint, the higher standards of living and welfare state benefits are having a marked and positive effect. Redundancy payments may be a misleading if not false palliative, but at least they now exist. More than a few West Cumbrians are having "one more good holiday just in case . . .". The general feeling is an anxious one, but I do know that it is nothing like as deadening and degrading as the means-testing of the 1930s was.

The West Cumberland Development Company Ltd no longer exists, but it laid foundations which have enabled the area at least to fight for survival. On Scottish Solway, the smaller Development Association has also gone, and sadly Colonel Robert Armstrong who built it has died.

Today the agricultural industries carry on, not unsuccessfully. My earlier comments on Carlisle and Dumfries still stand, including my description of the R.A.F. as a major employer in Carlisle. New organisations—particularly those designed to help small firms—work steadily on to help cushion the effects of the slump.

CHAPTER X

A JOURNEY ALONG THE COAST ROADS

My journey began in the Rhinns of Galloway. This hammer of land so close to Ireland has purposely not come into the story so far, but it seemed logical for me to begin at the Mull of Galloway, Scotland's southernmost point. Besides this feeling for logic, I wanted to visit some lonely relics of Solway's early greatness which live in this western peninsula.

The razor-jagged Silurian cliffs of the Mull bring Ireland very near, and before I turned my back on that dark horizon, I thought of prehistoric golden links between Ireland and the Solway and swung through time to 1947 when this North Channel was first officially swum—by Thomas Blower—the legendary crossing by St Patrick with his head held between his teeth must be classified as unofficial. The single dusty road north from the lighthouse soon branches into spreading veins, and I kept by the inner coast until I could take an inland lane a mile to the south of Sandhead. A winding road took me to the gates of the avenue which leads to the church of Kirkmadrine. It was a warm spring day with the land and sky washed clean by a sudden shower, and yet even in the sun the tree-lined avenue had a chill of loneliness. There were neither footprints nor wheel-marks in the grassy lane, for Kirkmadrine is empty and deserted. It was also locked, but that did not worry me, for the stones I had gone to see were preserved in a barred annex that is open to the world. The church and its tombstones seemed tilted on their little mound, but the sun was shining through the grill which repeated itself in shadow across stones made for an earlier church thirteen hundred years before that afternoon. They looked simple and impressive marked with a cross in a circle, with a cedilla at the top right hand of the cross's vertical. This is the Chi Rho symbol, an early mark of Christianity that had already been used by the Romans on lamps, tin ingots and silver plate. I went down to Sandhead, a sleepy half-holiday sort of place, with an impression of power and thoughts of the stones with me all the way. Later in my journey I was to think of them again, for this church falls into place as an offshoot of greater Whithorn.

The coast road swings around the sandy warrens at the head of Luce Bay, and though I did not stop, I thought of the great river that once flowed through this narrow neck, of the many prehistoric people who arrived here, and of the wildfowl, driven away by aircraft but now returning, becoming familiar with their rivals, and I remembered that here were found the only prehistoric stake-pit animal traps discovered, I think, in all Britain. I remembered too a pleasant by-way when I had gone away from the Solway to visit Stranraer. Although Stranraer is not the capital of the Shire, it is the most important town, and together with Newton Stewart is stealing many of the administrative functions, and rightly so. I remembered its sunshine and the rays of its ship-lights at night, and, strangely, sitting in polished sawn-barrel seats watching a barman experimenting with the aid of a little book in the manufacture of new and strange cocktails.

I did turn back a mile before I reached Glenluce to see the undistinguished rocky outcrop on the way to the House of Dunragit. Do not mistake this outcrop for the later motte, because the Dun of Rheged, as far as anyone knows, was the first capital of the Solway, a home of Dark Age Urien.

I cannot agree with those who delight so much in the appearance of Glenluce although I found it friendly enough, but I could use all their adjectives on the surrounding district. I stole inland for a few miles, breaking my journey along the coast road, first to look at the abbey and then to walk in the hills. The medieval plumbing at Glenluce found a place in an earlier chapter, so for this visit I concentrated on the more orthodox point of view. The Chapter House is as complete as any I have seen, although it is chipped and, having a roof, slightly depressing. I prefer my ruins to open into the sky. The rest of the abbey is open, and with its smooth lawns, clean grey walls relieved by tiny blue and white blossom, has all the atmosphere of the best ancient ruin.

A friend joined me then to take me over the moors in search of a Bronze Age settlement, and after bumping over stony roads, we were lucky and found two lots, but I must confess that I was not convinced that both were authentic or even which was more so; a herd with a bull appeared on the sky-line before we could decide. We went further up the main road past New Luce, and another stony track and a grassy walk led to the Caves of Kilhern, which are not caves but the chambers, now uncovered, of a great long cairn, a hundred feet by sixty feet. Four of the chambers are good and clear, and their blue-grey slabs and walls of rock against purpling heather give the essence of moorland colour. As we went back past Glenluce to the coast, the sun was still shining and the waters of the Luce looked very blue over bright yellow sand-dunes, and when the dunes had turned to rock, housing a reputed smuggler's cave, we came round the bend into Stairhaven. A few houses clustered round a hardly used harbour, and front basement windows that were almost portholes told of great westerlies, but the sea was calm as we passed the boathouse and scrambled along the rocky shore. As the tide was fairly well in, we had some energetic exercise over rocky struts to find the broch that I had to describe with a question mark in an earlier chapter. The size was right, the shape was right and the curves of the walls and their cavities clearly seen; perhaps some day excavation will provide the proof.

The road from Stairhaven took us away from the coast, but it led us past Whitefield where we saw a decayed mansion across the loch and we searched for Iron Age crannogs where once a flint javelin head had been found, before we got back on to the main road, A747, which hugs the coast for miles. This road runs close to the water and we stopped occasionally to look at the outline of the Rhinns, the misty darkness of Ireland, a still near Isle of Man, a strange Cumberland, and with glasses, the Scar Rocks in the bay, where the gannets breed. The shag we saw on a weed-covered rock probably had his residence there too.

Neither the houses fronting the sea around Port William nor Barsalloch Point—where there are traces of an Iron Age fort—held us for long, and the road led us inland again. After a few false stops, we found a turning to the right that led through wooded drives to Kidsdale, and landed in a little village that seemed miles from anywhere. The lady at her gate guessed what we were looking for and pointed out the path into a promising dell. That walk along the path behind high primrose-painted banks with birds skimming clear and rippling water still remains one of the most vivid experiences of the journey. It took us to a beach, pebbly and absolutely quiet except for a hawk that flew surprised out of a cleft in the cliffs. Our object was a cave, pale grey against the green slopes behind and sharp against the water. Climbing to its platform (carved by the twenty-five-foot sea?), we saw the writing on the wall.

There were two kinds of writing. The first we had gone to see, and it presented the same Chi Rho symbols that I had met at Kirkmadrine. These were protected by little metal cages that had the unfortunate appearance at a distance of baskets fixed for litter, but obviously they were necessary. Every other inch of the walls of St Ninian's Cave is covered with egotistical initials. May their perpetrators suffer or repent. This cave is said to have been the saint's first landing-place, but I think it more likely that it was his refuge, his place to sit and think. For many years it contained more than inscribed walls. It had carved stones both similar to and much later than those at Kirkmadrine, implying continued use, but these are now removed, preserved and well displayed in the little museum at Whithorn. A later association of the coast near St Ninian's Cave is less happy, for the *Rambler*, the last sailing-vessel from Creetown, ended her days on these rocks.

It was not far to Whithorn, but first we went to the Isle, and here got a delightful surprise, for the village really is beautiful. Solway has all kinds of villages and I am not going to judge between them, but I simply report that the Isle of Whithorn, with its fringe of buildings around the harbour, was white and shining over the bay, and a clean division between the different blues of sea and sky. We went over the foot-bridge on to the real island, which is just a dozen acres, and noticed first the mounded banks and entrances of one of the smallest promontory forts I know. The other building that interested us, halfway up the slope, was the small chapel that I have described as built for pilgrims. Plain and simple, it had little to hold us long except a Romanesque doorway, and we were soon on the way to the bigger House of God, the parent community of Whithorn.

Whithorn is simple and dignified, and we went through the shadow of the Pend to the museum and priory. There is no need to ask the way; the arch is prominent though plain, and it bears the old arms of Scotland above its semicircle. The stones in the museum, that old schoolroom which I have already commended, have a tale that speaks of five distant centuries. I have already mentioned the earliest stone; it had no Chi Rho and was erected for Latinus, aged thirty-five years, and his daughter, aged four, by the descendants of Barrovados early in the fifth century, perhaps while Ninian was still alive. The stones *with* the symbol, here and at Kirkmadrine, belong to the late sixth or early seventh century. Kirkmadrine has a stone to two bishops (sacerdotes), and Whithorn one to St Peter which *may* celebrate the peaceful transition from Celtic to Anglian forms brought about by the Synod of Whitby. Anglian ideas we know reached Whithorn. We have heard from Bede of its bishops, and decorated stones in this museum tell a story of its wandering sculptors up to the tenth century. Two of these later stones have wide links with others in Derbyshire and Yorkshire and St Bees, and as the last was probably carved by a man from Whithorn, we tore ourselves away from this inspiring little museum remembering a very early Solway unity. We went round the priory, admired the architecture and adventured into the crypts, sadly aware of the more recent church that watched us the while. The early Presbyterians, though no doubt strict, built many commendable churches, but some of last century's builders did not follow their example.

I looked at the map at Whithorn, and decided to make tracks along A746 for Wigtown, but my decision was reluctant. I could have gone to the east coast of the Machers down many a small road and found a worth-while ending. You can choose any of these coast lanes from the map (the surfaces are remarkably good), and the signs usually say "To So-and-so", which will be a farm although they never publicise that fact round here, but it invariably ends in a welcome surprise, a sheltered cove, twisted cliffs to wander about or shingle to sit on and watch the rarely disturbed birds. But I went to Wigtown. I can remember little good to say about this capital of the Shire. The square is certainly broad and open, but its openness was marred for me by part of a torn poster that flapped in the wind against my legs and advertised a concert long since applauded. I was sorry to feel depressed about a Galloway town, but I have used the word "shabby" for part of the English Solway, and Wigtown allows me to be impartial and use it again for Scotland.

From high points on the road, I saw the Wigtown sands, and the memory that accompanied this sight was one which the town will always bear, although that memory is grim. It was on these sands that a girl of eighteen, Margaret Wilson, and a woman of sixty-five, Margaret MacLachlan, were pegged out to drown on

11th May, 1685, because they would not conform to the Episcopalian Church. Margaret Wilson's tombstone, which names the "judges", can still be seen.* I thought a lot about the Covenanters on this stretch of my journey. They were not themselves always blameless, but certainly in south-west Scotland they underwent more suffering than ever they caused elsewhere. Old Mortality (Robert Paterson) died and was buried in Caerlaverock on Solway, and many a churchyard along my journey contains the carved stones whose inscriptions record his strange service to the memory of the Covenanters. I had so much to do on this journey that I could not explore every churchyard for Covenanters' stones, whether carved by Old Mortality himself or not.

My thoughts on the Covenanters carried me along to Newton Stewart, which should really on a geographical basis be the capital of the Shire. Thinking about things geographical reminded me—this is not original; it is often mentioned—that the boundaries of Dumfries, the Shire and the Stewartry are ungeographical and extremely awkward. In each case a river which joined people together is taken for the boundary, and so close was the contact in one case that Dumfries leaped over the Nith and took a bite, Maxwelltown, out of the Stewartry. Newton Stewart is similarly sited. It sits along a riverside and serves one half of a friendly and associated geographical region, whilst the other half comes under Kirkcudbright. I was going to recommend a watershed for boundaries, and then I remembered the Border ballads and should have held my peace.

I spent quite a time in Newton Stewart. It has pleasant inns and good cheap cafés, and it is a lively and happy little town set in lovely moors glimpsed through and over warm lines of trees. I had to move on, and went over its decorative but too narrow bridge across the flats and so to Creetown.

Creetown is small, granite and a favourite centre of mine. It shares with Newton Stewart a circle of lovely moors, the essence of the Galloway landscape, cloud-capped and ever alive. The miles between Creetown and Gatehouse are as interesting as any in Solway. I read before I first saw this road that it was one of the

---

* I doubt whether this sentence was ever carried out. The evidence for the actual drownings is by no means strong enough to convince all students of the period.

most beautiful in the world, and was told the whiskered story about it going both ways. I am sure it is not the most beautiful even in Solway, but to say it is one of them is saying much, and for me it has a friend at either end.

I broke my journey in Creet'n to meet Adam Birrell, for I felt he would sum up much that any book on the Solway must include. I have told stories of wildfowlers and salmon fishermen, but he could tell many better ones, for his life has been spent at the stake-nets or behind that punt gun whose reverberations became well known far outside the Solway. I chatted with him about the living coast as well, and learnt that his cottage is on the twenty-five-foot raised beach, and that from his boathouse he has seen the growth of half a mile of merse. Boats remind me of wrecks, and I know that Adam Birrell had hidden away amongst his books a medal of the Royal Humanitarian Society to remind him of the day, almost half a century ago, when he swam more than two miles ashore to get help for a boat on fire and out of control. That afternoon we talked about archæology, for he had found time to be a member and Vice-President of that Dumfries and Galloway Society whose *Transactions* I have used so often in making this book, and he acted as my guide to the stones, and there are many, around Creeside. We walked over the moors and climbed the fences, and when I first made this journey I was amazed at Mr. Birrell's fitness at the age of 87. Alas he died some years ago and Solway is the poorer.

The landscape above Creetown and its antiquities could easily fill a chapter. There is a stone circle, magnificently sited against Cairnsmore of Fleet, that represents the ritual of the Bronze Age. We approached it up the old military road that stands for another chapter in the history of south-west Scotland, passing on the way the sandpits that were robbed to build Cairnryan for the last war. As we crossed the burn—wondering why a granite bridge in a granite country should have a red freestone capping—we remembered a war six centuries before, for this is the "Englishman's Burn", and even the cautious Ordnance map marks by its banks a "supposed site of battle".

As I said good-bye to Adam Birrell and went by the coast road out of Creetown, I was reminded that I had been in a working town where ships still sail. The granite crusher, thrusting like a pier into the estuary, was shrouded by a cloud of dust, and I had noticed earlier in the town a precast-concrete-slab works which is typical of the smaller industries that the Development Association wants to encourage.

Further along I came to the first of this road's castles. There are three on this single stretch. Carsluith is a mixture of old and new with the grey castle sandwiched between whitewashed and working farm buildings. The guide-books give the details about Carsluith, but one is a special link: it was the home of Abbot Brown who presided over the dissolution of Sweetheart Abbey. You can climb spirally to the top of Carsluith and edge along its walls if you are careful and have a good head, but I left hurriedly as children were playing. I like climbing myself but watching the reckless scares me stiff. I walked along the road from Carsluith and found it a delight. Green meadows on my right sloped down to the cliffs and the sea, and behind yellow gorse and a woodland fringe, the moors rose to take thoughts inland. Every so often a bank of primroses splashed its colour, and the gardens of houses added vivid red and blue among the rocks to the general air of spring. Soon I came to a sawmill with its own little hydro-electric station, and had to decide between three explorations and I chose them all. First I went up the lane to Barholm. You can miss this castle if you are not careful; it hangs green and well hidden up and over a bend of the road. It claims to be the Ellengowan of Sir Walter Scott's *Guy Mannering*, and it is rapidly decaying. Ivy eats its walls and its steps are dusty and covered with twigs and leaves. The walls are thick so that their grassy tops are wide and soft enough for a picnic. All this may appeal to some adherents of the romantic age, but I prefer my castles to be preserved and displayed by a thoughtful Ministry of Works. As I left, I noted casually some long single trimmed rocks, and went my way back to the bridge where the road crosses the burn. Starting my second exploration, I struck up past the dammed water to Cairnholy. The map marks this spot as the site of another battle, and I could not suppose this was wrong as I did not know enough about it. Local traditions and two quite recent guide-books say that Cairnholy records the burial of the legendary king, Galdus. I can say that this is mere legend. The two great tombs up here tell any amateur that they are the remains of once great covered chambered cairns, and when I saw them I knew at once where the long stones at Barholm had come from. The two cairns up here are actually of the type classified as Clyde-Carlingford (or sometimes just as Solway) passage graves. They have a clear "horned", *i.e.* semicircular, platform at the entrance and are both imposing monuments. Cairnholy in the farm looks weird and striking as its rocks and cap stones crowning a little hill stand silhouetted against a cirrus sky, but the one behind the wall towards Barholm shows better the horns which distinguish this type. Two fields away beyond the farm are the remnants of a third of these long cairns, and near this is a cup-and-ring marked stone. As I walked down the lane—gently, for a huge white bull watched over a wall I could have sworn was fragile—I wondered why all this concentration of prehistoric peoples had come to this little spot. Perhaps they, too, had thought it as lovely as any in Solway. The cairns were built in the Neolithic age, but Professor Stuart Piggott has recently found evidence of later use, for the Bronze Age folk of less than four thousand years ago inserted a burial into Cairnholy, and in one of the chambers set up with ceremony a cup-and-ring marked stone.

I still had a third pilgrimage to make, and it was to the cave of Scott's Dirk Hatteraick. Although Dirk never existed, Jack Yawkins did. He adapted this cave for his smuggling activities, and it is almost certain that Scott had it in mind when he wrote *Guy Mannering*. I pushed to the cliff-top through the strongest, prickliest and closest woven brambles in the world towards a steep path (it is fairly safe, about a foot wide) which leads to the shore. I know this path exists because I came *up* it, but unfortunately I missed it in my haste to get to the cave, and had to climb down the cliffs. I do not recommend this, and mention it solely as a warning. The cave was there and I disturbed a couple of doves. What a cave! Most guide-books are strangely reticent and seem to repeat earlier descriptions of this Dirk Hatteraick's cave (there is another with less claim in Kirkcudbright Bay), and I must say that I do not blame them. The mouth is narrow, the floor slopes down very steeply and is also muddy. As you get into the cave, the walls close together around your shoulders and force you to caress the floor, which is steep and, may I repeat, muddy. A final twist, however, round a bit of rock brings you into the cave, and if your torch is still working you can stretch, walk about and see little cupboards hacked in the rock where the smuggled bottles were kept. I have never in my life been so pro-smuggling.

I could have used one of the bottles that day. If getting into the cave is difficult, climbing out is worse, and I recommend mountaineering tactics—a friend outside and a rope between the two. The explorer should be small and light. I turn the scales at thirteen stone.

I hurried from the shore as there were six crowded miles between me and Gatehouse. First I stopped after about a mile, and walked up over the heather and tufted grass above Laggan to look at another stone circle, this time one with jagged, slender, post-like stones. Onwards the road gave views across green meadows, with here and there the lightening brown of ploughland, to Fleet Bay and out to the misty islands. On this stretch I began to believe the raptures of the guide-books, for the next few miles brought the most surprising little adventures combined with the most charming sights. There were daffodils everywhere and primroses under the trees, the black and white of pintail ducks stood out clearly on the yellow sands, and then surprisingly were two little black rabbits playing in the road. I could take wild black rabbits in my stride, but I really began to have doubts when I swung round the corner, disturbed a pheasant and met a peacock face to face. I checked up later—it was really there.

This atmosphere called for another castle, and there it was presiding over the road from a rocky knoll, and I approached it between steep green lawns bright with daffodils and hyacinths. This is Cardoness Castle, and here I learnt about the McCullochs of Galloway, the Gordons of Lochinvar and, from another visitor, the activities of the Victoria League. From the castle-top, I looked out over the Water of Fleet and ruminated on the changes in the course of that river. There is now a straight cut close to the road, but old winding curves are still very obvious, ploughing their way through meadows now farmed, and there is still a hint of the stream that once defended the castle. In my imagination I saw Cardoness as redoubtable as Queen Elizabeth's intelligence report indicated when it said two hundred men would have difficulty in assailing it. On a peak above Cardoness is the Rutherford Monument to the memory of the great theologian who served twelve years (less two when he was banished) at Anwoth—and wrote such excellent prose—but my aim that day was something older than the seventeenth-century church or even its eleventh-century grey-stone cross slab. I had just seen three castles so I sacrificed the fourth of Rusco to the north and went in search of the rare fort that stands on Trusty's Hill.

I had asked a few local people exactly where it was because I was using that day the one-inch map which shows several forts in the district, but none named Trusty's Hill. I regret to say that no one had heard of it, but it is not difficult to find, and as it is well worth a visit, I shall be guide-bookish for a few minutes for the sake of fellow-travellers. I took a path that follows the burn which meets the road near the castle, and this led me between two hillocks. The more obvious one bears the Rutherford memorial, and to the north-east of it was a rocky eminence on which a close look showed a raised iron grill, on its southern slope quite near the top.

Trusty's Hill is one of the rare Galloway vitrified forts that I discussed in an earlier chapter (the Mote of Mark is another in the Stewartry). I found no vitrified rock on this occasion, and although some was obvious many years ago, I think excavation would now be required. The shape of the hill fort was quite plain, and I noticed that in parts the ditch had been cut in the solid rock. The hill fort represented an early Iron Age occupation, but I searched for the symbols of later visitors and found them easily, for the rusty grill protects them. Horned faces, weird lightning squiggles and many other grotesque devices join one or two of the inevitable modern initials on this small face of rock. These (apart from the initials) were the symbols known as Pictish, extremely rare in south Scotland and unusual anywhere on living rock. I have said very little about the Picts. The whole subject is full of pitfalls and the argument is still going on, but I think it is generally accepted that the once—and even recently—described "Picts of Galloway" were a phantasy based on a misconception from the *Ecclesiastica Chronica*. There were no "Picts of the Nith". There were Britons here and the Picts were British, but to paraphrase Professor Watson, all the Britons were not Picts. The ones who carved on Trusty's Hill were late and isolated arrivals; perhaps they came in the seventh century as remnants of the mixed force that had fought at the Battle of Nectansmere. However, it is a rare and thought-provoking place, and, incidentally, it looked to me as though one of the Pictish patterns had incorporated the signature of the earliest visitors of all, for the circular inscription at one end of its "dumb-bell" had a texture different from the other and reminded me vividly of a Bronze Age cup-and-ring.

It was with regret that I left Trusty's Hill, and walked down between flaming gorse to the old road that took me the long way round past Anwoth Old Kirk, the churchyard with its tomb of the Gordons and Covenanters' graves, and finally to Gatehouse.

Gatehouse nestles in a hand of the Solway and has a great reputation amongst those who travel Galloway. Though not out-standingly pretty, I found it a grand centre and noted its hos-pitable inns that cater for every taste. One of these, the Anwoth, has literary associations * and behind its luxurious rooms was a homely little back bar with a strange variety of pictures, of which the older ones set me thinking about the past. It used to be the "Ship Inn" of a bygone phase of Gatehouse, but the sailors and workers of a century ago would have difficulty in recognising this peaceful little town. The village around Fleet Street with its mills and factories, and ships sailing up to its quays, had hopes of being the industrial centre of the south-west; hopes that have disappeared as finally as the old "Ship Inn". Another Gatehouse hotel has two lives. Cally House was once the grand home of William Murray, the man who tried to industrialise Gatehouse. It is now an impressive hotel, still with acres of park, although the woodlands that surround it are now under the "Forestry". The road through the woods is public, and I walked up to the Cally, visited its snug bar (there is always some attraction in going down steps to get a drink), admired the old ceilings with the original seventeenth-century paint looking like miniatures of some of those at Blenheim, and was pleased to hear of one idea which seemed particularly sensible. One wing is completely set aside for visitors with children.

From "Cally Palace", I climbed up the hill on the next stage of my journey which was to take me to Kirkcudbright. There is a straight road across the promontory, but I avoided this and ex-plored the parish of Borgue, which lies to its south. There is enough in Borgue, apart from its honey, to fill a lifetime (or another book), and Robert Louis Stevenson used it in the *Master of Ballantrae*. Lazy roads thread its hillocks and go between innumerable mottes to a coast fringed with bays and cliffs and islands. I picked one of these roads—they all lead to the coast eventually—and went to look, or walk if the tide was right, across to the Isles of Fleet. Ardwell Isle has a particularly interest-

---

* *Five Red Herrings*, by Miss Dorothy Sayers.

ing atmosphere, is normally uninhabited these days and can be reached on foot. Little is known of its first occupants except that an inscribed cross was found some years ago that can be dated to about the twelfth century. Its forty or so acres were divided, much later, into three or four holdings and traces of dykes and buildings can still be found. There was even at one stage a licensed house, though it was probably built to excuse the comings and goings of smugglers. There were underground chambers on the island, which could be entered until some years ago, built by these smugglers in the great age of the "free trade". An inhabitant of the island of about a hundred years ago was an Irishman called Laurie (or Larry) Higgins, who lived there in poverty until he came into money by some dubious means concerned with a wrecked ship. He eventually got the public house, perhaps unwisely, for he was drowned one night crossing the narrow sands. Ardwell owes to him its other name of Larry's Isle.

Just south of the Islands of Fleet on a mainland headland overlooking Kirkandrews is a strange habitation that might possibly have been the fort of an Iron Age folk related to the broch people. When excavated, it provided bronze ornaments and blue and white beads of vitreous paste. Castle Haven is a dry-stone structure which has suffered destruction and reconstruction, both of which may make difficulties for those who try to interpret the past. A long walk around the coast (though it can be approached by devious roads) took me to Borness Point, south of Faed Sproat's farm, and on the cliffs near by, the highest in the Stewartry, is Borness Batteries, a well-marked promontory fort of the Iron Age. These cliffs shelter the Cave of Borness, which has had much to tell about the prehistory of south-west Scotland. It has specially illuminated the textile economy of the Iron Age peoples with its fine bone combs and needles as well as spoons and other tools. Further to the east, the headland sloped down, and I went on to hospitable Brighouse Bay with its old tiny landing-stage.

At last it was time to leave Borgue and go north along the coast, this time by the sands and merse of the Dee. From the coast road, I looked first across at St Mary's Isle, which is no island now, and then over the water to my next stopping-place, Kirkcudbright. Kirkcudbright is superbly spread with silhouetted roofs, castle dominated, across the river. Here you might see salmon nets of kinds I have not described, but I leave you to ask the locals how they work. There is nothing like asking questions in Galloway to meet some friendly folk.

No doubt this town works for its living, an out-of-place building at either end of an equally unsuitable bridge indicates that, but it always gives me a grand holiday feeling. It is light and open, brightly painted and has a flavour of history, slightly but not unpleasantly commercialised in cafés that go by the names of Paul Jones and St Cuthbert. It is a paintable town in a beautiful district, a fact that is proved by the thriving existence of its community of artists and craftsmen. One of the latter had an unusual job. Mr James Jeffs carved caskets for borough freedom ceremonies and printed by hand the illuminated scroll. He was a true craftsman and naturalist. Sadly he died in a sailing accident in 1975. James Jeffs was a Solway man and every aspect of the coast interested him and stimulated his life.

Kirkcudbright (pronounced Kirkoobree) is an historic town and preserves much of the material of its history in its present castle, the old tolbooth, its many records, the Hornel Collection and its museum. In recent years I have criticized Kirkcudbright Museum—it was so like a museum—and so I am happy to report that recently a complete and skilful reorganization has taken place. Kirkcudbright Museum is now well-planned and lively, attractive and therefore interesting.

This town has had a naval history. Adamnan's fleet for Ireland is said to have assembled here, and so perhaps did Alexander III's excursion against the Norse in Man, but apart from these doubtful two, it is known that this harbour, now muddy acres and half of it a bus station, sheltered the English fleet of Edward I, and was the destination suggested by Lord Maxwell for the Spanish Armada's invasion. Finally, it was raided by the great Paul Jones, who took the Douglases' silver from St Mary's Isle in spite of his earlier Freemasonry in the town.

Paul Jones was one of the greatest sons of the Solway Firth, and in some ways brings the two sides together—at least he treated them both in the same way. He was associated with other places on the estuary, but Kirkcudbright made me think most about him, and so I am halting my journey here to give a tiny sketch of this man who has suffered from biographers both too good and too bad. He was born John Paul in Kirkbean under Criffell's shadow, and his father was a gamekeeper on the estates of William Craik of Arbigland, the Improver we met in an earlier chapter. The young John Paul was apprenticed across the Firth to learn his trade at Whitehaven, but soon felt the pull of the sea as many another true Solway man has done. He could not stand his first ship; it was a slaver, and John Paul was never brutal, so he transferred to the colonial trade and brilliantly served his Solway masters on the *John of Kirkcudbright*. It was on this ship that he met a spot of trouble, was arrested when the *John* came home and put into Kirkcudbright gaol (the tolbooth) charged with having caused a seaman's death. He was later cleared of the charge, and it speaks well of his reputation that even while out on bail he was accepted as a member of the local High Lodge. Eventually, of course, as all the world knows, he became Paul Jones, threw in his lot with the newly-founded United States and built up for them the Confederate Navy. His return visit to the Solway united England and Scotland in fear if nothing else, for Paul Jones repaid his youthful training by raiding in the *Ranger* both Kirkcudbright and Whitehaven. Although he set fire to two ships in Whitehaven harbour, he did no great damage, but the letters of the time show how he scared the citizens, and as Norman Nicholson has pointed out, from that day onwards the girls have always rushed for protection to the arms of the nearest man at the sound of his name. His raid on Kirkcudbright also caused great consternation, though he later returned the Selkirk plate he had taken. Paul Jones's raids in 1778 represent the last invasion of these islands.

Paul Jones is sometimes wrongly called a pirate. In fact, he was a naval commander of a state with which Britain was at war. He was certainly a consummate seaman, but then coming from Solway, he would be. The details of his life give a picture of powerful brilliance which is supported by the strength of the features seen in Houdin's bust. There is a copy in Whitehaven. He died in Paris, and when his body was rediscovered in 1905 and identified (for one thing his ears were differently shaped), it was ceremoniously shipped back to the States with a naval escort. His memory in Solway was revived in 1945 when American naval men in Britain presented Kirkbean with a newly carved font in honour of "the First Commander of the U.S. Navy". It is an interesting touch that just as the Solway could not hold Paul

Jones, so this font, I was told locally, could not hold water. Its limestone was too porous.

Kirkcudbright had a pirate, a first-class bad character, in the person of Leonard Robertson, who finds his disreputable way into the documents of the years around 1570. He became a burgess and was finally banished for licentiousness, but I had to leave thoughts of Leonard Robertson, and move on from the most delightful town on Solway to what is for me the most beautiful ruin.

The coast between Kirkcudbright and Dundrennan, like other attractive parts of Britain, is not easily accessible because it is in the hands of the military. Why do they always choose places like Purbeck, the best of the Welsh coast and our own Solway to shoot at when there are elsewhere miles of uninteresting scene? I am told that the fishermen of Kirkcudbright—there are some, although I could not include them in a previous chapter—have been hit by restrictions on their activities off these shores, though at present there seems to be a certain revival. Perhaps this revival is general and indirectly follows the coming of Shell Mex, which is bringing more life to what is left of the harbour.

Going through the gate into Dundrennan (photograph 18), it was easy to forget the modern military age. I walked on across the lawns, passed foundations of massive pillars—now only inches high but still powerful—and from the Chapter House looked through one of the most exquisite doors in the world across the cloisters, where a vanished nave once trapped the warmth, and reflected on the lives of the monks and the even greater number of lay brothers who had squared this green and eaten to the sound of prayers in the fratry facing me.

The next stretch of road towards Dalbeattie with its many temptations to turn aside made me forget the Gatehouse stretch. The land south of Dalbeattie around the conglomeration of shallow inlets is as lovely as any in Galloway and less self-conscious than some. I had not gone far before I turned aside at the little village of Auchencairn and went threading between sand and stake-nets and trees and green hills towards Balcary, where there was plenty to fill my day. The hotel itself took my thoughts straight back to smuggling, for in the days before these buildings provided comfort for the traveller, they offered shelter and a hide to the smugglers along these coasts as still existing secret underground chambers testify. Climbing up to the point past the Tower, I found plenty to think about. There was the walled garden I had just passed with hardly any garden, but what walls! Apparently there was no trust among smugglers. There were the fulmars and herring gulls that shrieked in the wind that swept the cliffs below me, and out to sea was Hestan Isle. It is on the extreme left of the photograph facing page 70.

Many of us in these civilised days must sometimes envy *The Times* advertiser who wants to buy an island and retire to it, and here was an example before me of someone who had done so. Mr James Houston lived alone on Hestan, and lived among contorted rocks with only the lighthouse, his books, the Kippford mussel-men on the shores and the occasional grey seal for company. Mr Houston has died since I made this journey and his house is only used as a holiday cottage now. I acknowledge with gratitude the information he gave me about the Solway and his island. If you have read Crockett's *The Raiders*, you will recognise in Hestan "Isle Rathan", and Crockett's smugglers had their real-life counterparts. There are stories of secret caverns on the island, and James Brown, a Kippford man who worked as a boy for a previous owner, remembered finding several great foot-square beams that may have been their ceilings. I have not had space to say enough about Solway smuggling, but I recalled the fame of these inlets. The seventeenth century was the greatest period, and offered a life more exciting and more profitable than farm work to very many young men. The excitement was greater after the Union of 1707, when the revenue officers were mainly English, but there were too few of these officers and their boats were too slow. In 1710 there were twenty-one, costing £440 a year. Two fast sailing-skiffs from Whitehaven (£12 each) did not help much, although the later "well armed sloops" at Silloth and Annan Waterfoot cost £180 in the first year but saved more than that in duty. The end of this phase of smuggling came in 1760 when British revenue control was extended to the Isle of Man. In the early nineteenth century, whiskey smuggling brought the Solway waths again into use, and court cases in recent years have shown that the "free trade" still goes on.

Hestan was associated with Dundrennan and perhaps the remnants of fish traps or lobster ponds in the rocks were the lay brothers' creation. If we take it that the Estholm of the early charters is the Hestan of today, we can link with this island the McDowall family, and through them Balliol and the campaigns of Edward III.

Leaving these questions, I went north towards Dalbeattie. Before I got there, I was side-tracked twice. My first diversion took me to Orchardton Tower just north of the bay of the same name. I have already mentioned that its circular pele is architecturally unique. It looked peaceful and sedate on that day with nothing in sight but a single steading, and I noted the remains of the earlier, and independent, square building that once occupied the site. The loop past Orchardton took me on to a main road which led into Palnackie, where I was tempted to follow the sign saying "To the Harbour" and found that harbour still working. There was more mud than water when I passed, but there was a nice white yacht at the head of the winding river, a sawmill busily at work and trucks moving in and out, so I was glad I had gone there.

Dalbeattie—my next call—does not always get the credit it deserves, for although it is not a beautiful town, it is clean, neat and cheerful. It is, of course, a granite town, and when Londoners lean on their Embankment they are touching Dalbeattie stone, but even the quarry scars in the hills around do not jar this integrated landscape, and Dalbeattie with its forthright granite tower, square-built shops * and row of clean hotels is an excellent centre for the traveller. I made one excursion inland to Castle Douglas with its wide streets and its very Scottish look. There is always a different flavour even about the work-a-day houses of the two countries, and nowhere is it more apparent than here. Carlingwark Loch reminded me of crannogs and canoes and the wonderful Iron Age hoards that had been found dumped in two great bronze cauldrons. Castle Douglas is an important agricultural town, as is evident at the weekly markets and the great October sale of pedigree Ayrshires. I remembered, too, that the Levellers had first met at Kelton Hill Fair a mile to the south-west. Castle Douglas is named after the manufacturer who bought it (the same Douglas whose name had once replaced the Stewart in Newton Stewart). I did not linger in the town, but went through desperately muddy fields to Threave, a splendid tower secure on its island, its grey austerity contrasting with the daffodils around its

* Except for one round one which guards the street like a castle.

base. This was the home of the Black Douglases who had such an influence on the history of the Solway. The architectural details are impressive, and the prison and its sanitary arrangements thought-provoking, but these and other details can be found in the official pamphlet, and I left it, haunted a little by its sombre atmosphere if not by its custodian's ghosts, to return again to the coast.

South from Dalbeattie, I went this time on the east of the three inlets, Auchencairn Bay, Orchardton Bay and Rough Firth, that thrust like fingers into the land, noting as always their sandy shallowness. Then I turned off the road to go down to Rough Firth and call on Kippford and Rockcliffe (there are two Rock-cliffes on Solway; this is the first time we have met the Scottish one). I mention Rockcliffe first because personally I like Kippford better. Rockcliffe is delightful; I have nothing at all against it. Its hotels are pleasant and its rock gardens, threading the natural outcrops that stretch red into the bay, are unique and I would agree with the books that say they must be seen. Rockcliffe is a holiday centre and a popular one, but for me seems slightly artificial. Now Kippford, too, is a holiday centre, but it is some-how more down to earth, and to me more colourful even without rock gardens, perhaps because it has more history as a genuine fishing village. Rough Firth can be water or it can be sand and a winding channel, but whichever it is, I can think of no better occupation than to sit on this shore and talk to the musselmen, or to the yachtsman affectionately painting his boat.

I think Kippford is the only place on the Solway with a mussel industry. Three men co-operate and sail each day at about two hours' ebb to Hestan, where there is a pure and thriving bed. Quickly the mussels are plucked between the thumb and a two-pronged fork, and as soon as the tide is right, back go the boats to Kippford to get their catch off fresh to the towns that appreciate this delicacy. I think Newcastle is the main market at present, but the cost of transport alone is more these days than the price of the catch once was. Mussels are good in any recognised form, but the dubious newcomer to this food might like a hint to try them with mayonnaise.

Kippford was once the only Solway port with a yacht club, and as the yachts are fitted out for the twice-weekly summer meetings and more brought in for the August Kippford week, they com-plete the real atmosphere of this little Solway resort. Before I leave the sea and Kippford, I ought to mention a memory holding sadness. The traditions associated here with boats are not of pleasure yachting, and Kippford—or Scaur as it is called locally—has memories of a busy little harbour that saw both success and tragedy in the past. In 1836 the Kippford schooner, the *Dispatch*, was wrecked off this coast, and six Colvend men lost their lives within sight of their homes and families. The pleasure sailor has little to fear. He can choose whether to go out or not, and if high water does not last long enough for his adventures, the worst that will happen is that his boat will be grounded and he must walk to shore across the shallows or the sands.★

The whole of this coast—the Colvend coast—with its queerly named rocks (including Cow Snout and Lot's Wife) is rightly a favourite haunt of Dumfriesians on the Sunday afternoon or week-end jaunt, and as I went along the road, I looked down on Sandyhills Bay and thought that families with children would have to go far to find a happier spot. The road climbed to Southwick and then on to Kirkbean, and I naturally thought of my chapter on the living coast, for spread beneath me was its illustration. The Mersehead sands stretched out far and golden to the Goodwins of the Solway, graveyard of many a ship, whilst closer and amazingly big was Preston Merse showing three clear stages of economic and botanical history. There was the fertile and prosperous reclaimed land stretching out to the lines of plantations with Wreaths Tower, slender and very forlorn on the east. Then there was the land that was being reclaimed, and I wondered why more was not done generally on the Solway. East Anglia seems more go-ahead in comparison, but there, of course, a different crop is grown. Lastly was the new and growing edge of Preston Merse. Dead Preston village, with its rediscovered cross, reminded me of Jean Walker, wife of the poet Allan Cunningham, who has immortalised her as "The Lovely Lass of Preston Mill". Kirkbean was my next destination, but I could not resist the signpost which pointed to Southerness, and went down the lanes to the village that is almost all hotel. It is, of course, the Paul Jones Hotel. It was dusk when I got there so I went straight through and along a short lane which took me on to the shore at

★ This statement must be qualified. In August 1954 a canoeist, watching the yachts, capsized and he spent eight hours in the Solway and nine more clinging to rocks before being hauled up two hundred and fifty feet of cliff.

the foot of the old grim lighthouse, and there I wandered on the rocks until darkness fell, entranced by night noises over the water.

Eventually I got to Kirkbean, saluted the cottage where Paul Jones was born on 6th July, 1747, and called in at Carsethorn where the "Steamboat", once the "Ship Inn", revived memories of emigrant ships, cattle exports and wrecks. This tiny port could be attractive still. The grotesque shore-line of timbers and broken stones is not undignified, but the sordid hen-runs by the seafront are. Then I went north by the Nith to New Abbey (the "old" abbey, by the way, was Dundrennan). Sweetheart Abbey is not to me a very beautiful ruin. There is a slight hardness about the design, particularly about the wheel windows, and some lack of architectural maturity that takes the edge off my appreciation, but it is a place of atmosphere, and to stand in the nave in the evening quite alone is a rare experience. The millstones by the roadside in the village indicate an old domestic industry, but I fear that New Abbey is now in some danger of bulging out as a dormitory to Dumfries. However, the drive out of the village past the sign that points to Beeswing is one of the great joys of the Solway landscape in almost any season.

I almost passed Criffell without a mention. The truth is it looks better at a distance; in fact, from England, where it really dominates the Solway; but the energetic traveller might like to know that the grind up its eighteen-hundred-odd feet is well rewarded by a magnificent view of the whole of the Firth, the only view of its kind. Criffell does dominate the Solway, and when I look through the photographs in this book, I find that, without conscious design, it has crept into a fifth of them.

Dumfries marked the end of my Galloway adventures; and I came along the road through Maxwelltown, over the bridge and on to White Sands, once the scene of busy shipping—at Dockhead to the south—and of enormous cattle sales, and now a bus stop. This was a place to linger, contemplating the swans under Devorgilla's bridge or watching the water curling over the Caul. Watching this blue and swirling water reminded me of other days of watching even lovelier in Norway's "Skerrygard", for the town of Dumfries was the headquarters of all the Norwegians in Britain from 1940 to 1945, and I know is remembered happily by this second lot of Scandinavian visitors (we met the first in the tenth century). White Sands especially comes to life on high days and holidays when the fair comes to town and fills its broad expanse. White Sands is now a name, not a description, and the tarmac was solid under my feet opposite the line of snack-bars.

There is so much I must leave unsaid about this cheerful town, but I did feel, as always, that it retains a special atmosphere as the town of Robert Burns, though its more usual name is "Queen of the South" and all its history is rich and varied. Burns came to the district in 1788, after he had married his Jean, to farm Ellisland, but in 1791 he gave it up, confessing he had not been so lucky in farming. He moved into the town as an exciseman, commenting that fifty pounds a year and a pension for widows and orphans was no bad settlement for a poet. He died at Dumfries on 21st July, 1796, after writing nearly a hundred of his songs around the town. This is not the book for many words on Robert Burns or his work. That has been done elsewhere, though some of the latest biographies are scurrilously unbalanced. To those who know Burns, Dumfries is a hallowed city; to those who do not know him I would simply say, it is time they did.

I could think of no way better to celebrate Dumfries than by making a pilgrimage of Burns's haunts in company with a literary Scot. We went first to the "Globe Tavern" and sat in his chair and paid our shillings, and then moved on to the "Hole i' the Wa'", where we looked at the goblets (outsize), the books and the relics and had one ourselves. We stood for a moment in the fresh air to admire his statue, cream stone over yellow daffodils, before going round the doomed fountain and up to the old part of the town to see Burns's house with its plain rough-stone walls, its generous rooms (except for the wall bed) and its general collection of antiquities. We left the mausoleum for another day, and called in the room in the County Hotel where Charles Stuart had held a Council and we quoted the poet at each other.

Dumfries (with Maxwelltown incorporated since 1929) and its district is a grand place for gentle walking, and I just found time to go by the Nith, avoiding the road, to Lincluden, which incidentally was a favourite walk of Burns. He would not see the new suburb and grand milk factory that press round this ruin, which began in the twelfth century as a Benedictine nunnery and later became a Collegiate Church, but somehow I don't think he would have minded terribly if he had. The old and the new are incongruous, but this should not have worried a poetic exciseman.

I left Dumfries on the road to the south, passing the Crichton Royal, a large mental hospital built with money that might have gone to found the fifth University of Scotland if the hopes of the benefactor had been fulfilled. However, I thought in passing that Glasgow University Extra-Mural Department serves the County well and has even been known to import a Sassenach to lecture to its members, one who is grateful for the many things that groups in Gretna and Dumfries have taught him about the Solway.

The old coach road fringes the Nith almost to the estuary, but I stopped at Glencaple, the outport of Dumfries and proud of the boats it had built, and walked up the road past the village hall. Soon I stopped, for I saw a little cottage that even from the road cried aloud of the Solway. There was a punt outside and waders in the porch, and the name-plate, "Barnacle", advertised its connection with the geese of the Nith. Inside I was made welcome by Bill Powell, one of Solway's finest wildfowlers, and listened to yarns about his adventures and that rare livelihood which took him into the heart of the marsh.

I have said somewhere that Rockcliffe Marsh is the heart of the Solway, and so it is in the physical sense, but every time I stand under Caerlaverock's grim bastion, I feel straightaway the power of this castle to symbolise the history of the Firth in its divided phases. Its stones tell a tale of destruction and repair, of optimism and despair. As I looked at the double towers of the gatehouse, I guessed a little of its story. The west tower is slightly bigger than the other, and high up on its curve three or four layers of squarish blocks, out of phase like erratics in a different sphere, told their story of an old destroyed castle used to mend a later one. Caerlaverock is full of hints to the curious, and it outlines for the knowledgeable a long chapter in the history of fortification. It has its mysteries too; there is the obvious thrill of Murdoch's tower where the Duke of Albany was imprisoned, but a more subtle question lurks in the woods a hundred yards south of this immense triangle of stone. I wandered over the marsh to trace an outline, lozenge-shaped, which showed that once Caerlaverock had two castles. Which was the castle of the poem of the siege, the castle that held up Edward Longshanks? There is more than one view about the answer, and the official report manages to be discreetly vague and contradictory. Following Dr Douglas Simpson, I suggest that the present ruins are the first and famous castle, and that when this was destroyed, a temporary structure was built on the softer ground to the south to serve until the original could be rebuilt on its outcrop of solid rock. Whichever was built first, the "dainty fabric" of the dwelling-house was last. It was not lived in long, and I risk repetition when I say that it provides the most delightful contrast in Solway and it lifts the heart to see it in the sun.

Wardlaw, tree-crowned against the sky, watched me leave the castle, and reminded me that the Romans had unified Solway, as well as used it as a frontier. I passed Comlongon Castle, which once housed a Warden of the Scottish West March, shuddered at the muddy Brow Well that is said to have cured so many ills, including some of Burns's, and went on to Ruthwell Church. Ruthwell Cross has occupied much space and I did not linger long, but as the visitor will want to see it—he dare not miss—I would drop a hint that a call at the cottage for the key might save him retracing his steps, and he may get a book there that not only describes the Cross but tells how the Post Office Savings movement was born in this parish. Before the visitor worries about details of dating and style, might I humbly suggest that he just looks and looks to get in contact with the Cross. Even the faint Crucifixion panel in the sunken pit comes out in time. I broke the spell when I came out of the church and saw the stone marking the burial of an earlier vicar's family. I forget how many children he had, round about thirty I think, but I do remember that his wife died young.

Going home towards Carlisle, I thought that scenically the coast had lost some interest, and yet I remembered battles and stories of fishing and fording associated with the shallows, and found plenty to see between Annan and Gretna. I have talked about Annan as an industrial centre, and Powfoot on the seaward side looked efficient as I took the road into the town, and what a sudden-sweeping magnificent entrance this road makes over the bridge and into the Royal Burgh. I called to greet Joe Wilson on my journey through Annan. I had met him as pilot and fisherman —much of my knowledge of the shrimp fleet came from him— and he reminded me of past activity when he told me how the Wilsons together with the Nicholsons had been the boat builders who brought fame to Annan.

A by-way from Annan persuaded me inland. Everywhere from the English Solway, Burnswark questions the sky-line. It is the neat, flat-topped hill to the right of Criffell in photograph number 20, and the road to Burnswark is so pleasant that I made it my excuse for a visit. The river by Hoddom with goosanders rising is delightful under the elms. Repentance Tower broods high in the west. Hoddom Castle with its old history, and its recent function with its stock of pedigree bulls, will soon be nothing but a local memory, though the "broomstick"-flagged hedges still mark Hoddom and Kinmount estate and the bulls have not gone far.

Opposite the castle entrance, a path by the river led me to a churchyard with a shock of skull-and-crossboned stones, but I soon forgot this in thoughts of an earlier church. After Armterid in 573, Rhydderch brought St Kentigern here from Glasgow, and he preached for at least one season in the now vanished church of Hoddom against the pagan practices of the times. Old crosses and inscribed stones are all that remain of a great religious centre, and these are now finally removed and safely stored after some wantonness during the war.* No mark remains of a church that continued long into the Anglian period and was, in fact, only slightly later and lesser than Whithorn. I went on past the house in Ecclefechan's pleasant square in which Thomas Carlyle was born, and up the rough hill to the slopes of Burnswark. Earthworks here tell of a British Iron Age fort, a centre of resistance in the region, and of the Roman forts that were planted on the slopes to the north and south to attack, starve and defeat the British. These earthworks have a visible story for anyone.

King Athelstan fought the great Battle of Brunanburh in 937 when he defeated a great mixed army of Picts and Scots, of British from both sides of the Solway and of Norse under Anlaf of Dublin. This battle is described and commemorated in a long poem in the Anglo-Saxon Chronicle. Earls and kings were left dead and the Vikings fled west in their long boats to Dublin. I think that this battle was fought at Burnswark, but no one knows and perhaps they never will (my friend, Jim Ingram, claims it for the Wirral), and that is why I have called this hill intriguing. Much scholarship, some top-heavy and fierce with learning, has been spent on this battle, but whatever the outcome, Burnswark

* Though some of the finest pieces appear to have been completely lost.

retains its story of siege, of defence against the Romans and still calls question from all who watch north from the English shore.

I came from Annan on the road to England, but I tried to imagine how this road would look bringing a newcomer to Galloway. Most of it is delightful, especially in sunlight. The houses become Scottish—long and low—and there are surprise glimpses of Solway sandbanks and the English shore between long tree-lines of windbreaks. I did notice, however, a queue of women at the single tap outside a line of cottages, as if to remind me of imperfections still existing in the rural scene. The only villages of any size between Annan and Gretna are Eastriggs and Dornock. Eastriggs is inland, but it brought back pleasant memories of the stake-nets I know best, and Dornock reminded me of the battle, the bells and the shortest visit I have ever paid to another country.

I had begun that evening nearly a year ago by talking about the old waths to Bill Lawson in his Bowness garden that looks straight across the Solway. He had had the glasses on Scotland, and he took up my suggestion that the tides looked right for an experiment I had long wanted to make. So we set off to Scotland across the Solway Firth and it didn't look very far away. Soon the world of worm-cast, rippled and shining sand turned to water, and we left my wife holding our valuables and looking rather forlorn as the two of us splashed towards Scotland. Bill found the track fairly easily and we just kept on going and quietly talking. Scotland looked very near all the time, but not quite as near as it did from the sands. The time passed, however, without undue incident, without too-soft sand or too-deep water, although we had to scout a bit in parts, and in company with the birds we walked the Bowness wath. "We are in Scotland," I said, feeling pleased with life, but with an eye on the tide; Bill just said, "Yes, and now we had better get back." So we walked back to England, a mile and a quarter, to a relieved wife and a welcome pint. I seem to remember—for the record—that Bill stuck to lemonade, but then he was no newcomer to the sands of the Solway.

Reliving that adventure, I took up my journey and pushed on to Gretna. "Graitney" was a small village to Lord Scrope and, associated with Gretna Green, it stayed a small village until the First World War. I am quoting from memory, but I think that the population rose with the coming of the munitions industry from four hundred to four thousand almost overnight. Many of the incomers were housed in wooden huts, some of which lasted far too long after they had served their original wartime purpose. However, I *am* happy to acknowledge hospitality in both old huts and modern houses on more than one journey. Lingering in Gretna, I thought how often it had come into my story. The Lochmabenstane in particular had seen Solway history from pre-historic times up to the pageantry of the Wardens' meetings, and as I went down to see it again, and looked over the Sark and the Esk to the Sulwath, I was reminded that Gretna had once had sea, regular ships and almost as regular smugglers.

Most people associate the word "marriages" with Gretna, and although I could not forget the subject myself as I went past the blatant whitewashed "smithy", I decided to say little about it, as it has been dealt with so much to the detriment of other topics. It is not generally known, however, that until 1754 (Lord Hard-wicke's Act) "irregular marriages" could take place all over Britain—London's Fleet Prison was notorious—and that until recent years several forms of these marriages, including the Gretna kind (*per verba de praesenti*), were recognised as completely legal in Scotland. One personality came to mind when I thought of marriages. John Linton ran his marriage organisation at Gretna Hall with dignity and with personality, in contrast with some of the other "blacksmiths" and their touts. Many of the registers of Gretna marriages are still preserved, and though tourists in-variably find the district worthy of a visit, most of the incomers to Gretna these days are Carlisle workers who find the district a pleasant dormitory, and more English (or Cumbrian) can be heard, especially round the cinema, than good Scots tongue.

I would have liked to have gone from Gretna into Eskdale to survey Arthuret again, the Netherby of the Grahams which was the Castra Exploratorum of the Romans, see the lovely riverside round Canonbie and go on to Langholm where ended the power of the Douglases that had begun in the days of Bruce's henchman, the good Sir James, but instead I reversed Celia Fiennes' direction and went for Carlisle, this time by the new road. I am always tempted to turn from this road towards Greenbed or Rockcliffe and see what is doing on the marsh, but I had to get on to Carlisle with its history and its excavations and its industry and its problems.

As I crossed the Eden bridge, I paused to look over the parapet at some of the city's history, important in early strategy but only recently revealed by work affecting the river channel. Robert Hogg, Keeper of Archæology at the city museum, has sorted out and published the story of the historic Eden bridges. The river meander at Carlisle looks irregular on the map, and imagination can easily draw the original loop and picture the present cut as a breach made by a crossing floodstream. This actually happened in about 1571, and Carlisle became protected by *two* channels, the old loop and the new Priestbeck. This called for two bridges, and Priestbeck bridge was built (but not for more than twenty years), and a few years later in 1601 both were in need of repair. The Priestbeck wooden bridge had not lasted long, but the timber stakes and stone blocks of its piers were very plain for me to see close by the modern bridge on the western side. Crossing the bridge, I saw on the shingle upstream the solid stone foundations of a pier that had carried another bridge—one of the two that had, after much correspondence, replaced the wooden ones after 1601. Priestbeck bridge had lasted four years and Eden bridge "was falling down". Early in the nineteenth century the south loop was filled in and the river confined to the Priestbeck and a single new bridge built to take Telford's road to Portpatrick. Telford's bridge design was turned down for one by Robert Smirke (whose father the R.A. had been born at Wigton), and this was the bridge I stood on, though it was doubled in width in 1932.

There are at least three separate Carlisles built one on top of the other. All three have been and are being excavated with positive results at every convenient opportunity. The results can be studied in archaeological journals, and from time to time on the ground itself. A part of the Roman city is preserved outside Tullie House, Carlisle's museum.

Quite naturally, Tullie House reminded me of the family which named and occupied it. The story of mining in Keswick, so closely linked in Elizabethan times with the Germans from Augsburg, is beyond my scope, but one of the Tullies, descended from these German miners, is remembered for his commentary on a grim episode in the history of Carlisle, one that I have so far not mentioned. Isaac Tullie was eighteen when Carlisle was besieged during the Civil War, and he kept a journal through that amazing time. General David Leslie commanded the army against the royalist town—historians will remember the arrangement which had bought Scottish support for Parliament—and from his headquarters, a few yards from my home, besieged the town for nine months, whilst inside the walls heroism and stoicism vied with poverty, pain and hunger. At the end of the siege all the food and most of the animals, domestic and otherwise, had been eaten, and some of the women were prepared to surrender or be shot rather than continue under these conditions. The forced submission of Carlisle to the Parliamentary forces was honourably received. This contrasted with a later episode hardly more than two hundred years ago when inefficiency in the city and muddling by the central government brought about Carlisle's surrender rapidly and ignominiously to Prince Charles Edward. This latter story has often been told, but the facts have never quite satisfactorily been explained.

I soon forgot history in the bustle of the busy city and its present problems. One of these concerns the provision of a civic hall, and I mention it here as I believe it is more important than is sometimes thought and one which affects more than the English part of the Solway area. Carlisle is the biggest centre in the region and ought to be a cultural focus, but it has neither a theatre nor big concert hall. Professional orchestras have to perform in the Market Hall or the Cathedral, but the city is not without cultural life for there are fine performances in music and drama in many small halls. Carlisle should be proud of one of its musical associations; this city recognised a young and unknown singer who was living on the Solway at the time of her first public appearance at the Carlisle Musical Festival in 1937. Her name was Kathleen Ferrier, and many of us specially mourned her death because she had never forgotten the city, and was back to sing shortly before her last illness.

I could have lingered in Carlisle and written much more about it. It is the gateway to Scotland and the western key to Hadrian's Wall. A long and interesting stretch of this, though not the most scenic, lies in Cumberland west of Gilsland, and is conveniently sited for the visitor to take in Lanercost Priory and Naworth Castle on the way. In the city itself I found no lack of interest. Busy traffic contrasted with quiet squares, a salmon river ran only a hundred yards away and the sky-line was crowned with stone memorials of the city's two-sided personality.

Most of the Castle was occupied by the Border Regiment, but I visited the oldest part that is preserved and displayed by the ubiquitous and excellent Ministry of Works. Conscientiously I followed the guide-book, but lingered particularly around the cells of the strange carvings with their mixture of longings and loyalties. These carvings have been attributed to Major Macdonald (the original of Scott's Major MacIvor in *Waverley*), but they obviously are the work of much earlier prisoners.

I walked the short distance to the Cathedral, which in times past had been robbed both of masons and masonry for the more pressing work of strengthening the Castle. Wandering into its cool interior out of the heat and bustle of the town was like stepping into another world. The Cathedral needs a poet to do it justice and a poet luckily it has had, for Norman Nicholson has described it most beautifully in his County Book. I stood for a moment in the entrance looking at the simple arches contorted by subsidence soon after they were built but still upholding their burden, and wandered on to imagine the grace of the Cathedral before Leslie's men destroyed the nave, and to reflect how impressive a chapel the truncated nave had provided for the Border Regiment and its war-worn colours. Most visitors admire, and rightly, the capitals carved to represent the months of the year, but I neglected these to raise a few of the fifty-odd choir seats and meet the engaging little figures carved under them in the fifteenth century. I looked too, as always, at the stone heads on the pillars. I can never resist the most sinister one. It is the one over the pulpit, and as it is said to portray Piers Gaveston, perhaps my dislike is justified. I did not, of course, miss the east window; one cannot. It is one of the two finest in the north. The other is at York.

The Solway called me to the coast again, and I struck off west through over-pyloned country. There are several ways to look at this stretch, and I tried to include them all. First there is the Roman point of view. Although there is no dramatic stone line marching across crags as there is to the east, these Solway defences present an intriguing task. Much of the Wall and Vallum has been obliterated by buildings, engine sheds and in the country by farming, but the clues are there. The story can be pieced together by a mound or a line of hedge out of place in a field, a faint ditch, the reports of excavations, altars and inscriptions, new buildings using Roman stones, and, recently, by aerial photographs. I should have started this pilgrimage in Stanwix, north of the Eden bridge. The fort there, after masquerading for years under the wrong name, has now been proved to be Petriana, the home of the Ala of the same name, the only thousand-strong cavalry regiment to be stationed in Roman Britain (I had seen the tombstone of a trooper from Stanwix in Tullie House). Instead I joined the Wall at Grinsdale, site of a famous wath, and swung with it round two sharp bends past Kirkandrews-on-Eden to Beaumont (pronounced Beemont), where a great hoard of historic coins was found seventy years ago, and on to Burgh-by-Sands, where a fort was excavated some thirty years ago. The twelfth-century church at Burgh with its mid-fourteenth-century pele tower standing massive against the Scots was built within the area of the fort and almost entirely with Roman stones. I turned aside in Burgh to look at the clay dobbins, and wandered down to the Peatwath over Eden, looking back over the marsh to Edward I's memorial from the end of the lane. From Burgh to Drumburgh, I did not bother about the Wall, perhaps wisely, for there are few traces, but considered the marsh which must have grown from under Boustead Hill over many long centuries, but is now being eroded slowly back again. Swans were preening themselves on the little tarn and aristocratic Border Leicesters cropped the springy turf, and I walked to the edge of the marsh to see what is for me one of the loveliest views across the estuary with the outline of Burnswark, Criffell and even the Galloway hills mixed up with the riot of swirling clouds.

I joined the Wall again at Drumburgh where a small and peculiarly shaped Roman fort had been found, and I admired the old manor house, one of the most delightful on Solway, which, until recently, had to be propped up for safety. It was built about 1307 by Robert le Brun, and fortified by Lord Dacre in the time of Henry VIII to guard the English end of the Sandwath. As Leyland said four hundred years ago, "the stones of the Pict Wal were pulled down to build Dumbuygh", and as he went on, it is "a prety pyle for defens of the contery". I traced the path of the Wall as it went towards Port Carlisle, crossing the road where the bridges are being altered, having neither canal nor railway under them now. These bridges were a menace, swinging the road from side to side of the railway with right-angle turns, but they did give delightful surprise views. Near Glasson, several bends remain to do the same, and one in particular suddenly springs a blue and white house into a foreground for Criffell. I remembered what I had written about the canal and railway to Port Carlisle, and looked at the wreck of the harbour, which you can see in photograph number 19, as well as at a Roman altar built into the wall of a house, and I went on my way to Bowness.

Bowness is one of my favourite English villages, and I recalled with amusement the fantastic story of Aeneas Sylvius. This young nobleman, who later became Pope Pius II, was rather vague about his geography, but may have arrived in Bowness. He had crossed an estuary that separated two kingdoms and widened out from a high mountain (Criffell?). He came in 1435 or 36, and the village turned out to see him eat with the local priest, although they soon went "to flee to a tower a long way off for fear of Scots who were wont to pass over at ebb of tide". A false alarm was given by dogs and geese in the night, and even Sylvius's guide deserted with the rest. He implies that the women were left behind, but from many of his points, Canon Wilson suggested that the whole story of the raid was a hoax to get rid of an unwelcome visitor. Unlike Sylvius, I found Bowness hospitable and brave, and I wandered about the village, noting in a wall in the main street a faded Roman altar which records a dedication to Jupiter for the welfare of two emperors by Sulpicius Secundianus carved seventeen hundred years ago. I thought also of the other stone from this same site, now at Carlisle, which tells the optimistic story of a merchant's prayer for a profitable return so that his poem could be sanctified by gold letters. Almost the whole village occupies the area of the fort. In the fields opposite the church are the mounds and hillocks of the Roman bath, and crossing the road, I looked in the porch to see the bells, and then went inside the church, which always strikes me as bigger than its exterior promises.

I decided not to go along the coast, although the Roman close defensive line continued around Cardurnock. Anthorn, near by, once hardly more than a boundary cross, became one of the biggest population centres on this part of the coast; for a time it was a roaring, busy Naval Aircraft Station. I hoped these guests were getting to know the Solway, and thought of one airman who had well served the region and the Carlisle Natural History Society by his observations on the birds of the estuary made *from the air,* and of a modern Solway rescue attempt by naval helicopter. I cut across the peninsula through Kirkbride and Newton Arlosh, skirting the marsh of Moricambe. I had not time to linger in these two Solway villages, but I remembered a sad inscription placed on the wall of the church at Kirkbride by an early vicar who kept his faith though the dreaded cholera of 1746 had taken his wife and six children within three weeks. This church is associated with Roman, British and Anglo-Saxon remains, and from rising ground looks out to the water through misty trees.

Newton Arlosh Church with its sturdy square pele tower stands watch over Moricambe. Holm Cultram built this church about 1305, but it decayed in the sixteenth century, and remained in this state until it was restored just over a century ago. I looked inside. The sun was catching the daffodils which blazed against unusual decorations, and I noted the early windows, none more than twelve inches wide. There is a tradition locally that St Ninian had built here an earlier church, but tradition it remains.

Having written so much about peat, I thought it would be refreshing to see the work of digging going on. One of the biggest peat areas is nearby Wedholme Flow, and Henry Engelen, whom I met there, told me it is one of the best, and he should know; he is familiar with most of the peats of Britain. As we took a ride on a little train into the middle of the moss, I was interested to learn that Mr Engelen, although born in Britain, was of Dutch extraction, and that the Dutch method of cutting peat was the one employed here. The moss is criss-crossed by a series of big drains and each square subdivided by smaller ones, the faces of which are worked in slices about a yard deep. The turves are cut and piled between the drains, partially to mature before going into long stacks. Although the peat is cut by hand, the baling and distribution process is efficiently mechanised, and I learnt that peat from this flow goes to many parts of the country and even overseas. We talked, too, about the wild life of this flow. Mr Engelen has often seen deer, and he not only told me about the adders, but showed me one that had been killed a few days previously. I stepped more carefully then, but met nothing more dangerous than a pied wagtail flying cautiously round the door of its home in a stack of peat turves.

From the moss, I made a devious route towards Silloth, but I did not get there directly. The roads were pleasant in the sun, and I broke my journey twice. First I stopped at Holm Cultram, and tried without success to read the cards with faded ink transcriptions of the stones that stand in the porch, one of which may have covered Bruce's father. The porch was cool and delicate inside, the sandstone more green than red. Robert Chambers had it built early in the sixteenth century. A monk, Gawen Borrodaile, was suspected of poisoning the next abbot, and there is a good mystery story hidden here. He was tried, but powerful friends got him off, and he returned later as an abbot himself. He was renowned for kindliness and tolerance, although these qualities were probably matched by shrewdness, for he managed to remain as vicar long after the Reformation. The abbey was burnt down whilst being repaired in 1604, and the records tell how a lost chisel, a workman's candle and a jackdaw's nest combined to start the blaze. Since then different ages of reconstruction and restoration have done their worst. I can do no more than recommend *The Register and Records of Holm Cultram*, by Francis Grainger and W. G. Collingwood, which gives a detailed picture of the medieval life and unity of the Solway. In spite of its reconstruction, this fragment of the once great building and its nearby prior's house still retain an atmosphere. Perhaps Bruce's ancestor may have something to do with it, but more likely it is the spell of Michael Scott, the Wizard of the North, that lingers on.

As I neared Silloth I was tempted again from the main road, for the lane that led to Skinburness embodied the essence of the lowland Cumbrian country scene. It was tree-lined with spring-green leaves glistening against an anvil-clouded sky, and led to one of those massive Cumbrian farms, with great buildings round a square, solid walls and bright red doors and windows, that always look more like a village than a farm. Over the cattle grid and I was on the marsh, but I stuck to the road which curves under the protection of a huge earthen dyke, until it opens into a view of Skinburness, cream and white, bigger than remembered and as handsome as any village in Solway, even without a fleet. I was tempted, too, to go to my favourite spot at the end of the Grune, where the mysteries of raised beaches, the magic of birds and flowers and the suggestion of Roman remains do not break the loneliness, but combine with a view across the Solway to make an always memorable experience. I have never walked from the

Grune to Anthorn, though I know it can easily be done, but in case I tempt the unwary to experiment, I had better mention quicksands (though they are seldom as dangerous as painted; it is the panic that kills) and recall recent drownings, particularly one pathetic story of a hat that returned without its wearer. Grune is a place to linger, but, noting new glasswort marsh on the way, I went back with the road that passes almost through the hotel, and down a lively coastal stretch to Silloth.

I wrote about Silloth as the outport of Carlisle, but I visited it that day as the holiday place of the Cumberland Solway. The town is square and neat although its proportions are not distinguished, and the shops and hotels look out over a green—with ponies, putting, tennis courts and a small arcade—through a fringe of trees to a Solway kept at bay by a sea wall, shining and new. Unlike some holiday places, it has a thriving and friendly community life of its own, which reminded me in a personal way of its W.E.A. branch, which brings its people and their outside interests so successfully together through the quiet winter months.

From Silloth the main road south winds dangerously, passing the golf course and the dunes before it reaches the coast again not far from Wolsty Castle. I had to have a look at Wolsty Castle if only for its association with Michael Scott, who had the distinction of a mention by Dante, and a friendly farmer's wife took me across the fields to point out the fragments that remained. Cows wander round this square of raised earth with only a six-foot block of wall remaining. Around the square, the moat is clearly visible marked dark with reeds and patterned in marigolds. In dry weather it is damp and in wet weather it relives its earlier function.

The next little village on the main road is Beckfoot, and here I could have stayed for days. There is a Roman fort in a field over the wall, although you would hardly know it at first. A gentle mound marks the walls and gates, stones of which were visible until last century. This second-century fort for an auxiliary cohort of five hundred men—perhaps the Second Panonians—was most skilfully excavated by Joseph Robinson of Maryport about 1880, and has been wonderfully revealed in a recent aerial photograph. Even from the ground, the colour of the growing corn, especially in a dry season, hints at the position of the gates and roads. This fort was fortunate that Mr. J. R. Armstrong

resided in its corner. He was always ready to have visitors, and
there were many, and to watch for the discoveries that the
plough, and sometimes the sea revealed. Seawards and south of
the fort was a Roman cemetery and here the sea is still cutting
in at a yard a year revealing the structure of sand-dunes, the
strata of glacial sand and gravel and sometimes Roman burials.
Mr. Armstrong himself recovered three urns and I think that
his retirement with its archæology, its fishing—he knows these
sands and scaurs intimately—proved as exciting to him as did
his long career at Scotland Yard. He was born near here and
inevitably came back to the Solway where he died.

There is more than Roman interest hereabouts, and on my visit
I was delighted with my luck, for way out on the sands south of
Beckfoot the submerged forest was nicely exposed by a tide just
right. It was a little hard to find, being on the edge of a scaur, for
rocks and stumps look similar at a distance, but once found, even
a tiny area left no doubt. This was no submerged forest with a
question mark; the trees were all *in situ* growing out of the sand
though with little remaining height, but growing at a point that
was well below mean sea-level and three hundred yards out from
the present strand. I was told that from some of the remains, and
the *prone* trees are more than stumps, hazel-nuts are sometimes
found. This might indicate a time (though I do not think pollen
analysis has proved it here) at the end of the Boreal period, a time
which saw the beginnings of the New Stone Age. The bit of
wood from this forest, looking like yesterday, which lies on my
desk is perhaps six thousand years old.

I had to tear myself away from this shore, but found Allonby a
pleasant compensation. Sand-dunes, the green with its bridges
over a tiny river, and bright painted houses make this a quieter
holiday resort than Silloth, and one which might be more widely
known although the dunes are already car-crowded on a summer
afternoon. I thought I felt a threat near Allonby. Some of the
dunes are being extensively mined for sand and gravel, and not
only does this tend to spoil the appearance of the coast, but may
lead to unexpected erosion dangers both here and further along.
South of Allonby is another halting-place which also gave me
doubts. The caravans at Saltpans are sited quite pleasantly, but
there was a suggestion of the untidiness of shacks and corrugated
iron as I passed this little headland.

From Saltpans to Maryport the road swept round dunes and a delightful bay for bathing as well as a golf-course that has known the ravages of the sea. An earlier sea had cut into Swarthy Hill revealing glacial structure as well as old cliffs and raised beach material, but its face is now grassed over, and I did not go to search, but turned inland from the bay to visit a favourite village.

Crosscanonby is a little bunch of winding hilly bends and its church stands on the highest knoll looking splendidly across the Firth. From the first minute this church held me. Inside the gate was a hog's-back Viking stone, and inside the church was a combination of colour and friendliness that every church should have and so few attain. The arch stones—the three main arches vary from round to pointed—are left as a natural border to primrose-painted walls, and every corner, including the delightful nooks, is filled with flowers to welcome the stranger, and with all this goes polished wood and ancient stones in the porch telling of a pre-Norman church as well as the present one begun about 1100. As the records and its name tell, Crosscanonby was served by the canons of Carlisle Priory.

Having started inland, I went on, crossed the main road, passed quiet Bullgill with its "Main Band Inn", cottages and slag-heaps telling of old coal workings, and so to Dearham itself. I went to Dearham for two reasons. First to revive pleasant memories of carnival days, special to this part of Cumberland, when I had incautiously accepted invitations to judge decorated wagons, disguised children and even the dog with the prettiest face. They were grand days; the procession filled the village, as I found to my cost when I had to drive back through its length to rush reinforcements of food to the great tea that ended the bustle and provided the sit and talk before the grand evening dance in the British Legion Hall. If I may intrude an irrelevant personal memory, on one of those days, for the first time in my life, I literally helped a dog over a stile—not that it was lame; it was just a St Bernard, heavily overgrown and lazy.

Leaving thoughts of carnivals behind, I went to Dearham Church, combining, with its black-painted gates and pleasant lawns under the four-square pele-like tower, the atmosphere of a corner of an old university with that of a Border stronghold. I felt that this church—the present one with its Norman arch goes back to about 1300—was rightly proud of its even more ancient history, for the pre-Norman stones were shown with taste and labelled neatly, if dogmatically. A cross labelled "Viking, 700" faced me just inside the door, and its weird carvings under the wheelhead were most delightful, though I could not make out the inscriptions, which are supposed to represent the combined worship of both Christ and Odin, and 700 seemed a little early. There is a cross to "Kenneth", a dubious figure hereabouts, a grave slab with undecipherable runes to Adam and interesting stones clearly displayed on the inside walls of the porch.

From Dearham it was downhill to Maryport, and I went into the town past the new imposing "Bounty", by the end of Netherhall Estate with its woods, pele-towered mansion and collection of Roman antiquities from Alauna. This estate now sprouts a fine new modern school, one of several which were made overdue by the depressed days of West Cumberland. Maryport's story has briefly cropped up in many of my chapters, and for this recapitulation I chose to take two walks. The first took me up to the Promenade which looks impartially over harbour, lovely in the sunset, slums, and Galloway hills across the Firth, and from there I went on to the Roman fort, from Camden onwards the most celebrated site after Hadrian's Wall. So many things have been found here in the fort, in the civilian settlement and around the temple near where the altars were buried, that you feel almost intimately at home. Even the regiments are familiar names from the First Cohort of Spaniards under Hadrian's friend, Agrippa, to the Dalmatians and Baetasians. A mansion, now flats, overlooking the fort had been a shipbuilder's home, and this brought me up through the centuries, and so I crossed the valley of the town for my second walk.

The High Street is a hill—the fact that hardly a street is level adds to the attraction of the town—and from the bottom of the hill I could look over the harbour and swing my gaze from the site of the first house, built two hundred years ago, to a Workingmen's Club, now busy, but with memories of an unemployed workers' movement. Further up High Street I passed a house which a plaque marks as the birthplace of Isabella Harris, whose son became Joseph, Lord Lister, one of humanity's benefactors. Further up again is the house where the man lived who inspired the placing of this and other plaques in the town.

J. W. Crerar was a doctor, too, and as I looked at his house I remembered with feeling the hospitality, the information and the great friendship that I had found therein. Dr Crerar was the Grand Old Man of Cumberland medicine, a patient historical student and a citizen for whom the town had pride and affection. He retired from practice some years ago at the age of eighty-five, and I could not have written these words about him had he not died early last year. He searched out the town's history from all parts of the world, and his papers are now in the county archives. All his life he gave an example of integrity and tolerance that must have strengthened many people in some of the harder days. As I stood on the hill I thought of one item of his research, for he had shown how a sailor, perhaps as well known as Paul Jones, had probably watched the ships from this selfsame hill. Enough to say now that the Christian family had a mansion, Ewanrigg Hall, in Maryport and property in this High Street, and although Fletcher Christian was born near Cockermouth, there is no doubt that his love of the sea belonged to the Solway.

I continued the journey up High Street to its very top, for reasons partly historical, partly sentimental, and stood on Moat Hill. This hill was a Roman signal station, a Norman motte, whose fosse is still visible, and a machine-gun post in the recent war. So much for history. The land by Moat Hill is now occupied by the Educational Settlement, which is a centre for adult education and community activities unique in Cumberland. I did not linger for I always carry many pleasant memories of my years there as Warden.

From Moat Hill I looked inland across the valley of the River Ellen to Ellenborough, now part of Maryport, but a thriving community even before that town was born, and across the new housing estate which creeps up to Ewanrigg Hall, and I thought again of the Christian family. Although I had so far avoided family histories, I could not help remembering that from the union of Christians and Senhouses had sprung three remarkable men. I have already told of John Christian Curwen and Fletcher Christian; the third was Edward Law, first Baron Ellenborough and Lord Chief Justice of England. From my vantage point I could just see Flimby woods, the only considerable stretch of woodland near the coast. In summer its edges flame with broom and its leafy coolness hides the heron's nest and the badger's sett.

I took the bus to Whitehaven. It is by far the best way to see this stretch, but only from the upper deck. There is a geological fault through Maryport: the coalfield begins almost under Moat Hill and the life and landscape change to the south. So far on my coastal journey I had been through places to which people flock each year for holidays, but my next stage was in no obvious way through tourist country. There is delight in this coalfield coast, but it is delight in surprises and the knowledge of a peopled land-scape and not in the thrill of the tourist scene of lonely hills or coast. There is, however, a remarkable admixture of farming activity along these industrial roads.

The road swept past Solway Trading Estate, its white modern factories contrasting with the red sandstone of the town I had left, into almost open country—almost, because on my right I could see from the top of the bus a great slag-heap eroded into fantastic shapes by the wind. Then the bus bumped up the hill past a long row of cottages without a door facing the road, and down again to the slag-heaps of Risehow, concrete buttressed to protect the road, and on to the mining village of Fothergill. I wonder how many travellers along this road pause to think that hundreds of feet in the earth beneath them is a strange and second world. There is a city under this stretch of coast with as great a population as on top, and trains clang and men work and walk for miles along great tunnels, eerie to the stranger, but a second home to the men who get the coal from under the sea. As the bus went through Flimby, a string of children scampered across the road and plunged into a culvert beneath the railway, to emerge on to the shore where ringed plovers nest within sound of the trains. The road goes on dead straight for Siddick, and I had just noted the dead windows of a disused brick works, when a line of hounds, strung out and yelping, skirted a field of corn. These were trail hounds, and they reminded me of leisure features of this West Cumberland coast, some unique, but mostly shared with the parent county. The excitement of hound trails, the bookmakers, the lovely released dogs streaking like arrows to a target, the ten miles over moorland after a smell of aniseed and the whistling, rattling excitement of the finish is common to all Cumberland. The hound—don't mistake him for a foxhound—is an important being in the eyes of the public, the Press, the bookie and the owner, who preserves his secret recipe, that reads like the best of

Mrs Beeton, for the meal before the race. Common also to Cumberland—and Westmorland—is our peculiar form of wrestling. Slow to watch and even slightly amusing, it combines great skill and generous friendliness and could provide a thousand tales. The coast has its many good wrestlers, as I have found to my cost, and it was interesting to remember that at one Grasmere Sports (the Mecca) a European immigrant with an unpronounceable name was prominent in the ring: just another case of that earlier fusion. Thinking about pleasure and moving along this stretch reminded me of music. West Cumbrians sing and their singing is known afar, and I had just passed two pits whose names, Risehow and Gillhead, had travelled with their Male Voice Choir far outside the coalfield. I was approaching Workington where Charlie Johnson coaxes and drills to perfection the Ladies' Choir of the Steelworks, and was aiming for Whitehaven whose Grammar School Choir has been on the air on more than one occasion. The bus went on past Siddick and into Workington by an inauspicious approach. On one side of the road was the rubbish dump, seagulls in attendance, and on the other the stands of Workington Town, which reminded me that the greatest pleasure of all this coast is to follow Rugby League and to shout on a winter Saturday, "Give it to Gus". Gus Risman, captain and manager of Workington Town,* is largely responsible for the team's great reputation, but he is the hero of this stretch of coast not only for his skilful play and consistency but for his sense and personality as well.

I wandered through Workington's busy narrow streets, through quiet Portland Square with its cobbled roadway and dignified houses, which is shown in photograph number 21, and looked at the house that had belonged to the Curwens to see if the ghost peered out of the window. A friend of mine once owned this house, calmly taking the ghost for granted, and I must say that he was very reliable, as I had discovered on many a rock climb. At the top of the hill I came to Workington Hall, the old home of the Curwens, grandly grown around a central courtyard from a humble pele. Here Mary Stuart was received by Sir Henry Curwen after her voyage across the Solway. The Curwens had originally lived on the north of the River Derwent, but moved to the stronger site of the present hall

* Gus Risman has just (August 1954) resigned after twenty-six years playing Rugby League.

during the troubles of King John's reign. The earliest Curwens had stood astride the Solway with lands in Galloway granted by Roland, Lord of Galloway, and in fact it was from these lands that they took their first name of Culwen. I wanted to see the older site which is a strange mixture of the past, and toiled up a hill from the crossroads to Burrow Walls, an ancient ruin on a farm that has since become the scene of much archæological activity.* The original Curwens' castle was first a Roman fort, and in the right-angle of walls that stand in the shadow of a railway embankment I could see stonework in the medieval herringbone fashion on top of straight courses that still look suspiciously Roman. I remembered other people who had chosen this spot; the records tell of a bronze palstave and a Viking sword found in the vicinity.

With my thoughts still in the past, I temporarily left Workington and the Solway to go on a private pilgrimage up the valley of the Derwent in search of a "cross" which had been described as superlative. I found the church at Clifton, but failed to find the cross, although a bricked-up door was more than interesting with its hint of Saxon workmanship. So I asked in the village and no one had heard of it, but a mile towards the sea at Great Clifton I was told the way to the Market Cross, and I assumed that my first informant had been wrong. I found that the mistake, if such it was, was in my second directions, for the "Market Cross" is an inn overlooking an empty square, and although it provided compensation, by this time I refused to give up the search, and discovering the vicarage, pursued my enquiries there. I was received with kindness, and eventually the vicar, Mr Todhunter, set off back to the church with me in search of the cross. He had not been there long, but he knew the one I was after, and we found it and heaved it into the light from a corner of a tiny crowded vestry. Mr Todhunter and I spent an interesting half-hour studying the cross, tracing its weird dragons and other inscriptions. I should stop calling it a cross, for all that exists now is a four-foot slab, scroll-carved on its edges, that was apparently chosen for the red flake on the back of the grey rock, and though this may have been an excellent idea a thousand years or more ago, the *flake* has stood up so badly to its ensuing interval of wear, that its inscriptions are hardly discernible. I left as it was going dark with the hope

* See page 68.

that somewhere in the church, small and full though it is, Mr Todhunter will find a place to put this unique carving so that all may see it.

To return to Workington was to return to the present day and the most successful of the west coast towns. Engineering and iron and steel stretch in association from Chapel Bank to Moss Bay, and the town is proud that the Distington Engineering Company has perhaps the largest casting department in the country's engineering industry.

There are two roads to Whitehaven. The high one climbs through real country and overlooks the Solway grandly, distant Siddick tip looking like a child's sand-castle at the water's edge. The wind lashes here in winter and the trees permanently stream away before its remembered blast. I took the low road past old long streets of workers' houses and new housing estates around equally new factories. This coast is glowing steel, and smoke and dust drift inland across the town (especially when the sinter plant is working), but the names of the streets spoke of the older coal industry, and I did not forget that here is the great pit named after the Firth, whose adventure was told in that stirring documentary film, *The Cumberland Story*. This coast has seen a struggle under the sea from the days when Lady Pit was flooded even to today, and I have heard miners from this district expressing doubts about the outcome of "Solway's" present relentless search for coal. Although many of them regard this pit, the most efficient on the coast, as the white hope of the area, there are a few who sometimes wonder if "white elephant" would not be a better term.*

With such matters in mind, I came to the point where the low and high roads join at the old toll cottage, and paused for a moment to look first at the great works of High Duty Alloys with its vigorous engineering—and happy memory of Olympic torches—and then over the new grey houses at older Distington Hall, now decayed and roofless. Remembering that later I should be able to link High Duty Alloys more closely with an older life, I skirted Distington village and plunged down over the little river and up again to Common End. Soon I find myself strolling down a lane with a stream running by its side towards an old mill, now bereft of water, though I still could see the idle pulley above the old wheel socket. Close to the mill was a raised square of ground, damp-moated like Wolsty, but higher and more imposing. This

---

* Sadly their doubts were accurate and Solway Pit has failed in many respects.

was Hayes Castle, and as a reminder of strength now gone, one thirty-foot wall remained in the embrace of a beech that grows from its very foundations. I mentally agreed with Camden that it was "very venerable for its antiquity" and remembered that it had been owned in turn by the three great families of this district, the Moresbys, the Distingtons and the Fletchers.

A road from Common End took me away from the Solway for I thought it only fair to visit a stone circle on the south of the estuary as I had seen so many on the north. There are just two near the English coast: the first is near the head of Bassenthwaite and the one I sought is up on Dean Moor. I found the circle crossed by a plantation wall. It looked very poor and insignificant compared with the greater ones I had seen on the journey, but any disappointment I felt was more than offset by the view that I had in both directions from the moor. I looked inland across the valley of the Marron and saw the whole panorama of the Lake District spread before me hardly half an hour away, and I looked back towards the Firth beyond the industrial coast which was spread below me as neatly as on a map. I took a winding road back to the coast, and it led me through desolated country, past an old railway track in a deep rock gash and under the black furrowed slopes of the most malevolent slag-heap that surely could exist. I came out on the coast road above Parton near the point from which photograph number 4 was taken.

I decided to circle the plateau on which I could see the Roman fort and the church, and dropped down the steepest of lanes to the village of Parton, sheltered in a little bay and dominated by the railway track, which hugs this coast from here almost all the way to Maryport, surely one of the most interesting railway journeys in Solway. The cliffs at Bransty plunged steep into the sea to the south of me and the grassy slopes of Lowca under the smoking chimneys looked desolate to the north. Here again a trip under the railway embankment was necessary to get to the shore. I left this port, that once threatened the Lowthers' Whitehaven, and went up the hill to Moresby Church. The present church is not distinguished, except that it stands in a Roman fort, but there is one lonely chancel arch outside that commemorates a previous graceful building as well as the Fletcher family who lie buried in its precincts. I wandered round the Roman fort, which was built by the Second Legion and used for at least two hundred years, and

I thought of the place it had occupied in the defences of the Solway Firth. The line was based on Beckfoot, Maryport and Moresby, and although on my journey I had not had time to search out the known linking signal stations, I had seen the intermediate fortlet(?) of Burrow Walls * and was planning to go to St Bees Head where a final fortlet is suspected. Going into the church, I wondered if it contained any clues to Roman history, but all I found were a few stones, bits of pottery and quite a striking head, and I remembered a vicar of past centuries who had regarded the almost daily Roman finds as his own private perquisites. As I left the church I saw an old notice that spoke of qualified Christianity, for joined with the quotation, "The rich and poor. meet together, the Lord is the Maker of them all. Prov. xxii, ii", were the words, "All the seats on the ground floor of the church are free and unappropriated". I went up the stairs to find the balcony looked very little used in these modern times. Perhaps since the decline of the Lords of the Manor, we are all on the ground floor these days.

Crossing the road from the church, I found myself outside Moresby Hall. This graceful building, once the home of Moresbys and Fletchers, now belongs to High Duty Alloys and is run as a guest-house for their visitors. Its frontage is Palladian but round the side are Elizabethan chimneys and under the grounds is a secret passage to the church, now blocked up. I was fortunate enough to meet Mrs Simons, who now presides over the house, and she demonstrated to me that "guest-house" was no empty phrase, and I saw for myself that here was everything the modern guest could hope for, even to four-poster beds. I reflected how fortunate it is that many of the old buildings of Britain are being cared for by great firms or education authorities who keep them alive and useful when otherwise they would decay, not perhaps into ruins, but into dinginess and despair. I went on my way refreshed, and came down the hill through the glacial overflow channel into Whitehaven.

The modern town centre is busy and all of a piece although suburbs are spreading new over the hills that enclose it and even the sky-lines are chimneyed. The harbour with its complicated pattern of piers and railway lines sprawls across the water-front

* This section is now not accurate, but I have left it unchanged as an indication of the state of knowledge in 1954. The new position is summarised on page 68.

with its quayside inns, and from it straight streets push inland towards the Lowther mansion which is now a hospital. In the days of its early prosperity, Whitehaven must have been a gay and lively town. Graham Sutton has told in his novels how it was the centre of touring theatrical companies like those of Macready and his friends. Thoughts of the theatre led my steps to an inn that looks out over the harbour. On a Saturday evening one of the rooms in "The Royal Standard" is noisily crowded and customers enjoy the offerings of amateur talent from a small stage. This is no novelty to attract a modern generation; it is perhaps the last of the Restoration tavern theatres. This little room, shaped, painted and gilded like a theatre, recalls the days when visiting actors always did a turn at the "Standard". I was taken upstairs to the room above the theatre, and saw old and beautiful wallpaper that I guessed, although no expert, goes back to the early nineteenth century. I would recommend this to an expert before dampness finally strips the walls.* I could have stayed in Whitehaven; it has some lovely streets and gracious houses—it was John Wesley's favourite rendezvous—but I went on the last stretch of my journey up the hill out of the town and soon descended into a St Bees that crouches unspoilt in its sandy bay between the red cliffs like a toy between a lion's paws.

St Bees is still quiet. I walked past the Priory I have already described, and tried to photograph its lovely west door although some scaffolding made my view contorted. Across the road was the school which Edmund Grindal, a sixteenth-century Archbishop of Canterbury, had founded after the Dissolution to replace the one he had attended as a boy. There was a cricket match in progress as I looked back over the green lawns from the railway bridge, and I thought that, as an outsider, I could comment without prejudice on the fine reputation of this school, and I remembered the Everest film which had been photographed by Tom Stobart, one of its old boys. I found the shingle and sand crowded with holiday-makers, so I turned back along the Solway and walked up over Tomlin towards the lighthouse on the North Head. Halfway along I was tempted into Fleswick Bay, the existence of which is concealed from strangers using the One-Inch map, and there I searched for semi-precious stones and bathed

---

* Dampness and decay have won (August 1954), and the theatre has been demolished but there are hopes that it will be re-erected near by.

from the natural recesses in the cliff. Another pull took me almost to the lighthouse, and I sat on a jutting rock, the best place to see the thronging birds, and looked out from this Solway gatepost and thought how much I had been forced to omit from this survey of the Solway Firth. The towers of Sellafield to the south, symbols of the latest developments of science, reminded me how badly I had treated the scientists of the Solway. The study of atoms had begun with the work of John Dalton of Eaglesfield, near Cockermouth, and the mathematical foundations of its co-partner, radio and electronics, had been brilliantly laid by James Clerk Maxwell, whose family hailed from the Kirkcudbright-shire I could see across the water. As I thought of these two, lesser discoverers came back into my mind. Dumfriesshire had pro-duced Kirkpatrick Macmillan, who had made in 1839 the first bicycle to use levers to drive the back wheel and thus saved the footwear of succeeding generations, and Patrick Miller whose first steamboat had sailed on Dalswinton Loch (they are still dis-cussing whether Burns was on board or not), and a living though lesser-known man, Robert Waland, whose skill in making astro-nomical telescopes has taken him from a home-made observatory in Glencaple to St Andrews University. His first telescope was built round a lens from a cycle lamp, but his latest construction at St Andrews is the world-famous Schmidt-Cassegrain telescope with its tolerances to two millionths of an inch.

I felt it strange but somehow right that a journey along the Solway roads had led me to think of science. On both shores of the Firth appreciation of incoming modern ideas and men mingles with pride in local skills. Then I remembered the quiet and lovely stages of the journey, and gave thanks that, even in this time of great and complex problems, both Solway people and their guests can find by these shores richness of scene and story and quietness of marsh and lonely bay with only the call of the wild goose and the cry of the curlew for company.

POSTSCRIPT: 1973

The Solway Firth was written in 1954 and published in 1955. With this edition the book is being brought up to date but without major changes in the layout of the typescript. This last condition is to allow the book to be reprinted by modern copying methods so as to keep its price within reason.

I have found it desirable to make some small alterations in the text itself wherever this has proved possible without disturbing the general flow of the narrative.

On the other hand I have decided to leave the last chapter, "A Journey Along the Coast Roads", almost as it was originally written. This journey was made in reality, miles of it on foot, and it paints a picture of the region as a whole at one period in time. I am content to leave it this way if the reader will make allowances whenever the tenses seem a trifle strange.

In this postscript as well as making a few remaining detailed alterations I want also to try to cover a few of some of the less tangible changes that have taken place over the last 20 years. It seems right that I should do this in the form of a less leisurely but always fascinating, "journey along the coast roads".

This second journey has imprinted in me what I knew instinctively already; that essentially the Solway is eternal and unchanging. Life around the Solway still centres on the sea and the sky, on the landscape and on the deep feeling of history that permeates the buildings. There is as yet no threat of suburbia and even the hateful rashes of caravan sites and illegally scattered caravans shelter, I am certain, thousands of clear-eyed people who appreciate their setting and are, thank God, still too small to spoil it.

One major threat which has been hovering for a decade and which might have changed the Solway drastically seems to have been arrested; at least for a lifetime. There is little talk now of a Solway barrage and all that such a major construction would imply. Concentration on the problems of the possible barrage across Morecambe Bay may well have saved the Solway.

Industrially there have been changes which have dominated and are dominating the lives of many men. Only one coal mine, the Haig Pit at Whitehaven, is still working full-time, and the Solway Pit which was only "promising" 20 years ago has failed even to fulfil its promise and is now used mainly for training.

The fords of history can still be followed on foot as I followed them 20 years ago and here there is no change. They can, however, be by-passed now and many modern motorists speeding up the M6 are hardly aware that they have passed Carlisle and the estuary that is the pivot between England and Scotland.

One other industrial change foreshadowed twenty years ago is the building of the atomic power station at Chapelcross near Annan which has now been accepted by the landscape.

Retracing my steps along the coast roads my abiding feeling was one of permanence somehow more lit with brightness. Not only have new houses, especially on the English side been built but many of the old castles and towers, especially in Scotland, have been repaired and renovated, and derelict ancient buildings renewed. Two old buildings are, however, in a sadder state in 1973. The old house at Netherhall in Maryport is now a burned-out shell and the Roman altars it sheltered are now stored for safety in the coach-house. The old castle at Drumburgh was still shored up and the cracks in its walls looked wider as I walked by. But that is on the negative side.

The flats and houses around Maryport harbour, and even the harbour itself when the tide is in have a clean and prosperous look and most of the old "down-street" tenements are gone. The cottages leaning on Holm Cultram Abbey have been transformed into an active and attractive Arts Centre and the little village of Abbeytown is still proud to tell you about the visit of HRH Princess Margaret in June 1973 to open this new Arts Centre; which has already won prizes for outstanding tourist enterprise. (See page 88.)

There *is* plenty of new paint around the Solway and maybe this is a symbol of slightly more security. The shining shops and the polished cars lining the roads of the towns speak also of this confidence.

But when one comes to think about the people of the Solway my first thoughts are still of fishermen carrying on the traditions of centuries and still of wildfowlers like Bill Powell, and still, of course, of the seabirds and the wild-geese. Whilst they change not, new industries *are* coming again and perhaps typical is the growth of the new trading estate at Lillyhall between Workington and Whitehaven where lonely trees once leaned against the wind and now a British Leyland factory squarely stands. I have not much altered the chapter on industry; the pattern is slowly changing but this is a continuing change meriting a deeper and more detailed study than I can give it now.

Returning to the people; many of the individuals I met on my first journey are flourishing though Bill Lawson is content to watch the Solway rather than to fish in it these days. Adam Birrell of Creetown who was 87 when I first met him is gone; but mention of Creetown reminds me that a new museum has been built there and there is another new museum near Dalry designed to illustrate the deer of Scotland. Nature-trails are an established attraction now in Galloway as elsewhere. The Scottish Solway coast-lands are probably attracting more English than ever before, and I was told that 85% of the country cottages in Dumfriesshire and Galloway are now owned by "southern English" and certainly English voices are heard everywhere.

I cannot, in the space available, attempt to bring the archæology of the Solway up to date. Richard Bellhouse (although his work has taken him away to Lincoln) has been busy every holiday on the English side and there has been plenty of activity in Scotland too. All this work is well reported in the two series of transactions I referred to so often in the original survey: the "D. & G" and the "C. & W".

Silloth still lives up to the title I gave it—"an outpost of Carlisle" and is still pleasant though even busier in the summer when its new caravan sites are full; but it no longer has its railway. Another line has been crossed out and another negative paragraph added to the torturous story of Carlisle's thrust to the sea.

I think, as I write this, of my latest visit to the Solway, in September 1973, and I see and feel and hear immediately its beauty in my mind. My wife and I sat on the sea-washed turf near Bowness as the sun settled. The golden stones came back to remind us of great days and there fell the absolute peace that is made quieter by the sound of birds. The oyster-catchers stalked on the damp sand. The air, bright always, suddenly glowed as nowhere else it can, and once again, and forever, the cry of the curlew spoke for the Solway.

This postscript is intended mainly to record certain gains and losses experienced in recent years.

Prosperity is the most dramatic loss but it is now widely shared and I have commented on it earlier. Friends have died and none is a greater personal loss than Bill Lawson who epitomized the Solway to me and to many others.

In all other ways the book stands. Skinburness is as lonely as ever and the Scottish coastal lands are richer than ever in their varied attractions. Gains include Border TV and BBC Radio Carlisle, both serving Scottish as well as English Solway.

I have mentioned the Border Regiment in earlier editions. It is now, after amalgamation, the King's Own Royal Border Regiment; sadly its colonel, General Sir William Scotter, died just before taking up his appointment as Deputy Commander, Supreme Allied Command in Europe. He was a Carlisle man and a Solway man having been educated at St Bees.

I ended the second edition of *The Solway Firth* at Bowness on the English shore. This edition, I felt, should end on the Scottish shore and I chose Caerlaverock.

Dumfries was crowded and White Sands crammed with cars; it was a hot Saturday in August. Five miles south along the road by the River Nith, I came to the National Nature Reserve, six miles of lonely shore and merse. Here come each year the wild geese in their thousands. The Reserve embraces the Eastpark Refuge owned by the Wildfowl Trust, and Eastpark is open to visitors from September to February.

Caerlaverock Castle, open all year round, is but a stone's throw away. The sun burnishes red sandstone on both sides of the Solway, and here it can create a feeling of awe as one looks at the castle from its lovely undulating lawns and a feeling of utter delight as one looks up at the seventeenth-century house incongruously inserted inside the grim red castle triangle.

On this, my most recent Solway journey, I was greeted, not by my beloved curlew, but by Caerlaverock Castle's permanent garrison of Canada Geese. They circle the moat calling imperiously and, with the gigantic goldfish in the moat, provide a bonus—if one were needed. The journey around the coast roads of Solway is as magical in 1982 as it ever was.

BIBLIOGRAPHY

BOOKS AND PAPERS DIRECTLY CONCERNED WITH THE REGION

Annals of the Solway until A.D. 1307, George Neilson. This book may
  be difficult to find as only two hundred copies were printed, but
  it is invaluable in itself and contains many references.
*Transactions of the Cumberland and Westmorland Antiquarian and
  Archæological Society.*
*Transactions of the Dumfriesshire and Galloway Natural History and
  Antiquarian Society.*
Transactions of the Carlisle Natural History Society.

IMPORTANT BOOKS TOUCHING ON THE REGION

The Personality of Britain, Sir Cyril Fox.
The Coastline of England and Wales, J. A. Steers.
An Historical Geography of England before 1800, ed. H. C. Darby.
Prelates and People of the Lake Counties, C. M. Lowther Bouch.
The Lake Counties, W. G. Collingwood.

BOOKS DEALING WITH PARTICULAR SUBJECTS

Flowers of the Coast, Ian Hepburn.
Prehistoric Communities of the British Isles, V. Gordon Childe.
Roman Britain and the English Settlements, R. G. Collingwood and
  J. N. L. Myres.
The Roman Occupation of South-Western Scotland, ed. S. N. Miller.
Northumbrian Crosses of the Pre-Norman Age, W. G. Collingwood.
The Arts in Early England, vol. v., G. Baldwin Brown.
Ancient Emigrants—A History of the Norse Settlement in Scotland,
  A. Brøgger.
The Last Years of a Frontier, D. L. W. Tough.
The Border Line, J. L. Mack.
The Maryport and Carlisle Railway, Jack Simmons.
My Wild Goose Chase, Bill Powell.

SOME ORIGINAL SOURCES AVAILABLE IN TRANSLATION

Agricola, Tacitus. Most accessible and most readable in *Tacitus on
  Britain and Germany*, translated by H. Mattingly in the Penguin
  Classics.
The Ecclesiastical History of the English Nation, Bede; (Everyman's
  Library).

The Anglo-Saxon Chronicle (Everyman's Library).

The Journeys of Celia Fiennes. The only satisfactory edition is that edited by Christopher Morris and published by the Cresset Press.

The Chronicle of Lanercost, 1272–1346, translated by Sir Herbert Maxwell.

The Calendar of Border Papers, ed. J. Bain.

The above-mentioned books contain sufficient references to allow the reader to follow up most of the subjects discussed. They have led me to a great many sources of information and here I may acknowledge the help given in my search by the Librarians and Staff of the Cumberland County Library, the Ewart Library, Dumfries, and Carlisle City Library (Tullie House) with its wonderful collection (Jacksonian) of local material.

Plants Mentioned in Chapter III, Pages 31–36

BOTANICAL AND ALTERNATIVE NAMES

Sea-couch grass	*Agropyron junceiforme*	
Marram grass	*Ammophila arenaria*	
Rice grass	*Spartina Townsendii*	
Sea-manna grass	*Puccinellia maritima*	Glyceria
Eel-grass	*Zostera spp.* (usually *marina*)	Grass-wrack
Jointed glass-wort	*Salicornia spp.* (usually *stricta*)	Marsh samphire Sandforth
Annual seablite	*Suaeda maritima*	
Thrift	*Armeria maritima*	Sea pink
Sea plantain	*Plantago maritima*	
Sea aster	*Aster tripolium*	Star wort
Scurvy grass	*Cochlearia officinalis*	Sea scurvy
Obione	*Halimione portulacoides*	
Sea arrow grass	*Triglochin maritima*	
Sand fescue grass	*Festuca rubra;* variety *Arenaria*	
Buckshorn plantain	*Plantago coronopus*	

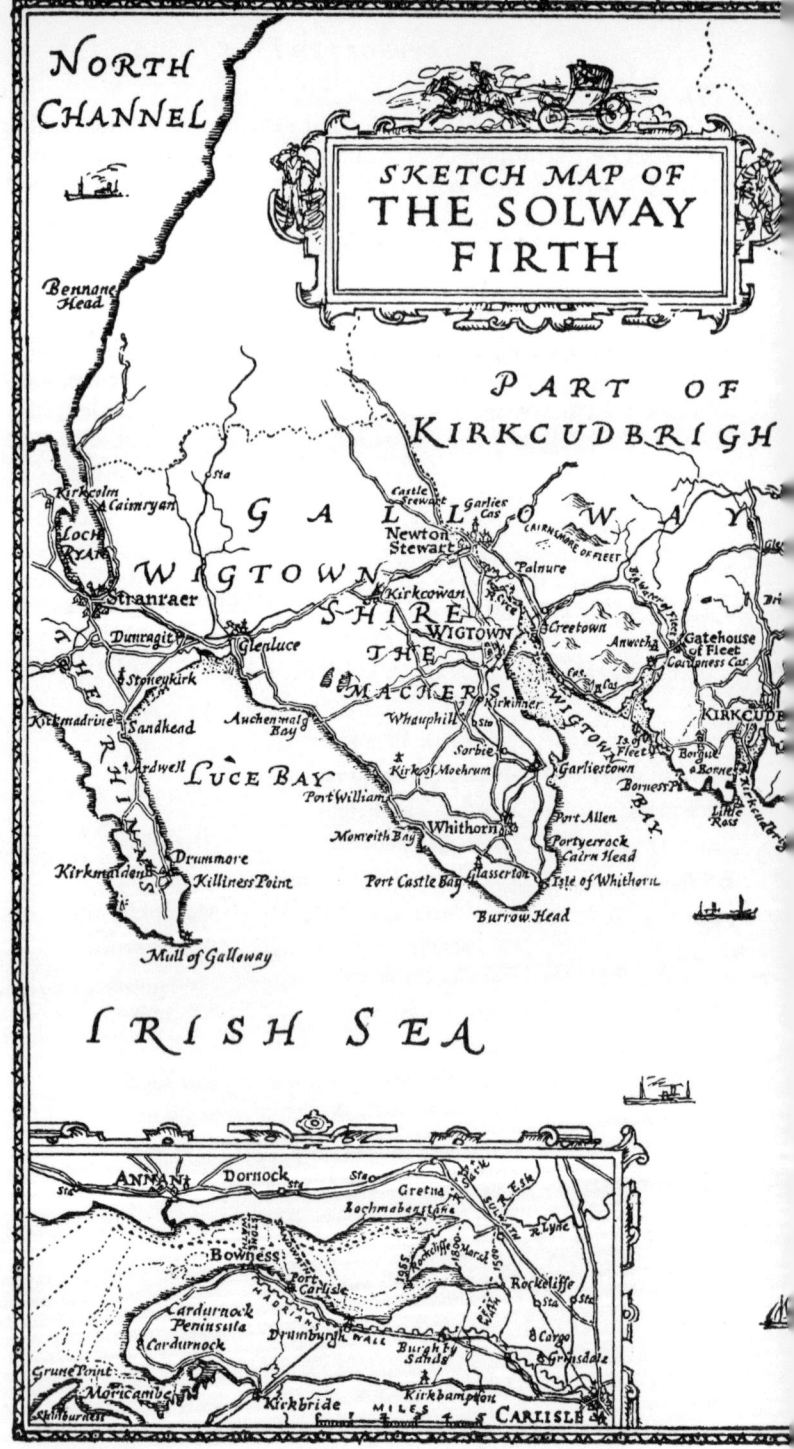

SKETCH MAP OF
THE SOLWAY
FIRTH

NORTH
CHANNEL

PART OF
KIRKCUDBRIGH

Bennane
Head

Kirkcolm
Cairnryan
Loch
RYAN
Stranraer
Dunragit
Stoneykirk
Kirkmadrine
Sandhead
Ardwell
Kirkmaidens
Drummore
Killiness Point
Mull of Galloway

Sta
GALLOWAY
WIGTOWN
SHIRE
THE
MACHERS
Auchenmalg
Bay
LUCE BAY
Port William
Monreith Bay
Port Castle Bay

Castle
Stewart
Garlies
Cas
Newton
Stewart
Kirkcowan
WIGTOWN
CAIRNSMORE OF FLEET
Palnure
Creetown
Kirkinner
Whauphill
Sta
Sorbie
Kirk of Mochrum
Garliestown
Whithorn
Glasserton
Burrow Head
Anwoth
Gatehouse
of Fleet
Cardiness Cas
Is of
Fleet
KIRKCUDE
Borgu
Borness
Borness
BAY
Little
Ross
Port Allen
Portyerrock
Cairn Head
Isle of Whithorn
Glenluce

IRISH SEA

ANNAN
Dornock
Sta
Sta
Bowness
Cardurnock
Peninsula
Cardurnock
Grune Point
Morecambe
Silloth Bank
Kirkbride
Gretna
Lochmabenstane
Port
Carlisle
Drumburgh
MIDLAND
WALL
Burgh by
Sands
MILES
Kirkbampton
Gretna
R. SUR Esk
Lyne
Rockcliffe
Sta
Sta
Cargo
Grinsdale
CARLISLE

INDEX

Abbey Burnfoot, 87
Abbeytown, 24, 88
Adams of Ennerdale, Lord, 157–158, 160
Aedan, 77
Aglionby, Edward, 113
Agricola, 61–66
Alard, Gervase, 100
Alexander II of Scotland, 97
Allonby, 42, 204
Almorness Point, 45
Anhydrite, 160
Annan, 13, 47
  castle, 12
  industries, 163
  poke-net fishing, 143
  port, 162
  river, 29
  shrimp fleet, 145–146
  Wath, 11
Annan Waterfoot, 11
Anthorn, 200
Antoninus Pius, 61
Anwoth, 178, 180
— Hotel, 180
Apollo, 11
Arbigland, 20
Ardwell Isle, 180 181
Armstrong, Johnnie, 109
—, J. R., 203–204
—, Colonel Robert, 164, 168
Arras culture, 58, 60
Arthur, 11, 75–76
Arthuret, 26, 27, 76, 193
Aspatria, 84, 158
Athelstan, 94, 193
Atomic Energy, 159
Auchencairn Bay, 45, 184, 187
Augustinian Order, 89

Balcary, 45, 184–185
Balliol, John, 89

Balliol, Devorgilla, 74, 89, 91, 92, 189
—, King John, 89, 98, 99
—, Edward, 12, 103
— College, Oxford, 89
Bann axe, 56
Bannavem Taberniae, 73
Barholm Castle, 176
Battle of:
  Arthuret (Armterid), 26, 27, 76, 193
  Brunanburh, 193 (and see Burnswark)
  Camlann, 76
  Degsestan, 77
  Dornock, 12
  Langholm, 109
  Nectansmere, 82, 93, 179
  the Sark, 110
  Solway Moss, 108
Bayle-fires, 114
Beacons, 114–115
Beaker folk, 54–55
Beaumont, 199
Beckfoot Fort, 68, 70, 203–204
Bellhouse, R. L., 68–70
Belted Galloway cattle, 128–129
Benedictine Order, 86
Berwickshire, Merse of, 20
Bessemer process, 166
Bewcastle Cross, 77–81
Birds, 43 et seq.
Birrell, Adam, 136, 141, 175
Birrens Fort, 63
Black Galloway cattle, 125–126
Blengairn, 45
Blower, Thomas, 169
Boniface VIII, Pope, 11, 101
Border laws, 97, 103–108, 111–113
Bore, 40
Borgue, 180–181
Borness Batteries, 181
— Cave, 59, 181
Borrodaile, Gawen, 202

Bowness, 67, 200
— Bells, 13, 200
— Wath, 11, 194
Brampton, 7
Brigantes, 60
Brighouse Bay, 41, 181
Brochs, 58–59, 171
Bronze Age, 54–56
Brow Well, 192
Brown, Mr James, 128
Bruce Family, granted land in Annan-
    dale, 95
— —, grant fishing rights, 138–139
Bruce,
    the Competitor for Scottish Crown,
        98
    Constable of Carlisle Castle, 98
    buried at Holm Cultram, 202
    Robert, 98, 101–102
    —, murders Comyn, 91
    —, crowned at Scone, 101–102
    —, attacks Carlisle, 102
    —, pillages Holm Cultram, 88
Buittle Castle, 116
Burgh-by-Sands, 102, 199
Burgh Castle, 116
Burke and Hare, 123
Burns, Robert, 122, 166, 190
Burnswark, 1, 93, 193–194
Burrow Head, 19, 147
— Walls, 69-70, 210, 213

Cædmon of Whitby, 80
Caerlaverock Castle, 100, 110, 117,
    191–192, 219
Cairnholy, 176–177
Cairnryan, 161, 175
Cairnsmore of Fleet, 19, 175
Camboglanna, 76
Camlann, 76
Cally House, 180
Canals, 165-166
Candida Casa, 73–74
Canonbie, 21, 195
Cardoness Castle, 178
Cardurnock, 200
Carey, Sir Robert, 112, 120
Cargo, 7

Carlingwark Loch, 60, 186
Carlisle, 196 et seq.
    Roman town of, 66, 83
    — fort at, 199
    St Cuthbert's visit to, 81–82
    and the Danes, 82, 83
    and William Rufus, 94
    Castle, 94, 198
    and David I of Scotland, 95, 96
    Cathedral, 22, 82, 89, 198
    Prior's houses of, 89
    Friaries, 90, 91
    Bishopric, 94, 95
    Edward I in, 102
    Defence by Andrew de Harcla,
        102–103
    Dormont Book of, 112
    Guilds, 112
    Civil War and siege of, 82
    Jacobite rebellions and, 7, 197
    Eden bridges, 5–6, 196
    industries of, 164–165
Carlyle, Thomas, 193
Carsethorn, 20, 161, 189
Carsluith Castle, 176
Castle Douglas, 186
— Haven, 181
Castles, 115–117
Castletown, 9
Cattle breeding, 128–130
— droving, 120–121
Celtic art, 58, 74 et seq.
— language, 74
— peoples, 55
Chambers, Abbot Robert, 119, 202
Charles Stuart (Bonnie Prince
    Charlie), 7, 190, 197
Charters, James, 120
Chesterholm Stone, 71
Chi Rho symbol, 169, 172
Choirs, 209
Christian Family, 207
—, Fletcher, 207
Church, Celtic, 71–75
—, Medieval, 85, et seq.
Cistercian Order, 87–89
— Wool Trade, 118–119
Clay Dobbins, 124-125, 199

Cl--tor Moor, 20
Clerk-Maxwell, James, 215
Cleveland Dyke, 24
Clifton Cross, 210
Coal-mining, 17, 20–21, 23, 150 *et seq.*, 208, 211
Coastal drift, 40–41
Coel the Elder, 72, 76
Collingwood, Professor R. G., 64, 67, 69
—, W. G., 81
Colvend, 19, 45, 188
Comlongon Castle, 192
Comyn, 91
Coroticus, 72
Covenanters, 119, 174
Crabs, 146–147
Craik of Arbigland, William, 121, 126, 183
—, Helen, 122
Crannogs, 60, 186
Cree, River, 138
Creetown, 100, 162, 174–175
Crerar, Dr J. W., 207
Crichton Royal Institution, 191
Criffell, 16, 189
Crosscanonby, 204
Crosses and slabs (pre-Norman):
  Acca's cross, 81
  Anwoth, cross at, 178
  Bewcastle Cross, 77–81
  Chesterholm stone, 71
  Chi Rho symbol, 169, 172
  Clifton Cross, 210
  Dearham collection, 206
  Gosforth Cross, 84
  Hartlepool slabs, 80
  Hoddom Cross, 193
  Kirkmadrine collection, 169
  Latinus stone, 73, 172
  Ruthwell Cross, 15, 77–81, 192
  St Peter Stone, 173
  Viking stones, 83–84, 205, 206
  Whithorn collection, 172–173
Cumberland Clydesdale horses, 130
— turf, 33
Cunedda, 72
Cunningham, Alan, 188

Curwen Family, 209–210
—, John Christian, 122, 151, 207
Cymry, 72

Dacre, Thomas, 12
Dairying, 129–130
Dalbeattie, 19, 130, 184, 186–187
Dalton, John, 215
David I of Scotland, 96
Dearham, 205–206
— Bridge, 205
Debatable land, 103–104, 110–112
Dee, River, 15, 116, 181
Distington, 211
Dominican Order, 90
Dornock, 12, 194
Douglas Family, 104, 108, 109
Dream of the Rood, 79–80
Drumburgh, 12, 116, 199, 217
Dumfries and district, 190
  urn burials, near, 56
  Grey Friars, 91–92
  Devorgilla's Bridge, 91, 189
  murder of Comyn, 91–92
  garrisoned by English, 99
  rivalry with Kirkcudbright, 160–161
  Robert Burns in, 190
  meal riots in, 123
  Burke and Hare at, 123
  shambles, 126
  White Sands, 189–190
  Norwegian headquarters at, 189
  Creighton Royal, 191
  Observatory Museum, 22
  Industries, 163–164, 189–191
Dumfries and Galloway Development Association, 164, 176
Dundrennan Abbey, 87, 184
Dunragit, 170

Eamont, 94
Eastriggs, 194
East Whinns, 44
Ecclefechan, 193
Eden, River, 4 *et seq.*, 37, 40
— fords, 7, 111
— bridges, 5–6, 196

Edgar, 93
Edmund, 93
Edward I, 97–98
  and the Competitors, 98
  and the Scottish War, 98 *et seq.*
  at Carlisle, 90
  and Solway fords, 8, 11, 12
  and fleet in Solway, 99–100
  at Caerlaverock, 100
  at Sweetheart Abbey, 101
  and Robert Bruce, 102
  at Linstock and Lanercost, 89
  holds Parliament in Carlisle, 102
  dies near Solway, 102
  memorial to, 199
Ehenside Tarn, 53
Elizabeth Dock, 153
Elizabeth of England, 111
Embleton Sword, 58
Engelen, Henry, 201
Esk, River, 4 *et seq.*, 15, 37
— fords, 6, 9
Estholm, *see* Hestan
Estrella de Chile, 38
Ethelfrith, 77
Etterby Wath, 7

Faed, John, 129
Faults (geological), 16–17
Ferrier, Kathleen, 197
Feudalism, 95–96
Fish-spearing, 52, 147–148
Fisher, Robert, 3, 155
Fisher's Cross, 165
Flax, 123
Fleet, Isles of, 18, 180–181
—, River, 178
Fleming, Mary, 154
Fletcher Family of Parton, 153
Fleswick Bay, 214
Flimby, 122, 207, 208
Floriston, 5
Floshes, 35
Flows, 36
Food-vessel People, 55
Fords, 6–14, 67, 194
— and Cattle droving, 121

Fox, Sir Cyril, 54
Franciscan Order, 91–92

Galdus, 176
Galloway Nag, 150
Garliestown, 162
Gatehouse-of-Fleet, 64, 180
Gilsland, 76
Glaciation, *see* Ice Age
Glencaple, 161, 191
— Merse, 15
Glenlochar Fort, 64
Glenluce, 53, 170
— Abbey, 88, 170
Gosforth Cross, 84
Graham, Sir James, 134
—, Dr Robert, 122
—, David, 139
—, Jack, 129
Granite, 19
Greenbed, 9
Gretna, 194, 195
— marriages, 7, 195
Grindal, Archbishop Edmund, 214
Grinsdale, 7, 199
Grune Point, 31, 32, 202, 203

Haaf-net fishing, 135–137
Hadrian's Wall, 7, 61, 66–70, 197
— —, Solway extension of, 68–70
Haematite ore, 20, 153, 155, 166
Halfden, 83
Hallstatt culture, 57
Harald Fairhair, 83
Harcla, Andrew de, 102–103
Harris, Isabella, 206
Hatteraick, Dirk, 177
Hayes Castle, 212
Herries, Agnes, 115
Hestan Island, 50, 185–186
Hills forts, 60, 179, 193
Hoddom, 115, 193
— Castle, 193
— Cross, 193
Hogg, Robert, 196
Holm Cultram Abbey, 9, 88, 118, 119, 202
Holy Cross of Lyme, 38, 100

Horse Isle, 45
Hound trailing, 208
Houston, James, 185
Howard of Corby, Philip, 122
Hydro-electric power, 163

Ice Age, 17, 24-27
Ida, 76
Improvers' Societies, 121
Inglewood, manors of, 97, 98
Iron Age, 56-60, 181

Jacobites, 7
Jeffs, James, 182
Johnson, Captain, 120
Jones, Paul, 182-183

Kelton Hill Fair, 120, 186
Kemble, J. M., 79
Kidsdale, 171
Kilhern, caves of, 171
Kinmont Willie, 106-108
Kinmount Estate, 47
Kirkandrews-on-Eden, 199
Kirkbean, 19, 183, 189
Kirkbride, 131, 201
Kirkcudbright, 100, 160-161, 181-184
— Castle, 116
— Harbour, 182
Kirkmadrine, 169
Kippford, 42, 45, 187-188

Laggan, 178
Lake Carlisle, 25
Lanercost, Chronicle of, 91, 98, 100
— Priory, 89, 91, 197
Langholm, 109, 195
La Tène culture, 57-58
Latinus stone, 73, 172
Law, Edward, First Baron Ellen-
    borough, 207
Lawson, Billie (Bill), 136 et seq., 194,
    219
Leslie, General David, 196-197
Levellers, 120, 186
Lewis, W. V., 41
Liddel Strength, 115
Lincluden, 190
Linstock, 89, 101

Linton, John, 195
Lister, Joseph, Lord, 206
Loan Wath, 10
Lobsters, 146-147, 185
Lochar Moss, 36
Lochmabenstane, 10, 11, 14, 195
Lollius Urbicus, 61
Longnewton Marsh, 36
Lougan Whale, 142
Lowther, Gerard, 150-151
—, Sir John, 151
Luce Bay, 170
Luguvallium, 83
Lyne, River, 8

Macmillan, Kirkpatrick, 215
Machers, 18, 173
Main Band, 17
Man, Isle of, 83
Maponus, 11
Mark, Mote of, 115, 179
Maryport:
    Roman fort, 68, 70, 206
    origins of, 138
    foundation of, 154
    Netherhall, 206
    docks and shipping, 153-155
    meal mob in, 123-124
    first secret ballot, 85
    Lord Lister and, 206
    Thomas Henry Ismay and, 154
    industry, 150 et seq.
    Dr J. W. Crerar and, 207
    Educational Settlement, 207
Maryport and Carlisle Railway, 157,
    166
Mary Stuart, 87, 111, 154, 209
Maxwell, John, Lord Herries, 115
—, Robert, 121
Maxwelltown, 174, 189, 190
Megalithic tombs, 53, 176, 177
Merin Rheged, 76
Metal Bridge, 5-6
Mezolithic man, 52
Middlebie, 13
Miller, Patrick, 215
Milton Loch, 60, 84
Mitchell, William, 38

Moresby Church, 212–213
— Hall, 213
— Roman fort, 68, 70, 212–213
Moricambe, 15–16, 33, 201
Mosses, 36
Mote of Mark, 115, 179
— — Urr, 115
Murray, William, 180
Mussel gathering, 187

Naworth Castle, 197
Neolithic man, 53
Netherby, 111, 123, 195
Netherhall, 206
New Abbey, 189
— Luce, 170
Newton Arlosh, 201
— Stewart, 170, 174
Nicholson, Norman, 14, 183, 198
Nith, River, 15, 29, 33, 34, 40, 47
Norman Conquest, 94 et seq.
Norse immigration, 83–84

Old Carlisle, 66, 68, 70, 75
Old Mortality, 174
Orchardton Bay, 45, 187
— Tower, 115, 186
Orkneying saga, 84
Oswy, 77

Palæolithic man, 52
Palmcaster, 75
Palnackie, 161, 162, 186
Papcastle, 66, 68
Parton, 151, 212
Paton, Dr T. G., 125
Peat, 131, 201
Peatwath, 8, 199
Pele Towers, 113–115, 199, 201
Petriana, 199
Picts, 179
Piggott, Professor Stuart, 177
—, Mrs, 60, 84
Plants, see Appendix
Platorius Nepos, A., 66
Poke-net fishing, 143–144
Port Carlisle, 146, 165–167, 199-200

Port Patrick, 161
Powell, Bill, 191
Premonstratensian Order, 90
Preston Merse, 188
— Mill", "Lovely Lass of, 188
— Village, 188

Rabycote, 119
Railways, 156, 157, 166–167
Raised beach, 29, 31, 175
Ravenglass, 50, 64
Redkirk Point, 138, 139, 140
Reid, Dr R. C., 65, 142
Repentance Tower, 115
Rheged, 76, 170
Rhinns of Galloway, 18, 161, 169
Rhydderch, 76, 193
Rigg and Rean, 119
Risehow Pit, 155, 208
Risman, Gus, 209
Rivers, 23
River terraces, 29
Robert of Ulm, Friar, 100
Robertson, Leonard, 184
Robinson, Joseph, 69, 203
Rockcliffe (England), 5, 7, 47
— Castle, 111, 116
— Marsh, 9, 15, 33, 35, 36, 45, 46
— Wath, 7–8
Rockcliffe (Scotland), 187
Roman coastal defences, 67–70, 198–199
Roman forts:
    Beckfoot, 68, 70, 203–204
    Birdoswald (Camboglanna), 76
    Birrens, 63
    Bowness, 200
    Burgh-by-Sands, 199
    Burnswark, 63, 193–194
    Burrow Walls (Workington), 69–70, 210, 213
    Carlisle, Town (Luguvallium), 66, 83
    —, Stanwix (Petriana), 199
    Dalswinton, 63
    Drumburgh, 199
    Gatehouse (near), 64
    Glenlochar, 64

Roman forts (*contd.*):
  Maryport (Alauna), 64, 68–70, 206
  Moresby, 68, 70, 212–213
  Netherby (Castra Exploratorum), 195
  Old Carlisle, 66, 68, 70, 75
  Papcastle, 66, 68
  Wardlaw, 65, 192
Roman occupation, 60 *et seq.*
Rough Firth, 18, 45, 187
Rugby League Football, 3, 209
Runes, 78–79
Rutherford Memorial, 178
Ruthwell Cross, 15, 77–81, 192
— Salt, 131, 132

Saint Bega, 86
— Congal, 90
— Cuthbert, 81–82
— Kentigern, 76, 193
— Ninian, 73–74, 172–173
— Patrick, 72, 73, 169
St Bees, 43, 86, 150, 214
St Joseph, Dr J. K., 63, 69–70
St Mary's Isle, 181
St Ninian's Cave, 172
Salmon, 133 *et seq.*
Salt marshes, 32–36
Saltpans, 204–205
Salt works, 131–132
Sandbanks, 37–38
Sand-dunes, 31
Sandhead, 169
Sandsfield, 8, 40
Sandywath, 12
Sark, River, 4, 10
Scar Rocks, 43, 171
Scaurs, 37–39
Scots Dyke, 111
Scott, Sir Lindsay, 59
—, Michael, 202, 203
— of Buccleuch, 104, 106–107
Scottish Wars of Independence, 98–103
Screel, 45
Scrope, Lord, 104, 105–106
Sea-level, 28–29, 31
Sellafield, 159, 215

Senhouse Family, 151, 153–4, 157, 207
— Dock, 15, 153, 155
—, Humphrey, 154
Severn Wildfowl Trust, 46
Sheep farming, 118, 130
Shipbuilding, 151 *et seq.*
Shrimping, 145–146
Siddick Ponds, 47–48
Silloth, 9, 42, 166, 203
Simpson, Dr Douglas, 192
Simpson, F. G., 82
Skinburness, 99–100, 156, 202, 219
Smiles, Samuel, 121
Smirke, Robert, 196
Smuggling, 177, 185
Solway Moss, 36–37, 56
— Pit, 17, 211
Southerness, 20, 132, 188
Sproat, Faed, 128–129
Sproat, George, 129
Stairhaven, 59, 171
Stanwick, 58, 60
Stanwix Fort, 199
Stake-net fishing, 138, 139–141
Stanegate, 62, 66, 76
Steel, 155
Stephenson, George, 156
Stobart, Tom, 214
Stonewath, 8
Stranraer, 64, 161, 170
Strathclyde, 76
Submarine geography, 37
Submerged forests, 28, 204
Sulwath, 8, 9, 10, 101
Sutton, Graham, 214
Swarthy Hill, 205
Sweetheart Abbey, 19, 89, 101, 189
Sylvius, Aeneas, 200

Tacitus, 61–62
Telford, Thomas, 4, 196
Teroy Broch, 59
Textiles, 159
Threave Castle, 109, 116, 186
Three-shilling Rab, 123
Thurstonfield Lough, 48
Tides, 39–40
Tomlin, 214

Tongland, 163
Torrs, 58
Torthorwald, 125
Tracht Romra, 76
Trading Estates, 158, 208
Trailtrow Hill, 115
Trusty's Hill, 179
Tullie House, Carlisle, 6, 22, 196

Urien of Rheged, 76, 170
Urn folk, 55
Urr, Mote of, 115

Venutius, 58
Viaduct across Solway, 6, 137, 166–168
Vikings, 82–84
Vitrified forts, 57, 179
Vortigern, 75

Waland, Robert, 215
Wallace, William, 95, 99, 101
Wampool, River, 40
Wardens of the Marches, 97, 104–106
Wardlaw Fort, 65, 192
Waths, 6–14, 67, 194
Wave action, 40–41
Waver, River, 119
Weather, 126–128
Wedholme Flow, 131, 201
Wesley, John, 214
West Cumberland Development Company, Ltd., 158, 163
Westoll, Captain James, 128
Wetheral, 86

Whales, 141–142
Whammel fishing, 144–145
Wheeler, Sir Mortimer, 58, 60
Whitby, Synod of, 77
Whitehaven, 213–214
    Coalfield, 151–152
    Colonial trade, 151, 152
    shipbuilding, 151–152
    Paul Jones raids, 183
    Royal Standard Inn, 214
    industry in, 150 et seq.
Whithorn, 73, 74, 90, 172
—, Isle of, 73, 161, 172
Wigton, 130, 196
Wigtown, 161, 163
— Martyrs, 173–174
Wildfowl, 43 et seq.
Willie o' the Boats, 9
Winchelsea, Robert of, 11–12, 13, 101
Wilson, Joe, 192
Wolsty Castle, 116, 203
Workington, 209–211
    Curwen Family of, 209–210
    Burrow Walls, 68, 210, 213
    St Cuthbert in, 82
    Mary Stuart lands at, 209
    Hall, 209
    Agricultural Show, 122
    industry in, 150 et seq.
Wreaths Tower, 188
Wrestling (Cumberland and Westmorland style), 209

Yachting, 187–188
Yawkins, Jack, 177
Youth Hostels, 162